The Armchair Economist

The Armchair Economist

Economics and Everyday Life

Steven E. Landsburg

THE FREE PRESS
A Division of Macmillan, Inc.
NEW YORK

Maxwell Macmillan Canada
TORONTO

Maxwell Macmillan International
NEW YORK   OXFORD   SINGAPORE   SYDNEY

The Free Press
A Division of Macmillan, Inc.
866 Third Avenue, New York, N.Y. 10022

Maxwell Macmillan Canada, Inc.
1200 Eglinton Avenue East
Suite 200
Don Mills, Ontario M3C 3N1

Macmillan, Inc. is part of the Maxwell Communication Group of Companies.

Printed in the United States of America

printing number
1   2   3   4   5   6   7   8   9   10

Library of Congress Cataloging-in-Publication Data

Landsburg, Steven E.
     The armchair economist: economics and everyday life / Steven E. Landsburg.
        p.   cm.
     ISBN 0-02-917775-8
     1. Economics—Sociological aspects.   I. Title.
HM35.L35   1993
306.3—dc20   93-4008
                                                                CIP

CONTENTS

INTRODUCTION

In November 1974, shortly after I arrived at the University of Chicago to begin my graduate studies, the *Wall Street Journal* published a list of "Ways to Stump an Economist." It was written by a man named John Tracy McGrath, who raised a series of embarrassingly simple questions about everyday life that he thought economists would be unable to answer: Why does a pack of cigarettes bought from a cigarette machine cost more than a pack of cigarettes bought from the man at the candy store? Why can't racetracks make change in less than 20-cent increments? Why does orange soda cost four times as much as gasoline?

That night over dinner, my friends and I—first-year graduate students all—had quite a laugh at McGrath's expense. With just a little knowledge of economics, all of his questions seemed easy.

Today, with nearly twenty years of additional knowledge, I think that all of McGrath's questions are both fascinating and difficult. In my recollection, the answers that came so easily over dinner consisted of nothing more than refusals to take the questions seriously. I believe that we dismissed most of them with the phrase "supply and demand," as if that meant something. Whatever we thought it meant, we were sure that it was what economics was about.

Here is what I *now* think economics is about. First, it is about observing the world with genuine curiosity and admitting that it is full of mysteries. Second, it is about trying to solve those mysteries in ways that are consistent with the general proposition that human behavior is usually designed to serve a purpose. Sometimes the mysteries themselves—like McGrath's—

are hard to solve, so we practice by trying to solve similar mysteries in fictional worlds that we invent and call models. If the goal is to understand why orange soda costs more than gasoline, we might begin by thinking about a world where the only things that anybody ever buys are orange soda and gasoline. If the goal is to understand why particular constituencies want to outlaw silicone breast implants, we might begin by thinking about a world where men choose their marriage partners exclusively on the basis of breast size.

We think about models not because they are realistic, but because thinking about models is a good warm-up exercise for thinking about the world we live in. The goal, always, is to understand our own world. The first step toward understanding—and the step that we had not yet taken when we started graduate school—is to admit that the world is not always easy to understand.

This book is a compendium of essays about how economists think. It is about the things that we find mysterious, why we find them mysterious, and how we try to understand them. It describes some mysteries that I think are solved and others that I think are not. There are a lot of good reasons to learn about economics, but the reason I have tried to stress in this book is that economics is a tool for solving mysteries, and solving mysteries is fun.

For most of the last ten years, I have had the splendid privilege of eating lunch every day with an extraordinary group of economic detectives who never fail to inspire me with their incisiveness, their whimsy, and their capacity for wonder. Almost daily, someone arrives at lunch with a new mystery to solve, a dozen brilliant and original solutions are proposed, and a dozen devastating objections are raised and occasionally overcome. We do it for sheer joy.

This book is largely a chronicle of what I have learned at lunch. I am sure that some of the ideas are original with me, but I am no longer sure which ones. Many others I learned from Mark Bils, John Boyd, Lauren Feinstone, Marvin Goodfriend, Bruce Hansen, Hanan Jacoby, Jim Kahn, Ken McLaughlin, Alan Stockman, and the others who have come and gone over the years. With profound thanks for taking me along on their roller coaster ride, this book is dedicated to the lunch group.

It is dedicated also to Bonnie Buonomo, the restaurant manager who created the perfect atmosphere for the group to thrive in, and to the Tivoli Coffee Shop in Rochester, which, in defiance of the laws of economics, allowed me to take up nearly permanent residence for the price of a daily cup of coffee while I wrote the final draft.

A NOTE ON THE CHAPTERS

These chapters give a sampling of how economists see the world. For the most part, they can be read in any order. Some chapters refer to ideas from earlier chapters, but these references are never essential to the flow of things.

The ideas expressed in this book are intended to give a fair representation of how mainstream economists think. Of course, there is room for disagreement over specifics, and any particular economist would surely want to dissent from some of the things that I say. But I believe that most economists who read this book will agree that it accurately reflects their general viewpoint.

Attentive readers will observe that this book applies economic reasoning to a vast array of human (and sometimes non-human) behavior. They will note also that when a question arises regarding the range of applicability of an economic principle, the author always prefers to risk error in the direction of being overly inclusive. I believe that the laws of economics are universal; they are blind to race and blind to gender. I am therefore confident that no attentive reader will mistake my repeated use of the generic pronouns "he," "him," and "his" for the exclusively masculine pronouns with the same spellings and pronunciations.

I

What Life Is All About

CHAPTER 1

THE POWER OF INCENTIVES

How Seat Belts Kill

Most of economics can be summarized in four words: "People respond to incentives." The rest is commentary.

"People respond to incentives" sounds innocuous enough, and almost everyone will admit its validity as a general principle. What distinguishes the economist is his insistence on taking the principle seriously at all times.

I remember the late 1970s and waiting half an hour to buy a tank of gasoline at a federally controlled price. Virtually all economists agreed that if the price were allowed to rise freely, people would buy less gasoline. Many noneconomists believed otherwise. The economists were right: When price controls were lifted, the lines disappeared.

The economist's faith in the power of incentives serves him well, and he trusts it as a guide in unfamiliar territory. In 1965, Ralph Nader published *Unsafe at Any Speed,* a book calling attention to various design elements that made cars more dangerous than necessary. The federal government soon responded with a wide range of automobile safety legislation, mandating the use of seat belts, padded dashboards, collapsible steering columns, dual braking systems, and penetration-resistant windshields.

Even before the regulations went into effect, any economist could have predicted one of their consequences: The number of auto accidents increased. The reason is that the threat of being killed in an accident is a powerful incentive to drive carefully. But a driver with a seat belt and a padded dashboard faces less of a threat. Because people respond to incentives, drivers are less careful. The result is more accidents.

The principle I am applying is precisely the same one that predicted the disappearance of gasoline lines. When the price of gasoline is low, people choose to buy more gasoline. When the price of accidents (e.g., the probability of being killed or the expected medical bill) is low, people choose to have more accidents.

You might object that accidents, unlike gasoline, are not in any sense a "good" that people would ever choose to purchase. But speed and recklessness are goods in the sense that people seem to want them. Choosing to drive faster or more recklessly is tantamount to choosing more accidents, at least in a probabilistic sense.

An interesting question remains. How big is the effect in question? How many additional accidents were caused by the safety regulations of the 1960s? Here is a striking way to frame the question: The regulations tend to *reduce* the number of driver deaths by making it easier to survive an accident. At the same time, the regulations tend to *increase* the number of driver deaths by encouraging reckless behavior. Which effect is the greater? Is the net effect of the regulations to decrease or to increase the number of driver deaths?

This question cannot be answered by pure logic. One must look at actual numbers. In the middle 1970s, Sam Peltzman of the University of Chicago did just that. He found that the two effects were of approximately equal size and therefore cancelled each other out. There were more accidents and fewer driver deaths per accident, but the total number of driver deaths remained essentially unchanged. An interesting side effect appears to have been an increase in the number of pedestrian deaths; pedestrians, after all, gain no benefit from padded dashboards.

I have discovered that when I tell noneconomists about Peltzman's results, they find it almost impossible to believe that people would drive less carefully simply because their cars are safer. Economists, who have learned to respect the principle that people respond to incentives, do not have this problem.

If you find it hard to believe that people drive less carefully when their cars are safer, consider the proposition that people drive *more* carefully when their cars are more dangerous. This is, of course, just another way of saying the same thing, but somehow people find it easier to believe. If the seat belts were removed from your car, wouldn't you be more cautious in driving? Carrying this observation to the extreme, Armen Alchian of the University of California at Los Angeles has suggested a way to bring about a major reduction in the accident rate: Require every car to have a spear mounted on the steering wheel, pointing directly at the driver's heart. Alchian confidently predicts that we would see a lot less tailgating.

It is in no sense foolhardy to take more risks when you have a padded dashboard. Driving recklessly has its costs, but it has its benefits too. You get where you are going faster, and you can often have a lot more fun along the way. "Recklessness" takes many forms: It can mean passing in dangerous situations, but it can also mean letting your mind wander, or temporarily diverting your attention from the road to look for a tape cassette. Any of these activities might make your trip more pleasant, and any of them might be well worth a slight increase in accident risk.

Occasionally people are tempted to respond that nothing— or at least none of the things I've listed—is worth any risk of death. Economists find this objection particularly frustrating, because neither those who raise it nor anybody else actually believes it. All people risk death every day for relatively trivial rewards. Driving to the drugstore to buy a newspaper involves a clear risk that could be avoided by staying home, but people still drive to drugstores. We need not ask whether small pleasures are worth *any* risk; the answer is obviously yes. The right question is how *much* risk those small pleasures are worth. It is perfectly rational to say, "I am willing to search for a cassette while driving if it leads to a one-in-a-million chance of death, but not if it leads to a one-in-a-thousand chance of death." That is why more people search for cassettes at 25 miles per hour than at 70.

Peltzman's observations reveal that driving behavior is remarkably sensitive to changes in the driver's environment. This affords an opportunity for some drivers to influence the behavior of others. Those ubiquitous Baby on Board signs provide an example. The signs are intended to signal other drivers that they should use extraordinary care. I know drivers who find these signs insulting because of the implication that they do not *already* drive as carefully as possible. Economists will be quite unsympathetic to this feeling, because they know that nobody *ever* drives as carefully as possible (do you have new brakes installed before each trip to the grocery store?) and because they know that most drivers' watchfulness does vary markedly with their surroundings. Virtually all drivers would be quite unhappy to injure the occupants of another car; many drivers would be especially unhappy if that other car contained a baby. That group *will* choose to drive more carefully when alerted to a baby's presence and *will* be glad to have that presence called to their attention.

This, incidentally, suggests an interesting research project. Economics suggests that many drivers are more cautious in the presence of a Baby on Board sign. The project is to find out how *much* more cautious by observing accident rates for cars with and without the signs. Unfortunately, accident rates can be misleading for at least three reasons. First, those parents who post signs are probably unusually cautious; they have fewer accidents just because they themselves are exceptionally careful drivers, independently of how their sign affects others. Second (and introducing a bias in the opposite direction), those parents who post signs know that the sign elicits caution from others, and they can therefore afford to be less vigilant themselves. This would tend to involve them in *more* accidents and at least partially cancel the effects of other drivers' extra care. Third, if Baby on Board signs really work, there is nothing to stop childless couples from posting them dishonestly. If drivers are aware of widespread deception, they will tend to suppress their natural responses.

This means that raw accident statistics cannot reveal how drivers respond to Baby on Board signs. The problem is to find a clever statistical technique to make all the necessary corrections. I do not propose to solve that problem here, but I offer it as an example of a typical difficulty that arises in empirical economic research. Many research projects in economics revolve around creative solutions to just such difficulties.

After this slight digression into the challenges of empirical research, let me return to my main topic: the power of incentives. It is the economist's second nature to account for that power. Will the invention of a better birth control technique reduce the number of unwanted pregnancies? Not necessarily—the invention reduces the "price" of sexual intercourse (unwanted pregnancies being a component of that price) and thereby induces people to engage in more of it. The percentage of sexual encounters that lead to pregnancy goes down, the number of sexual encounters goes up, and the number of unwanted pregnancies can go either down or up. Will energy-efficient cars reduce our consumption of gasoline? Not necessarily—an energy-efficient car reduces the price of driving, and people will choose to drive more. Low-tar cigarettes could lead to a higher incidence of lung cancer. Low-calorie synthetic fats could increase the average weight of Americans.

Criminal law is a critical area for understanding how people respond to incentives. To what extent do harsh punishments deter criminal activity? A case of particular interest is the death penalty. The deterrent effect of the death penalty has been studied intensely by innumerable government commissions and academic scholars. Often their studies consist of nothing more than examining murder rates in states with and without capital punishment laws. Economists tend to be harshly critical of these studies because they fail to account for other important factors that help to determine murder rates. (Often they fail even to account for how stringently the death penalty is enforced, although this varies appreciably from state to state.) On the other hand, the refined statistical techniques collectively known as *econometrics* are designed precisely to measure the power of incentives. This makes it natural to apply econometrics in examining the effect of the death penalty. The pioneer in this effort was Prof. Isaac Ehrlich of the University of Buffalo, whose work was published in 1975. His sophisticated analysis led to a striking conclusion: During the 1960s, on average, each execution that took place in America prevented approximately 8 murders.

The details of Ehrlich's methods have been widely criticized by other economists, but it is possible to make too much of this. Most of the criticisms involve esoteric questions of statistical technique. Such questions are important. But there is widespread agreement in the economics profession that the *sort* of empirical study that Ehrlich undertook is capable of revealing important truths about the effect of capital punishment.

In 1983, Prof. Edward Leamer of the University of California at Los Angeles published an amusing article called "Let's Take the Con Out of Econometrics," in which he warned that the prejudices of the researcher can substantially affect his results. Leamer used the death penalty as an example. He showed that a simple econometric test, with a prodeath penalty bias built in, could demonstrate that each execution prevents as many as 13 murders. The same test, with an antideath penalty bias built in, could demonstrate that each execution actually *causes* as many as 3 additional murders. Still, unless one goes very far in the direction of building in a bias against the death penalty, most econometric research reveals a substantial deterrent effect of capital punishment. Murderers respond to incentives.

How can this be? Are not many murders crimes of passion or acts of irrationality? Perhaps so. But there are two responses to this objection. First, Ehrlich's results indicate that each execution prevents 8 murders; it does not indicate *which* 8 murders are prevented. As long as some murderers can be deterred, capital punishment can be a deterrent. The second response is this: Why should we expect that people engaged in crimes of passion would fail to respond to incentives? We can imagine a man who hates his wife so much that under ordinary circumstances he would do her in if he thought he had a 90% chance of escaping execution. Perhaps in a moment of rage, he becomes so carried away that he will kill her even if he has only a 20% chance of escaping execution. Then even in the moment of rage, it matters very much whether he perceives his chances to be 15% or 25%.

(Let me mention a third response as well. Ehrlich did not just make up the number 8; he arrived at it through a sophisticated analysis of data. Skepticism is fine, but it is incumbent on the serious skeptic to examine the research with an open mind and to pinpoint what step in the reasoning, if any, he finds suspicious.)

There *is* evidence that people respond significantly to incentives even in situations where we do not usually imagine their behavior to be rational. Apparently psychologists have discovered by experiment that when you hand a person an unexpectedly hot cup of coffee, he typically drops the cup if he perceives it to be inexpensive but manages to hang on if he believes the cup is valuable.

Indeed, the response to incentives may be as innate as any other instinctive behavior. In a series of experiments at Texas A&M University, researchers have allowed rats and pigeons to "purchase" various forms of food and drink by pushing various levers. Each item has its price, such as three lever pushes for a drop of root beer or ten for a piece of cheese. The animals are given "incomes" equal to a certain number of pushes per day; after the income is exhausted the levers become inoperable. In some versions of the experiments the animals are able to earn additional income by performing various tasks. They earn additional lever pushes at a fixed wage rate for each task they perform.

The researchers have found that rats and pigeons respond appropriately to changes in prices, changes in income, and changes in wage rates. When the price of root beer goes up, they buy less root beer. When wage rates go up, they work harder—unless their incomes are already very high, in which case they choose to enjoy more leisure. These are precisely the responses that economists expect and observe among human beings.

Incentives matter. The literature of economics contains tens of thousands of empirical studies verifying this proposition, and not one that convincingly refutes it. Economists are forever testing the proposition (while perhaps secretly hoping to make names for themselves by being the first to overturn it) and forever expanding the domain of its applicability. Whereas we used to think only about shoppers responding to the price of meat, we now think about drivers responding to seat belts, murderers responding to the death penalty, and rats and pigeons responding to wage, income, and price changes. Economists have studied how people choose marriage partners, family sizes, and levels of religious activity and whether to engage in cannibalism. (This trend has gone so far that the *Journal of Political Economy* published a satirical article on the economics of toothbrushing, which "predicted" that people spend exactly half their waking hours brushing their teeth. "No sociological model," boasted the author, "can yield such a precise conclusion.") Through all the variations, one theme recurs: Incentives matter.

CHAPTER 2

RATIONAL RIDDLES

Why the Rolling Stones Sell Out

Economics begins with the assumption that all human behavior is rational. Of course, this assumption is not always literally true; most of us can think of exceptions within our immediate families.

But the literal truth of assumptions is never a prerequisite for scientific inquiry. Ask a physicist how long it would take a bowling ball to land if you dropped it from the roof of your house. He will happily assume that your house is located in a vacuum, and then proceed to calculate the right answer. Ask an engineer to predict the path of a billiard ball after it is struck at a certain angle. He will assume that there is no such thing as friction, and the accuracy of his prediction will give him no cause for regret. Ask an economist to predict the effects of a rise in the gasoline tax. He will assume that all people are rational and give you a pretty accurate response.

Assumptions are tested not by their literal truth but by the quality of their implications. By this standard, rationality has a pretty good track record. It implies that people respond to incentives, a proposition for which there is much good evidence. It implies that people will be willing to pay more for a 26-ounce box of cereal than for an 11-ounce box, that highly skilled workers will usually earn more than their unskilled counterparts, that people who love life will not jump off the Golden Gate Bridge, and that hungry babies will cry to announce their needs. All of these things are usually true.

When we assume that people are rational, we emphatically do *not* assume anything about their preferences. *De gustibus non*

10

est disputandum—there's no accounting for tastes—is one of the economist's slogans. There is an appalling population of otherwise literate adults who prefer the poetry of Rod McKuen to that of William Butler Yeats. We do not pronounce them irrational. Some McKuen lovers might purchase a volume of Yeats with no intention of reading it, because it looks nice on the coffee table or impresses their more sophisticated friends. We still do not pronounce them irrational. When we assert that people are rational, we assert only this: That by and large, a man who wants to read the poetry of Rod McKuen, and who does not care how his books look on the table, and who feels no urge to deceive his friends about his literary tastes, and who has no other good reason to buy the collected works of Yeats, will not go out and buy the collected works of Yeats. And most of the time, this is true.

Likewise, when a man pays a dollar for a lottery ticket that gives him one chance in ten million of winning $5 million, we see no evidence of irrationality. Neither do we see irrationality in his twin brother, who chooses not to play. People have different attitudes toward risk, and their behavior appropriately differs. If a lottery player chose to play for $5 million instead of $8 million in another lottery with identical odds but better prizes, *then* we would call him irrational. Our expectation is that such behavior is rare.

Still, much human behavior appears on the face of it to be irrational. When a celebrity endorses a product, sales increase even though the endorsement appears to convey no information about quality. Rock concerts predictably sell out weeks in advance, and would still sell out even if the promoters raised ticket prices, but the prices aren't raised. Sales of earthquake insurance increase following an earthquake, even though the probability of a *future* earthquake may be no different than it was before. People take time off to vote in presidential elections, even though there is no perceptible chance that one vote will affect the outcome.

How should we respond to such phenomena? One eminently sensible response is to say, "Well, people are often rational, but not always. Economics applies to some behavior, but not to all behavior. These are some of the exceptions."

An alternative response is to stubbornly maintain the fiction that all people are rational at all times, and to insist on finding rational explanations, no matter how outlandish, for all of this apparently irrational behavior.

We choose the latter course.

Why?

Imagine a physicist, well versed in the laws of gravity, which he believes to be excellent approximations to the ultimate truth. One day he encounters his first helium-filled balloon, a blatant challenge to the laws he knows so well. Two courses are open to him: He can say, "Well, the laws of gravity are usually true, but not always; here is one of the exceptions." Or he can say, "Let me see if there is any way to explain this strange phenomenon without abandoning the most basic principles of my science." If he takes the latter course, and if he is sufficiently clever, he will eventually discover the properties of objects that are lighter than air and recognize that their behavior is in perfect harmony with existing theories of gravity. In the process, he will not only learn about helium-filled balloons; he will also come to a deeper understanding of how gravity works.

Now it might very well be that there are real exceptions to the laws of gravity, and that our physicist will one day encounter one. If he insists on looking for a good explanation without abandoning his theories, he will fail. If there are enough such failures, new theories will eventually arise to supplant the existing ones. Nevertheless, the wise course of action, at least initially, is to see whether surprising facts can be reconciled with existing theories. The attempt itself is good mental exercise for the scientist, and there are sometimes surprising successes. Moreover, if we are too quick to abandon our most successful theories, we will soon be left with nothing at all.

So economists spend a lot of time challenging each other to find rational explanations for seemingly irrational behavior. When two or more economists meet for lunch, the chances are excellent that one of these riddles will come up for discussion. I've been at countless such lunches myself and have a few examples I'd like to share.

Rock concerts starring major attractions sell out long in advance. Everyone has seen news footage of teenagers camping out, sometimes for many days, to ensure their place in the ticket queue. If the promoter increased the ticket price, the queue might shrink, but there is no doubt that the concert would still be a sellout. So why doesn't he raise the price?

Over the past 15 years, I've probably participated in a couple of dozen heated attempts to resolve this question. The most common suggestion is that the long queues on the evening news are a form of free advertising, keeping the group in the public eye and prolonging its popularity. Promoters don't want to sacrifice the long-term value of this publicity for the short-term advantage of raising prices. I personally find this implausible. It seems to me that there is also valuable publicity to be had from letting it be known that you've sold out a concert hall at $100 a ticket. Why should long lines be better advertising than high prices?

Still, until very recently, I'd never heard a better suggestion. Last year, I finally did. It came from my friend Ken McLaughlin, and here it is: Teenage concertgoers tend to follow up by buying records, T-shirts, and other paraphernalia. Adults don't. Therefore the promoters want teenage audiences. The way to guarantee a teenage audience is to set low prices and watch the queues grow; adults won't camp out overnight to see the Rolling Stones.

This story rings true to me and provides a rational explanation of the promoters' behavior. Unfortunately, I think it fails to explain other similar phenomena: Hit Broadway shows seem to sell out predictably without prices being raised, as do blockbuster movies in their first week or two.* Can some variant of the same story work? I don't know.

Finding a theory like McLaughlin's is one goal of the game we play. There is also another goal. The unwritten rules specify that a theory must come packaged with a nontrivial prediction. In principle, the prediction could be used to test the theory. In this case, we predict low ticket prices and long queues for performers who sell a lot of records and T-shirts; high prices and short queues for those who don't. I do not know whether this prediction is borne out, but I am eager to learn.

My next riddle is about product endorsements. It isn't hard to understand why people might be more attracted to movies

---

*In the case of Broadway shows, it appears that prices are set in such a way that the best seats usually sell out before the cheaper ones do. Is this to prevent people from paying for cheap seats and then moving to unsold expensive ones?

that have been endorsed by Siskel and Ebert, whose careers depend on their reputations for accuracy. This explains why their comments are prominently featured in advertisements.

But it is also common to see products endorsed by celebrities who have no particular expertise, and who are obviously being paid for their testimony. Well-known actresses endorse health clubs; ex-politicians endorse luggage; in Massachusetts recently, a Nobel prize-winning economist endorsed automobile tires. People respond to these ads, and sales increase.

What useful information can there be in knowing that the manufacturer of your overnight bag paid a six-figure fee to feature a famous person in a television commercial? How can it be rational to choose your luggage on this basis?

Let me suggest an answer. A lot of people make luggage, and they pursue different formulas for success. Some go for the quick killing, turning out a cheap product and expecting to leave the market when its low quality becomes widely recognized. Others have a long-term strategy: Produce quality goods, let the market learn about them, and reap the eventual rewards. Those in the latter group want to be sure that consumers know who they are.

One way for a firm to accomplish this is to very publicly post a bond to guarantee its continued existence: It places $500,000 on account in a bank and is allowed to recover $100,000 per year for five years; but if the firm goes out of business in the interim, then the owners sacrifice the bond. Only the high-quality firms would be willing to post these bonds. The rational consumer would prefer to patronize those firms.

Hiring a celebrity to endorse your product is like posting a bond. The firm makes a substantial investment up front and reaps returns over a long period of time. A firm that expects to disappear in a year won't make such an investment. When I see a celebrity endorsement, I know that the firm has enough confidence in the quality of its product to expect to be around awhile.

This theory also makes a testable prediction: Celebrity endorsements will be more common for goods whose quality is not immediately apparent.

The same reasoning can be used to explain why bank buildings tend to have marble floors and Greek columns, particularly those that were built in the days before federal deposit insurance. Imagine a frontier con man who moves from town to town setting up banks and absconding with the money after a few months. Unlike the Wells Fargo Company, which plans to be in business permanently, he cannot afford to construct a magnificent building every place he goes. Other things being equal, rational townsfolk choose the bank with the nicer building— and a rational Wells Fargo company invests in a flamboyant display of its permanence.

This explains why banks have fancier architecture than grocery stores. It's a lot more important to know that your banker will be there next week than that your grocer will.

Here's an old favorite: Why are so many items sold for $2.99 and so few for $3.00? There is an enormous temptation to attribute this phenomenon to a mild form of irrationality in which consumers notice only the first digit of the price and are lulled into thinking that $2.99 is "about $2.00" instead of "about $3.00." In fact, this explanation seems so self-evident that even many economists believe it. For all I know, they could be right. Perhaps someday a careful analysis of such behavior will form the basis for a modified economics in which people are assumed to depart from rationality in certain systematic ways. But before we abandon the foundations of all our knowledge, it might be instructive to consider alternatives.

As it happens, there is at least one intriguing alternative available. The phenomenon of "99-cent pricing" seems to have first become common in the nineteenth century, shortly after the invention of the cash register. The cash register was a remarkable innovation; not only did it do simple arithmetic, it also kept a record of every sale. That's important if you think your employees might be stealing from you. You can examine the tape at the end of the day and know how much money should be in the drawer.

There is one small problem with cash registers: They don't actually record *every* sale; they record only those sales that are rung up. If a customer buys an item for $1 and hands the clerk a dollar bill, the clerk can neglect to record the sale, slip the bill in his pocket, and leave no one the wiser.

On the other hand, when a customer buys an item for 99 cents and hands the clerk a dollar bill, the clerk has to make change. This requires him to open the cash drawer, which he cannot do without ringing up the sale. Ninety-nine-cent pricing forces clerks to ring up sales and keeps them honest.

There are still some problems. Clerks could make change out of their own pockets or ring up the wrong numbers. But a customer waiting for change might notice either of these strange behaviors and alert the owner.

The real problem with this explanation is that it ignores the existence of sales taxes. In a state with a 7% sales tax, the difference between 99 cents and a dollar on the price tag is the difference between $1.06 and $1.07 on the checkout line; the likelihood of needing change is about the same either way. Might it be that in states with different sales taxes, prices differ by a penny or two so that the price at the register comes out uneven in every state? This, at least, is a testable prediction. Here is another: 99-cent pricing should be less common in stores where the owners work the cash register.

Much primitive agriculture shares a strange common feature. There are very few large plots of land; instead, each farmer owns several small plots scattered around the village. (This pattern was endemic in medieval England and exists today in parts of the Third World.) Historians have long debated the reasons for this scattering, which is believed to be the source of much inefficiency. Perhaps it arises from inheritance and marriage: At each generation, the family plot is subdivided among the heirs, so that plots become tiny; marriages then bring widely scattered plots into the same family. This explanation suffers because it seems to assume a form of irrationality: Why don't the villagers periodically exchange plots among themselves to consolidate their holdings?

Inevitably, this problem attracted the attention of the economist and historian Don McCloskey, whose instinct for constructing ingenious economic explanations is unsurpassed. Instead of asking, "What social institutions led to such irrational behavior?" McCloskey asked, "Why is this behavior rational?" Careful study led him to conclude that it is rational because it is a form of insurance. A farmer with one large plot is liable to be completely ruined in the event of a localized flood. By scattering his holdings, the farmer gives up some potential income in exchange for a guarantee that he will not be wiped out by a local disaster. This behavior is not even exotic. Every modern insured homeowner does the same thing.

One way to test McCloskey's theory is to ask whether the insurance "premiums" (that is, the amount of production that is sacrificed by scattering) are commensurate with the amount of protection being "purchased," using as a yardstick the premiums that people are willing to pay in more conventional insurance markets. By this standard, it holds up well.

On the other hand, a very serious criticism is this: If medieval peasants wanted insurance, then why didn't they buy and sell insurance policies, just as we do today? My own feeling is that this is like asking why they didn't keep their business records on personal computers. The answer is simply that nobody had yet figured out how to do it. Designing an insurance policy requires at least a minor act of genius, just like designing a computer. But there are those, more exacting than I, who think that McCloskey's theory will not be complete until this objection is answered. And they are absolutely right in demanding that we try to answer it. Theories should be tested to their limits.

There are a lot of riddles. Why does the business world reward good dressers to such an extent that there are best-selling books on how to "dress for success"? I suspect that fashionable and attractive dressing is a skill that those of us who incline toward jeans and T-shirts tend to underrate. The good dresser must be innovative without transcending the limits set by fashion; knowing the limits requires alertness and an eye for evolving patterns. These traits are valuable in many contexts, and it can be rational for firms to seek employees who exhibit evidence of them.

Why do men spend less on medical care than women do? Possibly because men are more likely than women to die violent deaths. The value of protecting yourself against cancer is diminished if you have a high probability of being hit by a truck. It is therefore rational for men to purchase less preventive care than women.

When two people share a hotel room in Britain, they often pay twice the single-room rate; in the United States they usually pay much less than that. What accounts for the difference?

A noneconomist might be satisfied with an answer based on tradition. The economist wants to know why this pricing structure is rational and profit-maximizing. If any reader has a suggestion, I'd be pleased to hear it.

Perhaps that same reader can tell me why people choose to bet on the same sports teams that they feel fond of. By betting against the team you like, you could guarantee yourself a partially good outcome no matter how the game turns out. In other areas of life we choose to hedge, but in sports betting we put all our eggs in one basket. What explains the difference?

Economists are mystified by a lot of behavior that others take for granted. I have no idea why people vote. One hundred million Americans cast votes for president in 1992. I wager that not one of those hundred million was naive enough to believe that he was casting the decisive vote in an otherwise tied election. It is fashionable to cite John F. Kennedy's razor-thin 300,000-vote margin over Richard M. Nixon in 1960, but 300,000 is not the same as 1—even by the standards of precision that are conventional in economics. It is equally fashionable to cite the observation that "if everyone else thought that way and stayed home, then my vote would be important," which is as true and as irrelevant as the observation that if voting booths were spaceships, voters could travel to the moon. Everyone else does *not* stay home. The only choice that an individual voter faces is whether or not to vote, *given* that tens of millions of others are voting. At the risk of shocking your ninth-grade civics teacher, I am prepared to offer you an absolute guarantee that if you stay home in 1996, your indolence will not affect the outcome. So why do people vote? I don't know.*

I am not sure why people give each other store-bought gifts instead of cash, which is never the wrong size or color. Some say that we give gifts because it shows that we took the time to shop. But we could accomplish the same thing by giving the

---

*André Weil, one of this century's greatest mathematicians, has written, "I could not count the times (for example, when I tell people I never vote in elections) that I have heard the objection: 'But if everyone were to behave like you . . .'—to which I usually reply that this possibility seems to me so implausible that I do not feel obligated to take it into account." The quotation is from Weil's autobiography, *The Apprenticeship of a Mathematician* (Birkhauser, 1992).

cash value of our shopping time, showing that we took the time to earn the money.

My friend David Friedman suggests that we give gifts for exactly the opposite reason—because we want to announce that we did *not* take much time to shop. If I really care for you, I probably know enough about your tastes to have an easy time finding the right gift. If I care less about you, finding the right gift becomes a major chore. Because you know that my shopping time is limited, the fact that I was able to find something appropriate reveals that I care. I like this theory.

I do not know why people leave anonymous tips in restaurants, and the fact that I leave them myself in no way alleviates my sense of mystery.

When we raise questions about activities like voting or gift giving or anonymous tipping, it is never our intention to be critical of them. Quite the opposite: Our working assumption is that whatever people do, they have excellent reasons for doing. If we as economists can't see their reasons, then it is we who have a new riddle to solve.

CHAPTER 3

TRUTH OR CONSEQUENCES

How to Split a Check or Choose a Movie

Thank goodness for smoking; it can help to keep insurance rates down.

There are two types of people in this world. Actually, there are as many types of people in this world as there are people in this world, but let me simplify to make a point. There are the cautious and the reckless. The cautious exercise at health clubs, drink in moderation, drive defensively, and never, ever smoke. The reckless are overweight, keep late hours, ride motorcycles, and smoke a great deal.

If everybody paid the same insurance rates, the cautious would be forced to subsidize the immoderation of their reckless neighbors. But if insurance companies can set premiums separately for each type of customer, then the reckless bear the full costs of their life-style. The trick for the company is to determine who is who.

Smoking habits are a quick and easy indicator of general health consciousness. They reveal your type in a publicly observable way. Insurance companies use that information by offering lower premiums to nonsmokers. If you take advantage of such an offer, your discount reflects more than just the health benefits of not smoking. It reflects also that, as a nonsmoker, you are more likely than average to be watching your cholesterol.

Insurance companies know that people cheat, and they account for that when they set the nonsmoking premiums. If you are truly a nonsmoker, you pay a little more because some "nonsmokers" are sneaking cigarettes where the insurance company can't see them. But do not jump to the conclusion that if cigarettes were banned, your insurance rates would fall. As a *voluntary* nonsmoker, you implicitly notify your insurance company that you are probably cautious in a lot of ways they can't observe. As a nonsmoker in a world without cigarettes, you might be indistinguishable from everybody else, and be charged accordingly.

Take away cigarettes and you could deprive the company of its only basis for sorting its customers. Everybody would be treated equally. You would no longer pay for the extra medical bills that smokers generate, but you would also no longer get credit for your generally prudent behavior.

Advocates of mandatory helmet laws for motorcyclists argue that a rider without a helmet raises everyone's insurance premiums. The opposite might very well be true. Those who choose helmets reveal a general safety consciousness that helps to keep their premiums down. Mandatory helmets deprive safe drivers of a mechanism for advertising their character.

If the insurance company can offer discount rates to helmeted riders, those rates account not just for the safety characteristics of the helmet itself but for additional safety characteristics of the sort of rider who is likely to choose a helmet—a disinclination to weave in and out of traffic or to drive under the influence of alcohol. If all riders are helmeted by law, premiums continue to account for the benefits of the helmet but not for the rider's cautious personality. When helmets become mandatory, the careful rider's premiums are liable to rise.

Insurance markets are odd, because the buyer almost invariably has better information than the seller. If you wire your den with extension cords and cover them with paneling, you know exactly what you've done, but your insurance agent does not. He is left to wonder why you suddenly want to triple your fire insurance. Asymmetric information typically yields surprising outcomes, driven by one party's efforts to guess what the other party knows.

In some cases, asymmetric information threatens to drive insurance markets entirely out of existence. Rank policyholders' risk levels from 1 to 10, with 5 being the average. If the insurance company sets rates that reflect that average risk level, the 1s, 2s, and 3s might feel overcharged and drop out of the market.

Now the average risk level is no longer 5 but 7. The company raises rates to compensate, which causes the 4s and 5s to drop out, which raises the average risk level to 8, which necessitates yet another rate increase. The vicious cycle can continue until everyone is uninsured.

If the insurance company could observe individual risk levels, it would charge each policyholder an appropriate premium and the problem would disappear. If policyholders could *not* observe their *own* risk levels, the 1s, 2s and 3s would not drop out of the market and again the problem would disappear. It is the *asymmetry* of the situation—policyholders knowing more about themselves than the insurance company knows—that can break down the market.

To make matters still worse, people are likely to take on additional risks just *because* they are insured. Insured homeowners forgo security systems and insured drivers drive faster. In the presence of full information, insurance companies could prohibit such behavior and discontinue coverage for the disobedient. Because insurers are not omniscient, they explore alternatives.

One alternative is for the insurance company to help its customers avoid risk. Your car insurance company might be willing to subsidize your purchase of an antitheft device; your health insurance company will undoubtedly provide you with free information on the benefits of diet and exercise; your fire insurance company can give you a free fire extinguisher. But there are limits to what can be accomplished. If you weren't inclined to buy a fire extinguisher to begin with, and if you get one for free from your insurance company, it might turn up at a garage sale.

Employers typically have less than perfect information about what their employees are up to. This makes it hard to get incentives right. You can't reward productivity that you can't observe.

Labor markets abound with mechanisms designed to address the incentive problem. The university where I teach "gives" me an office but does not allow me to sell that office to the highest bidder. In many cases, that rule is inefficient. I have colleagues who do all of their work at home and in the library, and would gladly accept lower salaries in exchange for the right to convert their offices to Dairy Queens (or, if Dairy Queens are disallowed because of their boisterous clientele, then travel agencies). The university would save money and productivity would not suffer. Presumably that outcome would be agreeable all around except for one little hitch. Even the professoriat harbors unscrupulous individuals, and some of those who *do* use their offices effectively would be willing to sacrifice some productivity in exchange for the right profit opportunity. If the university could identify and punish productivity declines, then the problem would vanish. In reality, information is asymmetric—*we* know whether we're producing, but we don't always tell the dean—so we end up accepting an imperfect rule.

Many firms provide their employees with more health coverage than is required by law, essentially giving an extra $500 worth of medical insurance instead of an extra $500 in wages. At first this seems mysterious: Why not give employees the cash and let them spend it as they want? A partial answer—and perhaps the entire answer—is that employees prefer nontaxable benefits to taxable wages. But another possible answer is that good health care enhances productivity. If productivity were easily observed and rewarded, there would be no issue here, because employees would have ample incentives on their own to acquire adequate health care. But in a world of imperfect information, employee benefit packages can be the best way to enforce good behavior.

If you are employed by the General Motors Corporation, it is not unlikely that sooner or later you will discover something that can save the corporation $100. If that something requires a little effort on your part, and if that effort is invisible to your supervisor, you might choose to let it slide.

The corporation wants your incentives to be right and seeks appropriate mechanisms. One mechanism is profit sharing among employees. But in a corporation with half a million employees, profit sharing is not a very good incentive. If employees share equally in 100% of the company's profits, your $100 contribution adds only about $\frac{1}{50}$ of a cent to your own income. Unless GM can observe its employees perfectly, only one mechanism gets the incentives exactly right: Each employee receives as his annual salary 100% of the corporate profits. If GM's profits are $1 billion this year, then *everybody*—from the chairman of the board down to the night janitor—earns exactly $1 billion. Now each dollar that you save the company is a dollar in your own pocket. You have just the right incentive to take every cost-justified measure to improve corporate productivity.

One tiny problem with this scheme is that if there is more than one employee, the books don't balance. A single billion in profits does not suffice to pay a billion each to 500,000 workers. But that's easy to handle. At the beginning of the year, each worker *purchases* his job by putting a large sum of money into a fund that is earmarked to make up the difference between the company's profits and its wage obligations. The price of a job can be set so that the books balance in an average year. Over time, the revenue from job sales just covers the discrepancy between profits and wages.

This arrangement is the ideal solution to a very substantial problem, yet it strikes everybody who hears about it as completely ludicrous. What is less clear is *why* it strikes us as ludicrous. The fact that no major corporation has implemented such an arrangement is good evidence that it is unworkable. But that is hardly enough reason to stop thinking about it. If we are to design better mechanisms in the future, we should pause to ask just where this one went wrong.

The most obvious answers are wholly inadequate. The usual first objection comes in the form of a question: "Where is an assembly-line worker going to come by $1 billion to buy his job?" The response is that he is going to borrow it. The counter-response is that he is unlikely to have access to quite that good a line of credit.

At first glance the counterresponse seems devastating, but on closer inspection it is completely insubstantial. If workers cannot borrow enough to finance the program in its entirety, they can at least borrow enough to finance a fraction of it. If GM can't sell you your job for $1 billion and give you the entire company profits at the end of the year, it can at least sell you your job for a *fraction* of $1 billion and give you the same *fraction* of the company profits at the end of the year. This is a poor approximation to the ideal, but it's better than no approximation at all.

If your theory is that the program is derailed by borrowing constraints, then your theory predicts that workers would be enrolled in a partial program that expands until every worker has borrowed every cent that he possibly can. But most workers have *not* borrowed every cent they possibly can. Your prediction is wrong, so your theory is wrong also.

Here is a another difficulty, less obvious but also harder to dismiss: The buy-your-job program gets the incentives just right for workers but gets them exactly wrong for stockholders. Once the workers have bought their jobs, stockholders root for financial disaster. Every dollar of earnings generates $500,000 in wage obligations. If the company earns nothing, no wages need be paid.

Insofar as stockholders can influence corporate decision making, the consequences of this incentive structure are plainly disastrous. Nobody would be willing to buy a job at a firm where wages depend on profits and managers are doing everything possible to keep profits low. Conceivably, this problem could be averted by a novel corporate structure that prevented stockholders from participating in any management decisions at any level. But the incentive would remain for unscrupulous stockholders to approach key workers and bribe them to work mischief in the plants.

There is a moral here. The system that you construct to solve one problem can be the source of another. It is true that stockholders cannot completely observe the behavior of workers but equally true that workers cannot completely observe the behavior of stockholders. When information is distributed unequally, we need to watch for unexpected consequences.

The buy-a-job program has a nice parallel in the form of a riddle. Ten people go out to eat at a restaurant that refuses to issue separate checks. Desserts are expensive, and nobody considers them worth the price. Unfortunately, each diner reasons separately that if he orders dessert he'll pay for only a tenth of it, and each diner orders dessert on that basis. Everybody gets dessert, so everybody pays for shares of ten desserts. The cost to each diner is equal to the high price that he was initially unwilling to pay. How can this tragic outcome be avoided?

The solution is for each diner to pay the entire bill. Now ordering a $10 dessert increases your share not by $1 but by $10, and you don't order unless you're really willing to pay that much. The restaurant, of course, earns an enormous profit by collecting the bill ten times over. Therefore, the manager pays you to come to the restaurant in the first place. The bribe to enter is set so that on average it just exhausts the excess profits. (If it didn't just exhaust the excess profits, competing restaurants would offer better deals.)

A perfect solution? Almost, but not quite. As one of your party returns from the rest room, the manager quietly steers him aside and offers him $20 to order dessert.

Why are executive salaries so high? Why do stockholders approve annual salaries in the vicinity of $40 million for some of the highest-paid corporate officers?

Harvard economists Michael Jensen and Kevin Murphy recently examined this issue and were led to reformulate the question to something more along the lines of "Why are executive salaries so *low?*" More precisely, Jensen and Murphy found evidence that executive salaries are tied only very loosely to corporate performance, so that on average an executive who saves the company $1,000 receives only a $3.25 reward. Their research, reported in an unusually broad spectrum of publications ranging from the abstruse *Journal of Political Economy* through the *Harvard Business Review* and *Forbes,* concludes that performance incentives are woefully inadequate and that much of the problem can be traced to insufficient upward flexibility in executive wages.* They have argued that stockholders might be far better off paying salaries that were higher on average but more closely tied to accomplishments. Rewards and punishments should both be greater.

It seems to me that on this issue two outstanding economists have lost their economic bearings. The Jensen-Murphy theory is that by not tying compensation more closely to performance, stockholders are making a bad mistake.† Even in a world where people make bad mistakes constantly, no economist should ever be satisfied with a theory that something happened because

---

*In real terms, executive salaries today are lower than they were in the 1930s.

†As a vague alternative to a pure "mistake theory," Jensen and Murphy have suggested that exterior political considerations might constrain stockholders' flexibility, but they have not revealed anything about the exact nature of these constraints.

somebody erred. The game is to *assume* that human behavior serves human purposes and to attempt to divine what those purposes might be.

To the stockholder, the executive is just another employee, and like any employee he must be prodded to perform. One area where a little extra prodding might be called for is in the area of risk taking. Stockholders are generally favorable to risky projects with high potential rewards. The reason for this is that stockholders are usually well diversified. If the project fails, your stock could become worthless, but that is a risk you might be willing to take if that stock represents only a small fraction of your entire portfolio.

Executives, by contrast, typically have large parts of their careers riding on the fortunes of a particular company and accordingly tread gingerly when risky projects come their way. From the stockholder's viewpoint, this is bad behavior and should be discouraged. The most direct form of discouragement is to monitor the executive's behavior and punish excessive caution. But if the stockholders were going to monitor every executive decision, they wouldn't need to hire an executive. In practice, stockholders don't have enough information to enforce their preferences directly.

This observation might go a long way toward explaining the uncoupling of rewards from performance. When the president of IBM undertakes a project to develop an inflatable full-sized computer that can be folded and carried in a shirt pocket, and when the project fails and loses millions, stockholders are unable to distinguish between two theories. One theory is that the idea was asinine from the outset. The other is that the project was a sensible risk that happened to fail. Because the first theory might be correct, they want to fire the president. Because the second might be correct, they don't want to punish him too severely—that would send the wrong message to future presidents. So failed corporate officers are retired with enormous pensions. That practice is often derided in the popular press as a simple failure of common sense, but the economist's insistence on looking for method within apparent madness yields more insight than the journalist's resort to ridiculing that which he cannot immediately understand.

The tension regarding risky projects might also help to answer my earlier question: Why are executive salaries so high? Remember that stockholders want executives to take more risks. One way to encourage a person to take risks is to make him wealthy. Other things being equal, multimillionaires are a lot mellower about losing their jobs than people who are worried about how to put their children through college. If you want your corporate president to be receptive to the inflatable computer project, you need to encourage that kind of mellowness. A high salary helps a lot in that direction.

The general level of executive salaries is as much a topic of journalistic scorn as the "inadequate" punishment of failed executives. I am appalled by the anti-intellectualism that underlies such scorn. All that separates us from the beasts is our ability to wonder *why* things are as they are. In the realm of economics, the answer to *why* often begins with the observation that information is asymmetrically distributed. The executive knows his own basis for making decisions, but stockholders can only guess. They are forced to mold his behavior through imperfect incentives. There are good reasons to think that a high salary, through its encouragement of risk taking, is a component of the optimal incentive scheme. This is hardly a complete analysis of the problem, but it is an indication that analysis is *possible,* and worth pursuing.

There is a class of logic puzzles where the speaker visits an island populated entirely by liars and truth tellers. Liars always lie and truth tellers always tell the truth. Unfortunately, the two are indistinguishable. The problem is usually to draw some inference from the utterances of various islanders or to formulate a question that will elicit some hidden information. The simplest problem is: When you meet an islander, what single question enables you to identify whether he is a liar? "Are you a liar?" doesn't work, because truth tellers and liars both answer "No." A common solution is to ask, "How much is two plus two?"

I tried this problem the other day on my four-year-old daughter. Her solution was to say, "I won't be your friend if you don't tell me the truth." I concluded that she was too young for logic puzzles.

When the person you are dealing with knows more than you do, there are two general approaches to mitigating your disadvantage. One is to design mechanisms that elicit appropriate *behavior.* The other is to design mechanisms that elicit the *information itself.* In recent years, economists have discovered that, contrary to all intuition, there are a fantastic number of mechanisms that can often induce people to reveal everything they know.

In Joseph Conrad's novel *Typhoon,* a number of sailors store gold coins in private boxes kept in the ship's safe. The ship hits stormy weather, the boxes break open, and the coins are hopelessly mixed. Each sailor knows how many coins he started with, but nobody knows what anybody *else* started with. The captain's problem is to return the correct number of coins to each sailor.

Does the problem seem intractable? Here is a simple solution. Have each sailor write down the number of coins he is entitled to. Collect the papers and distribute the coins. Announce in advance that if the numbers on the papers don't add up to the correct total, you will throw all of the coins overboard.

That solution is a simple manifestation of an elaborate theory whose slogan might be "truth is accessible." In this instance the captain had a key piece of information—he knew the total number of coins. It turns out that even when a decision maker has *no information at all* he can frequently design a mechanism that elicits absolute truth from all concerned.

Last night my wife and I could not decide which movie to see. She leaned toward *Cries and Whispers* and I to *Sorority Babes in the Slimeball Bowl-o-rama.* We agreed that the person with the stronger preference—expressed in dollar terms—should prevail. The problem was to determine whose preference was the stronger. The problem was compounded because we were both perfectly willing to lie to get our way.

Here is what we did. We each wrote our bid on a piece of paper. The high bidder got to choose the movie but was required to make a charitable contribution equal to the *loser's* bid.

It was worth exactly $8 to me to get my way. Because winning meant paying the amount of my wife's bid, I hoped that I would win if my wife bid less than $8 and that I would lose if she bid more. I was able to insure this outcome by bidding exactly $8. In other words, my own purely selfish motives led me to make an honest revelation. My wife did the same, and the person with the stronger preference won.

This worked so well that we are planning to use it regularly. Rather than make charitable contributions, however, we are going to make our payments to an economist couple we know. They are going to do the same, making their payments to us. On average, over time, we expect that the payments in one direction will be about as great as those in the other, so that nobody stands to lose financially from our arrangement.

An economist is somebody who thinks it is worth wondering why everyone doesn't choose movies in exactly this way.

CHAPTER 4

THE INDIFFERENCE PRINCIPLE

Who Cares If the Air Is Clean?

Would you rather live in San Francisco or in Lincoln, Nebraska? San Francisco offers extraordinary shopping districts, world-class museums, a temperate climate, and Golden Gate Park. Lincoln offers magnificent old houses that can be had for the price of a San Francisco studio apartment. You can have the world's finest seafood or you can have wall space.

Each year, the *Places Rated Almanac* and *The Book of American City Rankings* issue their reports on the best places to live in America. San Francisco gets credit for its cosmopolitan charms and Lincoln gets credit for the allure of its housing market. Weighing the importance of education, climate, highways, bus systems, safety, and recreation, researchers rank cities in order of overall desirability. The implicit assumption is that the researchers have identified features that most people care about, and that we all pretty much agree about their relative importance.

If that assumption is correct, and if your tastes are not atypical, you can save yourself the expense of purchasing the manuals. When all factors are accounted for, all inhabited cities must be equally attractive. If they weren't, nobody would live in any but the best.

If San Francisco is better than Lincoln, Lincolnites move to San Francisco. Their exodus bids up housing prices in San Francisco, bids down housing prices in Lincoln, and thereby magnifies Lincoln's relative advantages. Before long, either the two cities become equally attractive or Lincoln becomes completely deserted.

Call it the *Indifference Principle.* Except when people have unusual tastes or unusual talents, all activities must be equally
desirable. In Woody Allen's *Radio Days,* a character with no
particular skills contemplates a career engraving gold jewelry,
anticipating great wealth because he plans to hoard the shav-
ings. But in the absence of unusual tastes or talents, no career
can be more attractive than another. If gold engravers led better
lives than street sweepers, street sweepers would become gold
engravers, driving down wages and working conditions until
both occupations were equally attractive.

I took my family to an outdoor Renaissance Fair on a rainy
day. It was crowded, but less crowded than usual. Was the rain
a curse or a blessing? Actually, it was neither. There are a lot of
indoor activities in the area, and the crowd size always adjusts
so that a day at the fair is exactly as much fun as a day at, say,
the shopping mall. The rain doesn't make the mall any better
or worse, so it can't make the fair any better or worse either.

Sex scandals have become a routine feature of the modern presidential campaign. Even candidates who have not yet
been publicly humiliated must suffer sleepless nights wondering which details of their own private lives will remain private.
Commentators argue, plausibly but incorrectly, that this development is damaging to the candidates. They overlook the
fact that *something* has to make potential candidates indifferent
about whether to run for the presidency. Without sex scandals,
more candidates would enter, to the detriment of those who
are already in the race. Entry would continue until being in
and being out of the race are equally attractive, just as they are
today.*

Chicago Tribune columnist Bob Greene has reported on the
activities of the Brotherhood for the Respect, Elevation, and
Advancement of Dishwashers, which encourages restaurant patrons to deviate from tradition and tip the busboy. If the organization succeeds in changing public attitudes, who benefits? The
answer is certainly not "busboys." Busboys can never be happier than janitors, and janitors' fortunes do not change. When
busboys start collecting tips, janitors start becoming busboys.

---

*The argument fails to apply to candidates who are extraordinary in some
relevant dimension, such as having unusually much or unusually little to hide.

Wages respond and busboys' paychecks shrink. The janitors keep coming until everything the busboy gains at the restaurant table is lost at the payroll office.

Well, then, who benefits? If busboys' wages fall, you might guess that the big winner is the owner of the restaurant. But that can't be right either, because restaurant owners can never be happier than shoe store owners, and shoe store owners' fortunes do not change. When busboys' wages fall and restaurant profits increase, shoe stores start converting to restaurants. Menu prices fall and profits shrink. The shoe store owners keep coming until everything the owner saves in busboys' wages is lost at the cash register.

If each diner leaves a $5 tip for the busboy, then busboys' wages must fall by $5 per meal and then the price of a meal must fall by $5. If it fell by less, restaurant owners would be ahead of the game, and that isn't possible as long as there are shoe stores waiting in the wings to become restaurants. So who benefits? Nobody. Diners' tips are returned to them in the form of lower menu prices. Nobody's wealth has changed. Diners might genuinely want to be generous to busboys, but the Indifference Principle intervenes.

Only the owner of a resource in fixed supply can avoid the consequences of the Indifference Principle. An increased demand for actors cannot benefit actors, because new entrants are drawn to the profession. But an increased demand for Clint Eastwood *can* benefit Clint Eastwood, because Clint Eastwood is a fixed resource: There is only one of him. As Clint's earnings reach several million dollars per movie, starving actors strive to emulate his features, but their best efforts are imperfect. When scientists develop the ability to convert one person to a carbon copy of another, there will be just enough Clint Eastwood clones to make being Clint Eastwood a matter of indifference.

The Indifference Principle guarantees that *all economic gains accrue to the owners of fixed resources.* The odd fair goer who likes getting wet—or doesn't mind it as much as most people do— can benefit from rainy weather. His unusual preference is a fixed resource. The busboy whose atypically pleasant personality generates more than the ordinary level of tipping can benefit from a change in tipping customs. His personality is a fixed resource.

If *many* potential busboys had the same personality, it would generate no economic reward.

In 1990, President Bush signed into law a sweeping new Clean Air Act, which was expected to cost businesses (that is, owners, suppliers, employees, and customers) approximately $25 billion per year. If that estimate is correct, the cost to the average American family of four is about $400 per year in the form of lower profits, lower wages, and higher prices for consumer goods. On the other hand, clean air is a great benefit, which uncritical observers expected would be shared by everyone who breathes, which is to say everyone. But the ability to breathe is not a fixed resource. Universal skills do not ordinarily reap great rewards.

If breathers do not benefit from clean air, then who does? Theory tells us to look for the owners of fixed resources. The most obvious candidates are urban landowners, who are able to charge higher rents after the smog lifts.

The Clean Air Act of 1990 is a fantastically complicated piece of legislation imposed on a fantastically complicated economy, and to trace every one of its effects in detail would be a fantastically complicated task. But as Aesop discovered some time ago, the details of reality can disguise essential truths that are best revealed through simple fictions. Aesop called them fables and economists call them models. Let me share one.

FABLE 1: A TALE OF TWO CITIES

Somewhere in the heart of the Rust Belt are two small cities: Cleanstown and Grimyville. All of the activities of daily life—shopping, working, going to the park—are equally pleasant in both cities, with one exception: breathing. The Grimyville Steel Company accounts for that. No Grimyvillian ever wakes up and fills his lungs with the crisp morning air that Cleanstowners take for granted. Not only do the residents of Grimyville find breathing relatively unpleasant; they also do less of it. Life expectancy is ten years lower in Grimyville than in Cleanstown.

Why would anyone live in Grimyville? For one reason: it's cheaper. A house that rents for $10,000 a year in Cleanstown can be had for $5,000 in Grimyville. That $5,000 difference is just enough to keep folks in Grimyville. If it weren't, people would leave Grimyville and rents would fall even further. Young people deciding where to settle are indifferent between the two towns. They like the atmosphere in Cleanstown, but they like the housing prices in Grimyville.

Last week, the Grimyville Council passed a Clean Air Act that requires Grimyville Steel to adopt extensive antipollution measures. Soon the air in Grimyville will be as pure as the purest air in Cleanstown. And when that happens, the rents in Grimyville will rise to Cleanstown levels.

Eventually renters in Grimyville will be living in a clone of Cleanstown. Is this an improvement for them? Evidently not, because if they'd wanted to live in Cleanstown, they could have moved there long ago.

Those young people deciding where to settle gain nothing from the Clean Air Act. Earlier they had a choice between Cleanstown and Grimyville, and they were indifferent. Now they have a choice between two Cleanstowns. They're no worse off than they were before, but no better off either.

The only people who stand to gain from this entire affair are the property owners of Grimyville, who can now command higher rents than they did before. The Clean Air Act is equivalent to a tax on Grimyville Steel with the proceeds distributed entirely to Grimyville landowners.

The conclusion is stark, but, to be fair, the discussion is oversimplified. When we say that people are indifferent between Cleanstown and Grimyville, we implicitly assume that everyone shares identical circumstances. In actuality, the world is more complicated. There might be people with special reasons to want to live in Grimyville, and among those there might be some who consider cleaner air in exchange for higher rents a bargain. Such people win when the Clean Air Act is passed. On the other hand, there could equally well be others who considered the old Grimyville a bargain, because they are less disturbed by pollution than their neighbors are. Those people are net losers when Grimyville turns into Cleanstown. An unusual preference is a fixed resource, which renders its owner liable to share in economic gains *and* losses.

So if there are important differences among nonlandowners, then the Clean Air Act affects some of them positively and some negatively, with no clear presumption about which effects dominate. On the other hand, if the Grimyville Press was right when it editorialized that "clean air is something whose value we can all appreciate equally," then only landowners stand to gain. If clean air is worth $5,000 a year to everyone, then clean air legislation raises rents by $5,000 a year, making no net difference to anyone but the landlord.

The Grimyville Clean Air Act is expected to cost $10 million per year. It is an invisible tax, and to a first approximation the proceeds are distributed entirely to the landowners of Grimyville. Of course, it is a strange kind of tax, because the proceeds available for distribution need not be related in any direct way to the revenues collected. Land rents could rise by either more or less than $10 million.

It seems an odd public policy objective to enrich those people who happen to own property in polluted areas, but in view of the nearly universal enthusiasm for clean air legislation, I will take it as given. Then if Grimyville land rents rise by more than $10 million, the council has performed admirably. But if rents rise by only, say, $8 million, then the council has passed up an opportunity to do better. Instead of passing clean air legislation, they could simply confiscate $9 million a year from Grimyville Steel and give it to the landlords. This policy would be cheaper for the steel company, better for the landlords, and a matter of indifference to everybody else, who neither gains nor loses from clean air legislation anyway. It would also have the advantages of directness and honesty: Nobody would be able to claim that this special interest legislation serves the general public or a noble cause. And that would be a real breath of fresh air.

Grimyville landlords capture all the benefits of clean air legislation because their land is the only fixed resource. The fixity of land renders its owners unusually susceptible to changes in the economic environment and gives landowners an unusually strong incentive to lobby for favorable changes.

Throughout the world, farmers have managed to appropriate disproportionate shares of government largesse. In the United States, farmers are routinely paid to leave land uncultivated, whereas nobody would think of paying motel operators to leave rooms vacant. That's a riddle: Why the asymmetry? Some say that farmers have successfully capitalized on the romance of the family farm. But is the family farm inherently so much more romantic than the mom-and-pop grocery store? Why do we subsidize the vanishing life-style of the small farmer while allowing the corner grocery to fade into the mists of nostalgia?

The Indifference Principle suggests an answer. Motel owners and grocers don't bother mounting the kind of lobbying effort that farmers do because they are well aware that they stand to gain very little from government subsidies. If motels were paid to keep rooms vacant, room rates might rise initially but new motels would soon appear in response. Before long, the motel industry would be no more profitable than it ever was. Motels are not a fixed resource. But if there is a fixed quantity of farm-land, then new farms cannot arise to take advantage of farm subsidies. Farmers *can* gain from a change in economic conditions, and it is worth their while to work toward the changes they prefer.

My goal is to make an argument with three steps, and I have made two of them. First is the Indifference Principle: When one activity is preferred to another, people switch to it until it stops being preferred (or until everyone has switched, if that happens first). Second is its corollary: Only fixed resources generate economic gains. In the absence of fixed resources, the Indifference Principle guarantees that all gains are competed away.

The final step is a corollary to the corollary and the moral of my next fable: *When a fixed resource is not owned by anyone, economic gains are discarded.* If nobody owns the only source of benefit, then there can be no benefit.

FABLE 2: THE SPRINGFIELD AQUARIUM

The town of Springfield is blessed with a magnificent city park where townspeople spend their weekends picnicking, hiking, and playing softball. Although the park is popular—almost the entire population can be found there on a nice Saturday afternoon—it is large and never crowded.

Unfortunately, there is not much to do in Springfield, and although people enjoy the park, there's always been talk about the need for some variety. A few years ago, the City Council responded to popular demand by authorizing the construction of a municipal aquarium, funded by tax dollars and open to the public free of charge.

The Springfield Aquarium has been open for several months now, and it is truly a first-class establishment. The exhibits are beautiful, entertaining, and informative. The aquarium's only drawback is that it is always crowded.

There is not much diversity in Springfield. Everybody has pretty much the same preferences and the same opportunities in life. So if we want to understand how the aquarium affects Springfield, we can concentrate on how it affects a typical Springfield family.

The Simpsons are a typical Springfield family. On a recent Saturday, Homer Simpson suggested that the aquarium would be a welcome change from the family's usual weekend picnic. His son Bart, however, was quick to remind Homer that a visit to the aquarium meant a long and unpleasant wait to get in. After some negotiation, the family agreed to drive by the aquarium and see how long the line was. If the waiting time to get in was fewer than 45 minutes, they would stay at the aquarium; if it was more than 45 minutes, they would go on to the park.

The Simpsons, unschooled in economic theory, failed to reckon on the Indifference Principle. All over Springfield, families just like the Simpsons were willing to wait up to 45 minutes in the aquarium line. Whenever the wait grew slightly shorter, new families entered the line. Whenever it grew slightly longer owing to unexpected bottlenecks at the entranceway, people at the end gave up and went to the park. The line at the aquarium was *always* exactly 45 minutes long. This was the one contingency the Simpsons hadn't planned on. They couldn't decide whether to stay and ended up flipping a coin.

On special occasions, the aquarium line is not exactly 45 minutes long. Two Saturdays ago, for example, it rained. On rainy days, the park doesn't look so good, and the Simpsons were therefore willing to wait up to 90 minutes to get into the aquarium. When they got there, the line was exactly 90 minutes long. They flipped another coin.

The Springfield Aquarium makes *absolutely no contribution* to the quality of life in Springfield. When the Simpsons wait 45 minutes to visit the aquarium, their entire outing is neither more nor less enjoyable than visiting the park—which is an option that was available long before the aquarium was ever conceived. A choice between what you've already got and an equally attractive alternative is no improvement over what you've already got with no alternative at all.

The Simpsons cannot benefit from the aquarium because they own no relevant fixed resources. The only relevant fixed resource is the aquarium itself, and the aquarium "belongs" to the entire town, which is to say that it belongs to nobody. Nobody, therefore, is exactly whom it benefits.

It cost the people of Springfield $10 million to construct their aquarium. Every penny of that $10 million was pure social waste. If the town had spent $10 million to purchase gold bullion and throw it in the ocean, the residents would be no worse off than they are today.

The mayor of Springfield might well commiserate with his counterpart in the neighboring town of Grimyville; their recent experiences have much in common. Grimyville's Clean Air Act imposes costs on local businesses whereas Springfield's aquarium imposes costs on local taxpayers. In each case, the offsetting benefit failed to materialize as expected. The legislation in Grimyville was supposed to benefit everyone; instead, it benefited only landlords. The aquarium in Springfield was supposed to benefit all who took advantage of it; instead, it benefits nobody at all.

In that sense, Springfield's mistake is far worse than Grimyville's. In Grimyville, at least the landlords are happy.

This suggests a way to improve the situation in Springfield: Just as Grimyville landlords are entitled to charge rent for the use of their land, allow someone in Springfield to charge an admission fee for the use of the aquarium.

Suppose, for example, that the town of Springfield decides to give the aquarium to the mayor's cousin, in appreciation for unspecified acts of good citizenship. The cousin immediately sets a $10-per-family admission fee.

How does that admission fee affect the Simpsons? Obviously it makes the aquarium initially less desirable. The maximum time the Simpsons will wait to get in on a normal day falls from 45 minutes to 10 minutes. The same is true of all their neighbors, and consequently the actual waiting time falls to 10 minutes. A visit to the aquarium is now more expensive in terms of dollars and less expensive in terms of waiting time; on net the aquarium must remain neither more nor less attractive than the park. The Simpsons value the aquarium as much—which is to say, as little—as they ever did.

After allowing for the improvement in waiting time, *the admission fee costs the Simpsons nothing.* Nor does it cost their neighbors. The *only* way in which the admission fee affects anybody's well-being is that it enriches the mayor's cousin. If the choice is between maintaining the aquarium as a free but valueless municipal operation and allowing the mayor's cousin to operate it for his own benefit, it would be churlish to deny him.

Of course, there is nothing special about the mayor's cousin; any owner collecting admission fees could benefit at no expense to anyone. Perhaps the City Council would prefer to start charging its own admission fee, using the proceeds to improve city services or to lower taxes. This would yield a benefit to everyone in Springfield with no offsetting cost. Here is a rare occurrence of the most sought-after and frequently elusive goal in economic policy—a genuine free lunch.

Alternatively, the city could auction off the aquarium to the highest bidder. Once again the lunch is free. The proceeds of the auction can be used to do good while the new owner's profit-maximizing behavior is of no consequence to anybody but himself.

Fixed resources—land in a particular location, a unique aquarium, an unusual skill, or an unusual preference—yield economic gains to those who own them. If there are no owners, there are no gains. The Indifference Principle ensures that all gains are either transferred to a fixed-resource owner or effectively discarded. Economists tend to feel that it is better for *someone* to reap the benefits of a resource than for *no one* to reap them, and therefore tend to think that the institution of property is a good thing.

Economists love fables. A fable need not be true or even realistic to have an important moral. No tortoise ever really raced against a hare, yet "Slow but steady wins the race" remains an insightful lesson. Grimyville and Springfield are figments of the imagination, stripped of complications that would make any real-world analysis vastly more intricate. But when complications are stripped away, simple and important truths can be exposed. In any specific application, the Indifference Principle might require a host of qualifications—just as in specific circumstances, fast but erratic might vanquish slow but steady. Still, it provides a starting point. We begin by expecting people to be indifferent among activities. When we are right, we are able to derive remarkable consequences. When we are wrong, we are led to ask, "In what essential way does this situation differ from life in Grimyville or Springfield?" and the search for answers is enlightening. A good fable has a good moral, and a good moral is instructive whether or not it is always true to the last detail.

CHAPTER 5

THE COMPUTER GAME OF LIFE

Learning What It's All About

There is an idea going around that if you want students to learn anything these days, you'd better put it in a computer game. I just came from a meeting on designing a game about financial markets. Let each student run a fictitious business, raise capital by selling stocks or bonds as he sees fit, use the capital to purchase inputs, combine those inputs to produce output, and earn profits depending on his performance.

The question arises, How should you measure success in this Game of Economic Life? My idea is to measure it the same way economists measure success in the Game of Life Itself, not by asset holdings or productivity but by the amount of fun you have along the way.

Let the computer reward profitable trades by printing coupons that students can exchange for consumption goods of real value: movie tickets, pizza, a kiss from the graduate student of their choice. Students can spend coupons as they arrive, or save them for the future, or borrow them from other students who are willing to lend. For each student, there comes a randomly selected day when his terminal informs him that his character has died; his savings are transferred to a designated heir and his own consumption opportunities come to an end.

That's it. You receive no grade for playing this game. There is no instructor looking over your shoulder. Nobody ever tells you that you did well or did poorly. You live and you die, and if you play well you collect rewards. If you decide it's not worth the trouble to play well, that's fine too.

Students would learn a lot from this game. They would learn that your success in life is measured not by comparison with others' accomplishments but by your private satisfaction with your own. They would learn that in the Game of Life there can be many winners, and one player's triumphs need not diminish anybody else's. They would learn that hard work has its rewards, but that it also takes time away from other activities, and that different people will make different judgments about what to strive for. Most important, they would learn that consumption and leisure, not accumulation and hard work, are what Life is really all about.

I had a friend in college whose parents were concerned that his life lacked direction. Once his father came to visit him for a heart-to-heart talk and asked, "Mitch, do you have any vision at all of what you want to *be* in ten years?" Slowly and with deliberation, Mitch replied, "I want to be—a *consumer*. I want to consume as much as I can of as many different things as I can for as long as I can." I think Mitch would have been an enthusiastic player of my computer game.

I want to create another version of the game where students produce consumption goods for one another. In one class, students bake brownies; in another they do each others' laundry. Halfway through the semester, I would lower trade barriers and allow students from one class to exchange services with those in the other.

This "international" version of the game would convey two valuable lessons. One is that trade expands opportunities. The second, and more important, is that trade is beneficial not because of exports but because of imports. The export business is the *down*side of international trade. You don't enjoy doing the other classes' laundry but you do enjoy eating their brownies.

International trade was a big issue in the 1992 presidential campaign, and every candidate missed the point. When then-President Bush relaxed import restrictions on Japanese pickup trucks, then-Governor Clinton complained that the United States had gotten absolutely nothing in return. Bush responded that his action had helped open Japanese markets to American goods. Apparently both failed to notice that what Americans gain when they buy Japanese pickup trucks is—Japanese pickup trucks. Selling is a painful necessity; buying is what makes it all worthwhile.

Do not imagine that I am an outwardly crusty but inwardly mellow economist acknowledging that there is more to life than economic models admit. On the contrary, my Computer Game of Life is a loud affirmation of the values that matter to economists. All mainstream economic models assume that people strive to consume more and to work less. All main-stream models judge an economic policy to be successful only when it helps people to accomplish at least one of those goals. By the standards of economics, a policy that does nothing but encourage people to work harder and die wealthy is a bad policy.

We live in an age of "policy wonks" who judge programs by their effect on productivity, or output, or work effort. Wonkian analysis uses the jargon of economics while ignoring its content. Economists view the wonks' fixation on output as a bizarre and unhealthy obsession. Wonks want Americans to die rich; economists want Americans to die happy.

Ross Perot was infected with an extreme form of wonkism during the 1992 presidential campaign when he called for Amer-icans to produce computer chips rather than potato chips. Even if we grant the dubious supposition that producing computer chips is invariably more profitable, the prescription overlooks the fact that producing potato chips might be *less work* and hence more desirable.* If our goal is to maximize profits with-out regard to the effort involved, then most Americans should probably be in forced labor camps. The fact that camps strike most people as a bad idea should give pause to those who are quick to judge policies by productivity measures alone.

In his criticisms of the North American Free Trade Agree-ment, Perot was quick to cite estimates of its potential for re-ducing American wages and employment. His two opponents, declared supporters of the agreement, chose to play on Perot's turf by disputing his estimates. They never came close to ar-ticulating a truly appropriate response by citing estimates of

---

*The work involved in *learning* to produce computer chips should be counted as part of the work of producing them.

the agreement's potential for reducing the prices of consumer goods and expanding the array of goods available. If the effect of the agreement is that Americans work less and consume more, we win.

I will try to have my computer game ready before the next election rolls around. I hope we can get the candidates to try it.

II

Good and Evil

CHAPTER 6

TELLING RIGHT FROM WRONG

The Pitfalls of Democracy

My dinner companion was passionate in her conviction that the rich pay less than their fair share of taxes. I didn't understand what she meant by "fair," so I asked a clarifying question: Suppose that Jack and Jill draw equal amounts of water from a community well. Jack's income is $10,000, of which he is taxed 10%, or $1,000, to support the well. Jill's income is $100,000, of which she is taxed 5%, or $5,000, to support the well. In which direction is that tax policy unfair?

My companion's straightforward response was that she had never thought about the issue in those terms before and was unsure of her answer. I have no problem with that; I *have* thought about the issue in those terms quite a bit and am still unsure of my own answer. That's why I hesitate to pronounce judgment on the fairness of tax policies. If I can't tell what's fair in a world with two people and one well, how can I tell what's fair in a country with 250 million people and tens of thousands of government services?

With never a thought to what "fairness" might consist of in the abstract, my companion was prepared to pass judgment on specific instances, confident that if she couldn't define it, she could at least recognize it when she saw it. But if she could really recognize fairness when she saw it, she'd have been able to recognize it in the world of Jack and Jill.

What she lacked was a moral philosophy. There are many moral philosophies to choose among, and I believe that economic reasoning is the most powerful tool we have for evaluating their merits. The initial proving ground for any moral

philosophy is the artificial world of the economic model—a
world where everything is specified in the explicit detail that is
never available in reality.

That is why, if I could ask one question of every presidential
candidate, it would probably be something along these lines:

Which is better: A world where everyone earns $40,000 a year,
or a world where three-fourths of the population earns $100,000
a year while the rest earn $25,000?

I'm not sure how I'd answer this myself, and I wouldn't dis-
qualify a candidate for coming down on either side of it. But I
would like to see some evidence that he found such questions
interesting.

Those reporters who actually get access to the candidates
seem to lean more toward questions about health care delivery systems or industrial policy, probing for mastery of detail
instead of broad philosophical insights, exploring the intellectual territory that would have invigorated Herbert Hoover and
glazed the eyes of Thomas Jefferson. The candidate knows what
questions to expect and is prepared to answer them. He describes his health care plan and touts its benefits. But if you
allow me to ask the follow-up question, it will be this:

Why do you believe that your health care plan is a good
thing?

Thinking perhaps that I must have dozed off during his
recitation of his program's virtues, the candidate patiently re-
views the high points of his argument. In other words, he
ignores my question completely.

One of the first rules of policy analysis is that you can never
prove that a policy is desirable by listing its benefits. It goes
without saying that nearly any policy anybody can dream up
has some advantages. If you want to defend a policy, your task
is not to demonstrate that it does some good, but that it does
more good than harm.

And if you are going to argue that a program does more
good than harm, you must at least implicitly take a stand on a
fundamental philosophical issue. Put most succinctly, the issue
is: What does *more* mean?

Suppose it can be demonstrated that the candidate's health
care plan would deliver additional health care worth $1 billion
to the nation's poorest families. At the same time, middle-class

and wealthy taxpayers would see their taxes increase by a total of $1.5 billion. Does this program do more good than harm? It all depends on what you mean by *more*. What is the right standard for weighing one kind of cost against another kind of benefit?

In the real world, any meaningful policy proposal must entail a huge number of trade-offs involving innumerable gains and losses to innumerable people. Anybody with something substantive to say about how we should compare those gains and losses must surely have something substantive to say about a fictitious simple proposal that does nothing but enrich the poor by $1 billion and impoverish the rich by $1.5 billion. Anybody who has given reasoned consideration to the underlying issues must have some thoughts that bear on the ideal income distribution in an imaginary world.

Policymakers need a dose of abstraction to keep their heads out of the clouds. It is easy to get carried away making long lists of pros and cons, all the while forgetting that sooner or later we must decide how many cons it takes to outweigh a particular pro. We can commission experts to estimate costs and benefits, but when the costs are measured in apples and the benefits in oranges, mere arithmetic can't illuminate the path to righteousness. When all the facts are in, we still need a moral philosophy to guide our decisions. If we can't address a simple, abstract question about a mythical income distribution, how can we possibly have principles that are sufficiently well developed to guide our preferences about health care delivery?

Health care is not the only issue on which politicians pontificate with less moral foundation than is appropriate to a pontiff. During his presidency, George Bush was particularly fond of saying that it would be good to lower interest rates to ease the burden on young home buyers. For heaven's sake, everybody already knows that lower interest rates ease the burden on home buyers. Everybody also knows that lower interest rates can devastate people who are saving for their retirement. To call attention to one side of the cost-benefit ledger while ignoring the other is plain dishonest. If a politician wants to argue legitimately for lower interest rates, he needs to explain not why it is good to help borrowers, but why it is good to *simultaneously* help borrowers and hurt lenders. In other words, he needs to defend the view that one income distribution is better than another. If he has no general thoughts about what constitutes a "better" income distribution, then he has no business having an opinion about which way the interest rate should move.

Unlike Mr. Bush and my dinner companion, I do not yet know what justice is. But I do believe that economics illuminates the possibilities.

One approach to justice is the extreme democratic view that the majority should always rule. I doubt that anyone in human history has ever subscribed to quite so stark a majoritarian principle. I do not know anyone, or expect to know anyone, or want to know anyone, who believes that the majority should prevail when 51% of the populace vote to gouge out the eyes of the other 49% for their idle entertainment. Typically majoritarians temper their views with some concept of individual rights that are either inalienable or alienable only under special circumstances. This is roughly the approach of the United States Constitution, which institutionalizes a variation on majority rule while enumerating certain rights that are not to be abridged.

A problem with majority rule is that it provides no guidance on what to do about multiple options, none of which garners a majority. Few would want to choose a national economic policy on the grounds that it received 4% of the vote while its 32 opponents received 3% each.

Any voting procedure must include rules for what to do when there are many options. If several policies, or several candidates for office, are up for consideration, should we hold a preliminary election followed by a runoff among the two or three top vote getters? Should we hold a round-robin, pitting two candidates against each other and then a third against the winner and so on until only one is left standing? Should we let people vote not just for their first choice but for their first two or three or ten and see whether a clear majority winner might emerge?

To choose randomly among these alternatives would be at best unsatisfying. To choose on the basis of a vague aesthetic preference would not be much better. A more systematic approach is to list some characteristics that would be *un*desirable in a voting procedure, then narrow the list to those that avoid these shortcomings.

First, it seems uncontroversial to require that if everybody unanimously prefers Tinker to Chance, then Chance should not be able to win an election in which Tinker is a candidate. Any procedure that allowed Chance to defeat Tinker through some quirk in the rules ought not to be acceptable. This rules out silly procedures like "whoever gets the most last-place votes wins."

Second, the outcome of a vote ought not depend on arbitrary choices about the order in which things are carried out. This rules out the round-robin, where a candidate with the bad luck to be scheduled in an early round has more chances to be disqualified than opponents who enter later in the game.

Third, a third-party candidate with no chance of winning should not be able to affect the outcome of a two-way race. This rules out the simple "plurality wins" rule. With plurality rule, a candidate's prospects can improve when a third-party candidate draws votes from his opponent.

In the early 1950s, the economist Kenneth Arrow (subsequently a Nobel prize winner) wrote down a list of reasonable requirements for a democratic voting procedure. They all have the flavor of the three I've just listed. Then Arrow set out to find all of those voting procedures that meet the requirements. It turns out that there aren't many. Arrow was able to prove—with the inexorable force of pure mathematics—that the *only* way to satisfy all of the requirements is to select one voter and give him all the votes. The only "democratic" procedure that meets the minimal requirements for democracy is to anoint a dictator!

Arrow's discovery must give at least a moment of pause to anybody who imagines it is possible to conduct an ideal democratic voting system. But it seems to me that there is a far more fundamental reason to be skeptical of democracy, or even of democracy coupled with a charter of inalienable rights. The reason is that we have absolutely no justification for the expectation that democracy leads to good outcomes. How can we, when we have continued to skirt around the issue of what "good" means?

Is it good for a majority's mild preference to overcome a large minority's passionate opposition? Most people think not and prefer a system that can avoid such outcomes. It is often asserted that our system of republican government works well in this regard, because the passionate minority can organize to exert more pressure on their representatives than the sluggish majority can muster. This assertion has the ring of plausibility, but a ring of plausibility is not a proof.

What would it take to prove that republican government leads to good outcomes? First, you would need a positive theory of politics, politicians, and pressure groups. (By a *positive* theory I mean one that makes predictions about outcomes without judging their desirability.) Your theory would specify assumptions about how politicians behave; for example, "politicians act to maximize their reelection prospects" or "politicians act to maximize their power while in office" or "politicians act to enrich their friends" or some combination of these. Economic theory could guide you from your assumptions to their logical consequences, enabling you to predict what kinds of legislation would be enacted under various circumstances. Presumably you would want to test your theory against real-world observations before putting too much confidence in it.

Second, you would need to state quite precisely which outcomes you consider desirable. Just how large or passionate must a minority be before it ought to be allowed to block the desires of the majority? Answers such as "reasonably large and fairly passionate" will not do; your specifications must be stated with mathematical precision. Such specifications constitute a *normative* theory as opposed to a positive theory; they describe what is desirable, not what will necessarily occur.

Finally, you can compare your positive theory's predictions about actual outcomes with your normative theory's carefully stated criteria for desirable outcomes, and try to prove something about the frequency with which they coincide. Once again, you will need a lot of theory, probably in a reasonably mathematical form.

The positive theory of pressure groups is in its relative infancy. In the last 15 years or so, several papers have appeared that attempt to deal with the problem; many are interesting but none is definitive. Even if we had the (presently unthinkable) luxury of a fully developed and well-tested positive theory, we would still need a separate normative theory to tell us whether our system is desirable. We keep returning to the same point: It takes a moral philosophy to distinguish right from wrong.

Now a simple preference for democracy, or for limited democracy, or for some variation on democracy, already *is* a moral philosophy, at least a rudimentary one, and it is quite enough philosophy for some tastes. It is not, however, a *consequentialist* philosophy; it judges the political system by an arbitrary standard of intrinsic merit ("democracy is good") rather than by its consequences for human happiness. The research program I've just outlined can be summarized as follows: determine the consequences of democracy, and then decide whether those consequences (as opposed to the idea of democracy itself) are desirable.

Much of the philosophy that finds its way into common political discourse is nonconsequentialist. Any assertion of "rights" appeals to our preferences for specific rules as opposed to the consequences of those rules. Both sides in the abortion debate—whether lobbying for the "right to life" or the "right to choose"—appeal to something that goes beyond consequentialism.

Economics offers no objection to a philosophy of rights. But consequences matter also and it pays to consider them in a systematic way. Because the consequences we care about concern human happiness, it is convenient to believe that happiness is measurable at least in principle, so that, for example, we know what it means to say that Jack is happier than Jill. Many economists scoff at such comparisons, contending that Jack's happiness and Jill's happiness are entirely different commodities incapable of being weighed against each other. But for the sake of advancing the discussion, let's suspend our disbelief.

If happiness is measurable, then it is easy to list a menu of consequentialist moral philosophies (or in economic jargon, normative criteria). One is, Pursue the greatest good for the unhappiest person. If happiness can be equated with income, this means that a world of middle-income earners is better than a world where some are rich and some are poor. But it also means that inequality is tolerable provided that it benefits even those at the very bottom. A society with a wide range of incomes where even the poorest have enough to eat is preferable to one in which we all starve equally.

A different normative criterion is, Maximize the sum of human happiness. Our philosophical baggage gets a little heavier now, because we are required not just to compare Jack's happiness with Jill's but to assign each of them a number. A system that gives Jack 4 units of happiness and Jill 10 (for a total of 14) is better than one that gives Jack 6 and Jill 7 (for a total of 13).

Once you've accepted the possibility of numerical measurements, there is nothing special about maximizing the *sum*. An alternative normative criterion is to maximize the *product* of human happiness. This reverses some judgments. Now a system that gives Jack 4 units of happiness and Jill 10 (for a product of 40) is *inferior* to one that gives Jack 6 and Jill 7 (for a product of 42).

Whatever their merits, each of these criteria takes an unambiguous moral stand, as opposed, for example, to the oft-repeated but utterly meaningless "seek the greatest good for the greatest number." (When you compare an income distribution of $40,000 for all with one of $100,000 for three-fourths and $25,000 for the rest, which constitutes "the greatest good for the greatest number"? Your guess is as good as mine.) They are also thoroughly abstract and strictly applicable only in highly stylized artificial examples. But as I've said before, if we can't understand highly stylized artificial examples, we have no hope of understanding the world.

The problem with all these criteria is that the choice among them seems entirely arbitrary. Who is to say whether it is better to maximize the sum of happiness or the product? I am aware of two approaches to overcoming this difficulty.

One approach is to begin by writing down some reasonable requirements that a normative criterion ought to satisfy. For example, we might require that whenever there is an opportunity to make everybody better off, our normative criterion ought to approve it; this rules out criteria like "always try to make the unhappiest person as unhappy as possible" or "minimize the sum of human happiness." We might require that our normative criterion treat everyone symmetrically; we should not be allowed to care more about the welfare of whites or of women than about that of blacks or of men.

Once we've agreed on a few such requirements, it becomes an exercise in pure mathematics to list all of the normative criteria that qualify for the job. Unfortunately, even for short lists of uncontroversial requirements, the most frequent result is that *no* normative criterion satisfies them all at once. This shifts the focus of the debate to: Which of your reasonable requirements are you most willing to abandon? Do we care more or less about interpersonal symmetry than we do about approving every opportunity to make everybody better off? The mathematics guides our understanding of the trade-offs; it tells us that *if* we want a criterion with certain properties, then we must be willing to abandon certain others.

Although this approach does not settle the issue, it moves the argument to higher ground. We have no obvious basis for preferring a sum-of-happiness approach to a product-of-happiness approach, but we seem to have deep visceral preferences for requirements like symmetry. A clear vision of those preferences, plus some pure theory, dictates the normative criterion we are forced to choose.

There is a second approach to the problem, first introduced by the economist John Harsanyi but associated primarily with the name of the philosopher John Rawls, who made it the basis for his monumental work on the theory of justice. In Rawls's or Harsanyi's vision, we must imagine ourselves behind a *veil of ignorance* where even our own identities are concealed from us. Behind the veil, we know that we are destined to *someone's* life, but all earthly lives are equally probable. According to Rawls, the just society is the one we would choose to be born into if forced to choose from behind the veil.

Rawlsians argue that if we were stripped of all knowledge of individual circumstances, we would all agree on how the world should be. Observations of actual behavior can even help us guess what we would agree to. We know that when people can insure at fair odds against catastrophic diseases, they typically do so. It is reasonable to infer that if we could insure against being born untalented or handicapped or otherwise unlucky, we would do that as well. Behind the veil, such insurance would be available: we could all agree that those born smart and healthy would share their incomes with the rest. Because we all would want to sign such a contract behind the veil, Rawlsians argue that it should be enforced in real life.

Rawls himself goes further. He believes that after agreeing on certain fundamental liberties, we would concentrate our efforts on improving the welfare of the least happy person. In its extreme form, this means that we would prefer a world in which everyone barely subsists to a world of billionaires where one unfortunate soul starves to death.

Others who accept the veil setup have quite different expectations about what we would agree upon. Harsanyi gave an argument—just slightly too technical for reproduction here—demonstrating that under certain reasonable conditions we would be forced to agree on a sum-of-happiness formula. I am very fond of this argument because I discovered it myself and believed for a few days that it was original. During those few days I shared it with my friends, of whom some found it marvelously clever and others found it entirely silly. Eventually our better-educated colleague William Thomson informed us that the argument had been discovered by Harsanyi several decades previously and widely repeated since.

The veil criterion seems inadequate for dealing with some critical moral issues, because it fails to specify who exactly is behind the veil. The usual answer is "everybody," but there are circumstances in which "everybody" is more ambiguous than it sounds. Should people be allowed to slaughter seals to make coats? I might give one answer if I knew that I was going to be born a random person; quite another if I thought I might be born a seal. Should abortion be legal? My answer behind the veil might well depend on whether "aborted fetus" was one of the identities I thought I might be assigned. To decide whether fetuses stand behind the veil with the rest of us is to ask whether we consider them fully human; this seems to me to bring us full circle back to the question we were trying to solve.

I believe that arguments from basic properties or from behind the veil can be enormously helpful in clarifying our thinking and warning us about hidden inconsistencies. I suspect though that the choice of a normative criterion is ultimately a matter of taste. And that very fact is the source of an intriguing paradox.

Let me illustrate the paradox in a case so extreme that it seems almost frivolous. Suppose that we agree to make policy based on a normative criterion that calls on us to maximize the welfare of the world's least happy person. Following a massive search, we locate that unfortunate soul and ask what we can do to make him happier. His reply is that he would prefer to live in a world where the normative criterion did not involve the welfare of the least happy person.

Given this preference, it is literally impossible to apply our normative criterion consistently. The only way to apply it is to abandon it.

Alternatively, suppose that we have agreed to maximize the sum of human happiness and discover we can increase that sum by agreeing *not* to maximize the sum of human happiness. Our goal is again self-contradictory.

Under various circumstances, we can prove mathematically that almost all normative criteria must become entangled in paradoxes of this sort. If we discard these paradoxical candidates, the choice among normative criteria is automatically narrowed down to a manageable number long before we start philosophizing.

This might be the most delicious paradox of all. It is sometimes maintained that moral behavior is so much a matter of personal taste that pure theory can contribute very little to the discussion. In fact it is precisely *because* moral behavior is a matter of personal taste that pure theory is able to uncover paradoxes that rule out a host of normative criteria as literally impossible to enforce.

If you took a poll of economists, you would probably find a clear preference for a normative criterion that I have not yet mentioned. The criterion goes by the deceptively callous-sounding name of *economic efficiency* or *cost-benefit analysis*. I think it deserves a chapter to itself.

CHAPTER 7

WHY TAXES ARE BAD

The Logic of Efficiency

On a windy day in New Orleans, the dollar bill I was holding got away from me. As it headed for a sewer and oblivion, I started to grab for it. David Friedman—my companion, my fellow economist, and temporarily the guardian of my soul—stayed my hand. I had just been arguing that economic efficiency is an appropriate guide to personal conduct. By that standard, David's interference saved me from thoughtlessly committing an immoral act.

Suggesting that the moral value of an action can be judged by its contribution to economic efficiency might sound as incongruous as suggesting that the aesthetic value of a sculpture can be judged by its utility as a doorstop. If that is your reaction, it may be partly because I haven't yet told you what economists mean when they talk about efficiency. For example, if it isn't clear to you that rescuing the dollar is inefficient, then you and I are using the word *efficiency* in different ways.

I'll say more about that dollar later in this chapter, but first I want to explain what efficiency is and why economists are so enamored of it. I will start by explaining why taxes are bad.

The most obvious sense in which taxes are bad is that it's no fun to pay them. But this is not conclusive; one could equally well argue that taxes are *good* because it's *great* fun to *collect* them. As each tax dollar paid is a tax dollar collected, the accounting so far shows that the good exactly cancels out the bad.

Let me make this more concrete. Suppose that the tax collector takes a dollar from you and gives it to my grandmother as a part of her Social Security payment. If I care more about my grandmother than I do about you, I will tend to approve of this arrangement. You and your friends, who have never met my grandmother, will probably have a different point of view. But there is nothing in the science of economics that can reveal whether you or my grandmother is more deserving. A completely disinterested observer must be silent about whether the transfer is desirable.

It is remarkable, then, that there *is* a sense in which economists agree that taxes are unambiguously bad. Briefly, taxes are bad because they can be avoided. The avoidance of taxes causes economic losses that are not offset by any gains.

Almost everything you purchase is a bargain, in the sense that you get it for less than the absolute maximum that you would have been willing to pay. Just this afternoon I paid $20 for a shirt that I would have been willing to buy for as much as $24. In a very real sense, I walked out of the store $4 richer than when I walked in. Better yet, my $4 gain came at nobody's expense, so not just I but the *world as a whole* is $4 richer. That $4 gain is what economists call a *consumer's surplus.*

If a sales tax had driven the price of that shirt up to $23, my $3 loss would have been the tax collector's $3 gain. But if a larger sales tax had driven the price up to $25, something quite different would have happened. To avoid the tax, I would have chosen not to buy the shirt. Now my $4 consumer's surplus simply vanishes. I have been made $4 poorer, and nobody has gotten any richer in the process.

Of course, *some* people will still buy shirts at $25, and the losses that those people experience are offset by gains to the tax collector (or to whoever gets the benefits of his collections). But *my* loss, and the losses of people like me, is what economists call a *deadweight* loss. It goes not to the tax collector but to nobody.

Taxes nearly always do more harm than good. To collect a dollar, you need to take someone's dollar; almost inevitably, in the process, you discourage somebody else from buying a shirt, or building a house, or working overtime. When a policy does more harm than good—that is, when it creates deadweight losses—we call it *inefficient* and tend to deplore it.

The only sort of tax that avoids deadweight losses entirely is a *head tax,* according to which everybody pays some fixed amount that is determined without reference to income, assets, purchases, or anything else over which he has any control. In theory, economists love head taxes, though in practice we recognize that they represent a rather drastic solution to the problem of inefficiency.

This means that if we are going to have any kind of government at all, and if we are not willing to go to the extreme of financing it entirely by head taxes, then we're going to have to accept some amount of deadweight loss. However, the deadweight losses that arise from different tax policies can vary enormously in size. When a policy creates a particularly large deadweight loss, economists usually start looking for an alternative.

This mode of analysis—weighing individual gains and losses—is characteristic of economists. When asked to assess the impact of, say, a tariff on foreign cars, policy analysts not trained in economics are wont to discuss the effects on employment in the automobile industry, on General Motors's profits, and even on the government's trade and budget deficits. One problem with this kind of analysis is that it provides no criterion for weighing the good against the bad. (Is a 4% increase in employment among auto workers worth a 3% increase in the price of cars? What about a $1 billion decrease in the trade deficit?) It doesn't even provide a criterion for deciding whether a given consequence is to be counted on the positive or the negative side of the ledger. (Is an increase in domestic car production—with its attendant consumption of valuable resources—a good or a bad thing?) Economists proceed in an entirely different way. We consider only the impact on *individuals* (of course, because individuals are affected by auto industry profits and government deficits, we might still have to consider such factors, but only as an intermediate step). For each individual in the economy we ask: Will this person gain or lose as a result of this tariff, and how much? Gains and losses include changes in consumers' surplus, changes in producers' profits, gifts that the government makes out of the tariff revenue, and anything else that any individual values. We add up all the gains to the winners and all the losses to the losers. If the winners gain more than the losers lose, we tend to view the policy as desirable. If the losers lose more than the winners gain, we label the difference a deadweight loss, pronounce the policy inefficient, and take the deadweight loss as a measure of its unattractiveness.

It is important here not to make the traditional noneconomist's error of overemphasizing that which is purely material. We mean it when we say that we count everything people value.

Suppose that the Exxon Corporation acquires drilling rights in a remote area where it is generally agreed that drilling will cause only negligible environmental disruptions in the traditional sense. Nevertheless, a group of militant Mineral Rights activists, contending that their personal serenity is threatened by the knowledge that oil is being removed from its natural resting place in the ground, files a lawsuit to prevent Exxon from proceeding. By the logic of cold-blooded economic efficiency, who should prevail?

By the logic of cold-blooded economic efficiency, we do not yet have enough information to say. If Exxon proceeds, the winners will be Exxon's stockholders, who will see a rise in the value of their shares; local laborers, who will see a rise in their wages and employment prospects; and perhaps motorists, who might see a fall in gasoline prices. The losers will be the Mineral Rights activists, who will sleep less soundly. The efficiency criterion dictates that we measure all gains and all losses in terms of *willingness to pay* and measure one total against the other.

A stockholder who stands to gain $50 from the project would presumably be willing to pay up to $50 if it would take that to elicit a ruling in Exxon's favor. That counts as 50 votes on the prodrilling side. A determined opponent might be willing to pay up to $3,000 to prevent that ruling. That counts as 3,000 votes against.

One of the local unemployed, who expects to earn $30,000 working for Exxon if the deal goes through, also casts votes in favor—but fewer than 30,000 of them. He'd be willing to pay something to get that job, but he surely wouldn't be willing to pay all of his expected wages to get it. Perhaps, though, he'd be willing to pay up to $10,000 to get the job (in other words, he would be willing to work for $20,000 but no less). Count another 10,000 votes in favor of drilling.

In principle, every person with an interest in the outcome should be allowed to cast a number of votes proportional to his willingness to pay for the outcome he desires. The efficient decision is the one that gets the most votes.

Let me use the battle between Exxon and its detractors to get to the heart of why economists deplore inefficiency. An inefficient decision *always* entails a missed opportunity to make *everybody* happier. Suppose that the total willingness-to-pay of the pro-drillers is $10 million, and the total willingness-to-pay of the antidrillers is $5 million, but the judge rules (inefficiently) to disallow drilling. Then here is an alternative ruling that *both sides* would have preferred: Allow drilling, but make the pro-drillers collectively pay the antidrillers $7.5 million to assuage their disappointment.

Under the alternative ruling, the prodrillers get $10 million worth of benefits for a bargain price of $7.5 million, while the antidrillers get paid $7.5 million to compensate them for a $5 million loss. In fact, the collections and payments can in principle be orchestrated so that each individual prodriller pays exactly 75% of his drilling-related gains and each individual antidriller receives exactly 150% of his drilling-related losses. If a referendum were held, with this and the judge's actual ruling as the only alternatives, the vote to overturn the judge would be unanimous.

Any proposal that manages to garner zero votes in a two-way election has got to be viewed as seriously flawed. And any proposal that is economically inefficient will always garner zero votes in a two-way election against an appropriately designed alternative.

An argument that inefficiency is always bad is not quite the same as an argument that efficiency is always good. But because efficiency is the only alternative to inefficiency, economists tend to favor it.

There are two obvious objections to this line of reasoning, of which one is entirely beside the point and the other is substantive. The first is that a judge endowed with anything short of omniscience is in no position to guess what a laborer would be willing to pay for his job, much less what a Mineral Rights activist would be willing to pay to maintain a pool of oil in

its natural habitat. This is partly true but wholly irrelevant.*
Judges, being human, are doomed sometimes to miss their targets. This does not relieve them from the responsibility to choose
their targets appropriately. The question is not "Should policies
always be efficient?" but "Should we in general strive to de-
vise efficient policies, doing the best we can with the limited
information at our disposal?"

The more important objection is that it is not necessarily a fatal flaw for a candidate to lose an election—even unanimously—
to an alternative who is not even in the race. In my example, the
judge has to either allow drilling or forbid it. To allow drilling
and simultaneously order a complicated collection of side payments may not be an option. Should the antidrilling position
be eliminated just because it is inferior to a plan that is not
even under consideration? And if this eliminates the argument
*against in*efficiency, what argument *for* efficiency remains?

These questions are troubling to many economists and constitute one reason why most of us are reluctant to embrace
pure efficiency as a vision of the ultimate good. Yet I think
it is a fair statement that a great many economists are generally agreed that efficiency should play a significant role in
formulating social policy.

The logic of efficiency dictates that economists bring an un-
common viewpoint to common debates. Consider the chronic
debate about military manpower. Comparing the draft with a
volunteer army, commentators frequently opine that one advantage of the draft is that it's cheaper. Those commentators
are wrong. The wages paid to volunteer soldiers exit from the
pockets of taxpayer's suits and overalls to enter the pockets
of military uniforms. These wages are not lost; they are simply transferred from one segment of society to another. By the
economist's reckoning, such transfers are not net costs.

The cost of maintaining an army is equal to the value of
the opportunities that young people forgo when they become
soldiers. The value of those opportunities is measured by what

---

*It is only partly true because economists have devised some most ingenious
mechanisms for eliciting true responses from people who are being questioned
about their willingness to pay.

the soldiers would be willing to pay to retrieve them. When a mechanic or a student or a beach bum joins the army, he loses the opportunity to repair automobiles, or to pursue his studies, or to catch the big wave. Those opportunities really do vanish; the world becomes a place with fewer working automobiles, or fewer trained scholars, or less fun.* Vanished opportunities are costs in any reckoning. In the economist's reckoning, they are the *only* costs.

Imagine a young man who would require $30,000 as an inducement to volunteer. If he is drafted and paid nothing, then he has lost a quantity of freedom valued at $30,000. If he is drafted and paid $18,000, then he has lost $12,000 and the taxpayers who pay his wage have lost $18,000; the total is still $30,000. If we hire the same young man into an all-volunteer force, then those taxpayers must come up with $30,000; the total is no different than before.

The best way to see the absurdity of the allegation that a draft is cheaper is to imagine taxing *the young man himself* $30,000 and then offering it back to him as a wage for joining the army. Surely this proposal does not differ from the draft in any meaningful way. If your accounting system tells you that paying wages to soldiers is always more expensive than drafting them, this example should convince you that you need a new accounting system.

Let me turn to another recurring controversy: congressional pay raises. A raise has two effects. First, it redistributes income by enriching sitting congressmen at taxpayers' expense, and second, it attracts a better class of candidates in the future.[†] The usual noneconomist's view is that the first effect is bad and the second is good. But if we take efficiency seriously, the first effect is neutral and the second might well be bad.

---

*A new mechanic may arise to take the old one's place, but then the world loses whatever it is that the new mechanic would otherwise have been producing instead.

[†]Actually, this second effect is far from certain. Higher salaries guarantee that future contests will be more hard-fought. The costs of participating in tougher campaigns might completely erase the benefits of higher salaries. On net, it could become either easier or harder to attract high-quality candidates. But for the sake of argument, I will assume that higher salaries really do draw forth better candidates.

As to the first effect, the logic of efficiency requires that we be neutral regarding pure transfers of income—even when the beneficiary is a congressman. As to the second effect, keep in mind that our new improved congressmen must come from the ranks of some other profession, so that if we attract a better class of officeholders, we must also have a poorer class of judges or lawyers or doctors or economists. The true cost of a good congressman is not his salary but the forgone opportunity to bring his excellence to bear in other fields. Is that cost worth the benefit? I have no idea.

The logic of efficiency drives the economist's distaste for inflation. Inflation is costly for those who receive fixed nominal incomes; but it is beneficial—and in exactly the same amount—for those who *pay* those fixed nominal incomes. An unexpected inflation can be a boon to the borrower who repays his loan with inflated dollars; it is simultaneously a curse—and of exactly the same magnitude—to the lender who is being repaid. These effects, which are so often cited as the primary economic consequences of inflation, cancel each other exactly and have no net effect on efficiency at all.

The true economic cost of inflation, like the true economic cost of a tax, is that people take costly actions to avoid it, and these actions benefit nobody. In times of inflation, people carry less cash, because cash loses value just by sitting in their pockets. This makes it more difficult to buy a sweater on a whim, to hail a cab in an unexpected rainstorm, or to get through the day without a trip to the ATM. Retail stores keep less cash in the till and run out of change more often. Large firms keep less cash on hand to meet unexpected emergencies and have to deal with those emergencies via expensive financial transactions. These losses are all deadweight losses—they come with no offsetting gains. They might sound unimportant in the grand scheme of things, but the deadweight losses due to inflation are estimated to total about $15 billion per year in the United States, or $60 per American—hardly devastating, but hardly trivial either.

In times of very high inflation, the deadweight losses can become enormous. In the Hungarian hyperinflation of 1948, workers were paid three times a day and their spouses were employed full-time running back and forth between the work-place and the bank, trying to deposit paychecks before they became worthless. During the German hyperinflation that fol-lowed World War I, John Maynard Keynes reported that tavern-goers frequently ordered several beers early in the evening—before the price went up. Drinking warm beer can be a hidden cost of inflation.

Hollywood screenwriters and denizens of the college lecture cir-cuit periodically rediscover the dramatic potential of a burning dollar bill. Typically the torching is accompanied by impass-sioned commentary—issuing from a sympathetic character on the movie screen or an aging cultural icon in the college gym—about how a dollar bill is nothing more than a piece of paper. You can't eat it, you can't drink it, and you can't make love to it. And the world is no worse off for its disappearance.

Sophisticated audiences tend to be uncomfortable with this kind of reasoning; they sense that it is somehow dreadfully wrong but are unable to pinpoint the fatal flaw. In reality, it is their own discomfort that is gravely in error. The speaker is right. When you spend an evening burning money, the world as a whole remains just as wealthy as it ever was.

Let me suggest a probable source for the audience's false feeling that something is amiss. The audience recognizes—correctly—that by the end of the evening the money burner is poorer than at the beginning. If *he* is poorer, and he is part of the world, must not the world as a whole be poorer, too?

The answer is no, because somebody else is richer. All we have to do is discover who that somebody else is.

The key to the mystery is the observation that the supply of money determines the general level of prices. When the money supply increases, prices rise, and when it decreases, prices fall. When a dollar bill turns to ashes, the money supply falls ever so slightly, and prices throughout the economy fall. If only one dollar bill is burned, prices fall only imperceptibly, but they do fall. The beneficiaries of that event are *those people who are holding money at the moment when the dollar bill is burned*. As prices fall, the money in their pockets gains value.

An imperceptibly small reduction in prices creates an imper-ceptibly small increase in wealth for each of the many millions who have money in their pockets at the time of the change. Many millions of imperceptibly small increases in wealth can add up to something perceptible. In this case, they add up to exactly one dollar. After all, we know that the total value of real goods in the world is unchanged and we know also that the speaker has lost a dollar; we are therefore entitled to conclude that exactly one dollar has been gained somewhere else.

Every now and then, some eccentric altruist gathers up his assets and donates them to the United States Treasury. As a result, our current or future tax bills must fall.* The beneficiaries are the many millions of U.S. taxpayers, each of whom experiences a tiny reduction in his tax burden. But we do not all benefit equally. Those of us in the highest tax brackets—by and large, the richest Americans—collect disproportionate shares of the gift.

An alternative strategy for the altruist would be to convert his assets to cash and, instead of giving them to the Treasury, hold a bonfire. The result is essentially the same. Tiny benefits accrue to millions of Americans (this time in the form of falling prices rather than falling tax bills), and the total of all those benefits is equal to the altruist's sacrifice. In the bonfire scenario, your share of the benefits is proportional not to your tax bill but to the quantity of cash you happen to be holding at the moment of the bonfire. This still tends to favor the rich, but probably less dramatically. So if you are thinking of remembering the Treasury in your will, and if you are something of an egalitarian, consider a bonfire instead.[†]

Now let me return to that dollar bill whisked away by the New Orleans wind. I knew that if I let that dollar get away, it would land in a place where it would never be found—it would be as good as burned. What were my options?

---

*The most plausible scenario is that the Treasury reduces its current borrowing, so that its future obligations and the future tax burden are reduced. Under *any* scenario, unless the gift causes the government to revise its spending plans, a gift to the Treasury must lower taxes one way or another.

[†]It might be worth noting, however, that when you make a gift to money holders, the biggest winners of all are likely to come from that class of people who frequently travel with suitcases containing several million dollars.

Option One is to kiss the dollar good-bye. The cost-benefit accounting: I lose a dollar, the rest of the world gains a dollar through falling prices, and the world as a whole is neither richer nor poorer than before. The consequence for economic efficiency: None.

Option Two is to grab the dollar, exerting approximately three cents' worth of effort. (That is, three cents is about what I would have been willing to pay my friend David to retrieve the dollar for me instead of grabbing it myself.) The cost-benefit accounting: I lose three cents, the rest of the world neither gains nor loses, and the world as a whole (including me) is three cents poorer. The consequence for economic efficiency: A decline.

By a purely selfish accounting, losing the dollar is costlier than grabbing it. But if I let the dollar go, my losses are offset by others' gains. If I grab it, my (substantially smaller) losses are not offset by anything. The logic of efficiency compels me to let it go.

Or does it? Let me distinguish between two quite different propositions. One is that economic efficiency should be an important consideration in resolving issues of *public policy*. The other is that economic efficiency should be an important consideration in resolving issues of *personal conduct*. It is only the first of these propositions that economists frequently defend. Like most people, economists are vocal when they criticize governments but coy when they criticize each other.

The efficiency criterion treats everybody equally. A cost is a cost, no matter who bears it. In the realm of public policy, this is an appealing feature. But in our private affairs, it seems odd to insist that we should behave as if our own concerns carry no more weight than those of distant strangers.

There are times—as on that day in New Orleans—when I think that efficiency fails entirely as a guide to how I should behave. But there are other times when it serves me pretty well. When my lawn gets shaggier than the neighbors would prefer, I have to ask myself whether I am morally obliged to take action. In the process, I think about what it would cost me to get the lawn mowed, and how unhappy I think the neighbors really are. If it seems likely to cost me $30 worth of effort to save the neighbors from $20 worth of grief, I pour myself a lemonade and stop worrying. If I believe that with $30 worth of effort I could save the neighbors from $50 worth of grief, then I feel like a jerk until I mow the lawn.

That's an efficiency calculation, and it leads me to conclusions that feel right. I'm not entirely consistent about this. When I decide whether to operate an internal combustion engine or an aerosol can, I *do* care about the harm that I might do to others by damaging the air quality. I emphatically do *not* care about the psychic harm that I might do to others who are morally offended by the very idea of my operating an internal combustion engine or an aerosol can. I think that this distinction would be very hard to justify philosophically. If my driving makes you unhappy, then I have made the world a less happy place in a way that is independent of *why* my driving makes you unhappy. The strict logic of efficiency would say that if I am prepared to stay home rather than cause $10 worth of damage to your lungs, then I should also be prepared to stay home rather than cause $10 worth of damage to your moral sensibilities.

I infer that although my moral philosophy is incomplete, efficiency considerations play a major role. But my last trip to Boston shook my faith a bit.

I flew from Denver, with my wife, and our round-trip tickets totaled just under $2,500. I offered alternatives to the publisher who was footing the bill, but he insisted that we come anyway. Still, I'm sure that if I'd been paying my own way I would have canceled the trip.

This led me to formulate the following moral dilemma: Suppose that getting to Boston and back is worth $300 to you. It costs the airline $200 to provide that transportation. But because of some extraordinary degree of monopoly power, the airline charges $1,000 for the ticket. Should you fly?

If you care only about efficiency, then you certainly should. If you fly, you are worse off by $700 (the difference between what you pay and the value of the trip), while the owners of the airline are better off by $800 (the difference between what they collect and the cost of flying you). There is a net gain of $100 and the efficiency criterion pronounces the trip a Good Thing.

Yet I am sure that I would not buy the ticket and I am equally sure that I would lose no sleep over it. I am sure that I would reach the same conclusion no matter how much the airline owners stood to gain, or how little I stood to lose. So while I still

believe that efficiency is usually the right general guide to government policy, and often the right general guide to personal
behavior, I now think that we need a much subtler criterion
before we can really know what it means to be good. I believe
that there are times when I ought try to behave efficiently and
other times when I need not. I just haven't figured out the rules
for knowing which times are which.

I did retrieve that dollar, without a moment's concern for its
effect on the general price level. I feel no guilt, though I'm not
sure why.

CHAPTER 8

WHY PRICES ARE GOOD

Smith Versus Darwin

I recently attended a party where a learned man—a prominent physicist—held forth. His topic was the analogy between Darwinian evolution, advancing the species biologically by allowing only the fittest to survive, and the Invisible Hand of the marketplace, advancing our species economically by eliminating all but the most efficient producers.

I suspect that he didn't know much about biology. I'm sure that he didn't know much about economics. And his analogy, though familiar, was profoundly wrong.

In biology, there is no equivalent of the Invisible Hand. Survival of the fittest is a different thing altogether. Nothing in evolutionary theory either promises or delivers the spectacular efficiency of the competitive marketplace.

Male birds of paradise have ridiculously long tails. Evolution has cursed them with tails far too long for any practical purpose, and in fact long enough to be a substantial hindrance in locomotion. Their bodies expend precious resources to grow and maintain these tails, increasing the birds' food requirements while simultaneously rendering them more susceptible to predators.

How could such a handicap have survived natural selection? In fact, Darwinism requires us to ask something far more perplexing: How could such a handicap have been a *consequence* of natural selection?

Remarkably, the biologists have answers. Male birds compete for female birds, who want mates capable of fathering healthy offspring. By growing a tail slightly longer than his rivals', the male demonstrates that he is robust, that he eats well, and perhaps that he is sufficiently athletic to survive even when burdened with an absurd encumbrance. These are just the qualities that the female wants in her sons, and so she seeks a mate who evidently has them. Long tails are a reproductive advantage and are therefore rewarded by natural selection.

Now let us be fanciful: The male birds of paradise, concerned about escalating competition, have called a peace conference. Some of the more scrawny-tailed birds have made a radical proposal: universal "disentailment," by which all will agree to immediately and permanently discard all unnecessary plumage. Their literature emphasizes advantages in the area of fox-avoidance but underplays the possibility of a redistribution of females.

The bird now occupying the podium is the bearer of a particularly magnificent specimen (he needed three assistants to carry it as he ascended the stage). He rejects the radicals' proposal out of hand but offers a grand compromise: "Let each and every one of us cut the length of his tail by half. To this there can be no objection. The tails that are now the longest will remain the longest. Those who are now most attractive to females will remain most attractive to females. At the same time, each of us will benefit from reduced maintenance costs, improved aerodynamics, and decreased visibility to our friends the foxes."

What is remarkable about this proposal is not just that it benefits the birds as a *species;* it actually benefits each and every individual bird. The scrawny-tailed birds like it less than their own proposal, but that one never had a chance of adoption anyway. The compromise is a game in which every player wins. Only the foxes might object.

For birds of paradise, it is an unfortunate truth that such a compromise can never be enforced. By the time the proposal has been moved, seconded, and adopted, unscrupulous males (and what male is not unscrupulous in such matters?) will be scheming to avoid the shears. Any bird who suspects widespread cheating must cheat in order not to be outdone by his rivals. Any bird who does *not* suspect widespread cheating is *still* likely to cheat, hoping to gain unfair advantage over his more honest fellows.

An economist would describe this outcome as *inefficient* because of the lost opportunity to make a change that is unanimously seen as desirable. The outcomes of biological processes are often inefficient, for the simple reason that there is no reason why they should not be. The outcomes of economic processes can be inefficient also, but they are efficient remarkably often, and thereby hangs our tale.

The best way to appreciate the spectacular efficiency of the competitive marketplace is to see some examples of outcomes that are *in*efficient. For such an example, let us make the pessimistic hypothesis that students learn nothing of any value in college. Nevertheless, employers prefer to hire college graduates, because grads are smarter, on average, than nongrads. Going to college did not make them smart; rather, being smart enabled them to survive college. Still, if employers have no other way to distinguish between the smart and the not-so-smart, then they will be willing to pay higher salaries to those with more education.

In this example, students are like male birds of paradise, employers are like female birds, and getting a college education is like growing a long tail: It is an expensive way to acquire something useless that nonetheless signals your inner qualities. Suppose that students could all agree to attend only half as much college as presently: Those who now graduate from four-year schools will attend two-year schools instead; those who now spend eight years getting a PhD will spend four years and get a bachelor's degree. With this plan in effect, the employers' ranking of the students would not change, and each student would save half his tuition costs (as well as being able to enter the work force earlier). Every student would benefit and nobody would lose.

But college students, like male birds of paradise, are notorious cheaters, and the agreement breaks down as each decides to violate its provisions and gain an advantage over his fellows. The result is an inefficient return to the status quo.

Examples abound, both in the animal kingdom and in human affairs. Consider a population of cattle that graze in a restricted area. If they all agree to eat a little less this year, the grass will replenish itself faster and all will have more to eat in the future.

Perhaps every cow and bull can agree that this trade-off would be worthwhile. Yet each animal cheats, eating a bit more than his allotment this year, secure in the knowledge that his own extra portion will have only a negligible effect on next year's crop. Alas, the herd is large and these negligible effects add up. Next year, everyone is hungry.

Rational behavior is no vaccine against inefficiency. In each of our examples, every individual acts rationally—the male bird who grows his tail long, the college student who extends his years of schooling, the cow who eats a little more than she promised to. If rationality cannot save us, what can? Remarkably—incredibly—miraculously—there is an answer. Under quite general conditions, when goods are produced and exchanged in competitive free markets in which people trade at market prices, economic activity leads to efficient outcomes. This fact is what economists have in mind when they talk about the Invisible Hand.

In the eighteenth century, Adam Smith described the economic actor who "intends only his own gain" but is nevertheless led "by an invisible hand to promote an end which was no part of his intention," that end being the welfare of society, which economists call efficiency. The metaphor endures, having survived countless misinterpretations. It has been said that Smith was expressing a religious sentiment, a faith that Providence oversees our affairs. It has been said more often—most recently by my physicist friend—that Smith meant something like this: Individual rationality, coupled with the ruthless pressure of natural selection (in the marketplace as in the biosphere) must necessarily serve the social good and the ultimate advancement of the species.

But if Smith had meant that, then he would have been wrong. Any bird of paradise could tell you so. What he did mean was something far more subtle, and far more remarkable: Individual rationality, coupled with competition *and prices,* leads to efficient outcomes; that is, outcomes in which there remain no unexploited opportunities to improve everybody's welfare. This is so even though individual rationality and competition *without* prices rarely leads to such desirable outcomes.

The Invisible Hand Theorem is not at all obvious, but it is true. In the 1950s, the economists Gerard Debreu and Lionel

McKenzie, working separately, successfully translated the Theorem into a statement about pure mathematics and rigorously proved that statement. Their accomplishment is one of the triumphs of modern economics.

Along with its modern formulation, the Invisible Hand Theorem has acquired a modern name. It is now called the First Fundamental Theorem of Welfare Economics, and it can be stated succinctly: Competitive markets allocate resources efficiently. There is also a Second Fundamental Theorem of Welfare Economics, which deals with the fact that there are many different ways to allocate resources efficiently. The Second Fundamental Theorem says this: No matter which of the many efficient allocations you want to achieve, you can always achieve it by first redistributing income in an appropriate way, and then letting competitive markets function freely.

The critical feature in the formulations and proofs of these theorems is the existence of market prices. Without prices, there is no reason to expect efficient outcomes. I see no analogue of prices in the origin of species, and conclude that evolutionary biology bears only the most superficial resemblance to the economics of the marketplace.

I cannot hope to explain completely why the Invisible Hand Theorem must be true. However, I do think that I can give enough of its flavor to clarify the crucial role of prices. The next few paragraphs will be just slightly rougher going than the rest of this chapter, but with a little close attention I think you'll find them understandable. Your reward will be a glimpse of one of the great intellectual achievements of humankind.

Suppose that I appoint you the czar of American agriculture. It has been determined that 1,000 bushels of wheat will be produced in America this year, and your job is to ensure that it is produced in the cheapest possible way.

Your ultimate concern is with the total cost of all the wheat grown in America. But to achieve your goal, you must take account of a different notion of cost, which we call the *marginal* cost of producing wheat on any given farm.

The marginal cost is the additional cost that would result if the farmer grew one more bushel. This is not the same as the farmer's average cost per bushel, because marginal cost tends to vary from one bushel to another. A farmer has a limited amount of land to work with, and coaxing this land to yield 2 bushels of wheat can cost more than twice as much as coaxing it to yield 1. For concreteness, let's say that growing 1 bushel costs Farmer Brown $1, while growing 2 bushels costs him $3 and growing 3 bushels costs him $7. If Farmer Brown plants 1 bushel, his cost is $1, and his marginal cost is $2 per bushel (because planting one more bushel would raise his cost by $2, from $1 to $3). If he plants 2 bushels, his marginal cost is $4 (because a third bushel would raise his cost from $3 to $7).

Now let's return to your problem as czar: Produce 1,000 bushels as cheaply as possible. Suppose that Farmer Brown's marginal cost is $4 per bushel, while Farmer Smith's marginal cost is $9 per bushel. Then here is something clever you can do: Tell Farmer Smith to grow one fewer bushel (reducing his costs by about $9) and tell Farmer Brown to grow one more bushel (increasing his costs by $4). Between them, the farmers grow just as much wheat as before, but their total costs are reduced by $5.*

Now that Farmer Smith is producing less wheat, his marginal cost will no longer be as high as $9 per bushel; perhaps it falls to $7 per bushel. Farmer Brown is producing more, so his marginal cost rises, say to $5 per bushel. Repeating your clever idea, you can save another $2 by having Farmer Smith cut back another bushel while Farmer Brown expands by the same amount.

You can continue to play this game until Farmers Smith and Brown both have the same marginal cost of production; at that point there is nothing more to be gained by this method. The next step is to look for other pairs of farmers with differing marginal costs and play the same game with them. The total cost of production is not minimized until you have exploited every such opportunity, at which point every farmer's marginal production cost is the same as every other farmer's.

---

*If you are following the arithmetic closely, you might object to my statement that Farmer Jones can reduce his costs by $9 if he grows one less bushel; I had assumed that $9 is the cost of his *next* bushel, not his *last* one. A complete answer to the objection is available but requires more mathematics than is appropriate here. The basic idea is to measure wheat not in bushels but in some much smaller unit, so that the cost of producing the *next* unit and the cost of producing the *last* unit are so close that they can be treated as equal.

This is worth emphasizing: *Efficiency in wheat production requires that all farmers face the same marginal cost.*

Now let's put aside the issue of efficiency and look at the choices made by an individual farmer seeking to maximize his own profits. On Farmer Jones's farm, the marginal cost of production happens to be $1 if he grows 1 bushel, $2 if he grows 2, $3 if he grows 3, and $4 if he grows 4. The going price of wheat is $3 per bushel.

Farmer Jones currently has 1 bushel of wheat in the ground and is thinking of expanding his operation. He notices that if he grows a second bushel, he can sell it for $3 while incurring a marginal cost of only $1. That sounds good, so he plants a second bushel. Should he plant a third? If he does so, he can sell it for $3 while incurring a marginal cost of only $2. Again a wise move. With 3 bushels already in the ground, the marginal cost of growing a fourth is $3, which is no more than the wheat can be sold for. So Farmer Jones stops planting when he has 3 bushels in the ground and faces a marginal cost of $3.

Like Farmer Jones, each farmer keeps planting until his marginal cost is equal to $3 per bushel (the market price of wheat) and then stops. Some farms will be bigger and others smaller (on Farmer Smith's farm, the marginal cost does not reach $3 per bushel until there are 7 bushels in the ground, so he plants 7 bushels), but at each farm the marginal cost is equal to the market price.

Now the remarkable part: Each farmer, seeking only to maximize his own profits—or, in Adam Smith's words, intending only his own gain—plants until his marginal cost is equal to the market price. Because all farmers face the *same* market price of $3 per bushel, farmers plant until they all face the same marginal cost. But this—the equality of marginal cost at different farms—is exactly what was required to produce wheat as cheaply as possible.

Let it be emphasized that no farmer cares about minimizing the total cost of everybody's wheat production—it is "an end which was no part of his intention". Yet he is led to this end as if by an invisible hand.

Notice the key role of the single market price that every farmer faces. In the pursuit of personal profit, each farmer plants until his marginal cost is equal to that price. Only because all farmers sell at the same price do all farmers end up with the same marginal cost. Only that equality of marginal costs guarantees that the economywide wheat crop is produced as cheaply as possible.

Now an economy consists of far more than a wheat market, and economic activity consists of far more than just production. The gist of the Fundamental Theorems of Welfare Economics is this: Even when we consider a complete economy, with many goods and many activities, all of which interact with one another in complicated ways, the existence of competitive markets and market prices is exactly what is required to guarantee efficient outcomes.*

The world abounds with inefficiency, and to the untrained eye much of it seems to be the result of "cutthroat competition" or "markets run amok." But the Invisible Hand Theorem tells us that if we seek the source of inefficiency, we should look for markets that are *missing,* not for markets that exist. We should look for goods that are not priced, which often means that we should look for goods that are not owned.

Consider pollution. A factory emits noxious smoke, causing discomfort to its neighbors. This might or might not be inefficient. The factory benefits some (its owners, people who buy its products, perhaps others who interact with it more indirectly) while hurting others (the neighbors). In principle, we can measure all of the gains and losses in dollar terms (for example, by asking the neighbors, How much would you be willing to pay to get rid of the factory? or, How much money would the factory have to give you before you were glad it was there?). The factory might, on balance, do more good than harm, in which case it is efficient for it to be there, pollution and all. But it is equally possible that it does more harm than good. If so, its existence is inefficient.

What is the ultimate source of this inefficiency? Some might say it is the consequence of too much market capitalism and the

---

*Some other conditions must be satisfied as well. For example, when different groups of people have access to significantly different information, the Invisible Hand Theorem may fail. This is essentially what went wrong in the earlier example with the college students, who know more about their own abilities than employers do.

unenlightened pursuit of profits. Actually, it is the consequence of too *little* market capitalism: There is no market for air.

Suppose that somebody owned the air around the factory and could charge for its use. The factory would have to pay for the right to pollute, while the residents would have to pay for the right to breathe freely. This creates a powerful disincentive for the factory to continue polluting. Even if the air belonged to the owner of the factory, there would be the same powerful disincentive, because by polluting he forgoes the opportunity to sell clean air to the neighbors! Regardless of who owns the air—the factory owner, some of the neighbors, or an absentee "airlord"—the factory is likely to stop polluting. In fact, it is not hard to show that the factory will continue to pollute if and only if that is the efficient outcome.

None of this is meant to imply that it would be easy to organize and maintain a market for air, or that this is a practical way to deal with the problem of pollution. What it is meant to illustrate is this: Inefficiencies arise from missing markets. Wherever there is an inefficiency, it is a good bet that a missing market is lurking (or, more precisely, failing to lurk) in the background.

African elephants are hunted for their ivory at far too great a rate, and these magnificent animals may be headed for extinction. While this problem may have no simple solution, it *does* have a simple cause: Nobody owns the elephants. An owner—any owner—would want to be sure that enough elephants survive to keep him in business. The demand for beef is far greater than the demand for ivory, but cattle are not threatened with extinction. The key to the difference is that cattle are owned.

Similarly, paper companies have every incentive to replenish the forests they own, and these forests are in no danger of disappearing. Concerned environmentalists advocate recycling paper so that fewer trees are harvested. Ironically, the companies respond to the reduced demand for trees by maintaining smaller forests. Evidence indicates that recycling causes the world to have fewer trees.

Roy Romer, the governor of Colorado (and the father of a prominent economist), recently spoke amusingly about leaf blowers. He told of going for a walk on an autumn day and watching each Denver homeowner blow his leaves into the next homeowner's yard. He concluded that the problem consists of too *many* markets—we'd all be better off if nobody bought a leaf blower. Perhaps his son could have told him that there are also too *few* markets: If there were a way to charge the neighbor for using your yard as a trash can, the problem would vanish.

The governor was onto something, though: two missing markets can be better than one. We know from Adam Smith that it would be best if there were markets for everything. But *given* the fact that there is no market for yards-as-trash-cans, it *can* be better to eliminate the market for leaf blowers as well.

On the other hand, the governor's description does not ring true to me. In my neighborhood, you don't blow leaves on your neighbor's lawn. Or if you do, then you don't count on him for favors, like taking in your mail when you're away. In fact, there is something very like a market, with a going price to be paid for violating unspoken rules. Even without any formal organization, markets tend to develop, precisely because they are such powerful tools for improving everyone's welfare.

Today we are everywhere enjoined to respect the delicate ecological balance of nature, in which each creature is so miraculously designed to fill its special niche, and in which each part interacts in glorious intricacy with the whole. Let us save some respect, too, for the equally delicate structure of the marketplace, which routinely accomplishes feats that even Nature dares not attempt.

CHAPTER 9

OF MEDICINE AND CANDY, TRAINS AND SPARKS

Economics in the Courtroom

Bridgman made candy in the kitchen of his London home. He got along well with his neighbors, including Dr. Sturges, who lived and practiced medicine in a house around the corner.

In 1879, Dr. Sturges built a new consulting room at the end of his garden, adjacent to Bridgman's kitchen. Only after the construction was complete did the doctor discover that Bridgman's machinery made noise—so much noise that the consulting room was unusable. Sturges brought suit in an attempt to shut down Bridgman's business.

The judges who heard the case thought they were deciding more than just the fortunes of Sturges and Bridgman. They were also deciding—or so they believed—between medical services and chocolate candy. If they granted Dr. Sturges's request, he would be able to treat more patients and to do so more effectively; the downside of such a decision would be the disappearance of Bridgman's candies from the marketplace. If they ruled in Bridgman's favor, his candy would survive while Sturges's medical services vanished.

The judges ruled for Sturges. He was granted the unconditional right to demand that Bridgman halt the use of his machinery. In justifying their decision, the judges explicitly referred to its effects on the production of various goods and services. But the judges were wrong. Despite their deeply held illusions, they were in fact powerless to affect the production of candy or of medical care.

Consider a simple example. Suppose that Bridgman earns $100 per week in the candy business, and that Sturges can

83

earn $200 per week by operating his consulting room. If the
court rules in Sturges's favor, he shuts Bridgman down, and
the neighborhood gets more medical services but less candy.

On the other hand, the court could rule for Bridgman, enti-
tling him to make noise. But the game is not yet over. Having
lost in court, Sturges now offers a deal: "I'll pay you $150 per
week if you turn off your machines." This leaves Bridgman with
$50 more per week than he can earn in business and leaves
Sturges with a net profit of $50 per week—not as good as $200,
but still better than the $0 per week that he will earn from
the consulting room if he doesn't deal. Each party benefits, the
bargain is struck, Bridgman shuts down, and the neighborhood
still gets more medical services but less candy.

In other words, Bridgman shuts down *regardless* of the judges'
decision. Their ruling has no impact on this question.

Here is a different, equally simple example. Suppose that
Bridgman earns $200 per week in the candy business, and
that Sturges can earn $100 per week by operating his consult-
ing room. If the court rules against Sturges, then Bridgman
continues to make candy and Sturges does not practice.

If, on the other hand, the court rules *for* Sturges, he has the
power to shut Bridgman down. But now it is Bridgman who
offers to deal: "I will pay you $150 per week if you let me
stay in business." This gives Sturges $50 more than he can earn
from consulting; it still leaves Bridgman with a positive net
profit; and it is therefore mutually agreeable. The deal is struck,
Bridgman still continues to make candy, and Sturges still does
not practice.

In this example, as in the previous one, the court's decision
has no effect on whether Sturges operates his consulting room,
and no effect on whether Bridgman continues to operate his machinery. Economists are fond of summarizing this observation
by saying that the court's decision "does not matter."

Bridgman and Sturges might not agree with this wording,
because the decision matters very much to them. In the first
example, a ruling for Sturges leaves him operating his consulting room and ignoring Bridgman's existence, while a ruling
against Sturges leaves him operating his consulting room but
paying Bridgman $150 per week. In the second example, a rul-
ing against Sturges leads him to close down his consulting room

and curse Bridgman for his noise, while a ruling for Sturges leads him to close down his consulting room and happily collect a weekly check from his neighbor.

If we were being more precise, then, we would say that while the judges' decision *does* matter to Sturges and to Bridgman, it doesn't matter to anyone else. The decision does not affect the allocation of resources. That is, it does not affect what gets produced, or the means of production. Economists are usually far more concerned about the allocation of resources than they are about transfers of income between individuals. We reveal our priorities when we say that judicial opinions don't "matter."

The conflict between Sturges and Bridgman is a conflict over who should control a resource. The resource in question is the air surrounding Sturges's consulting room, which Sturges wants to use as an atmosphere conducive to contemplation and Bridgman wants to use as a dumping ground for noise. The court can grant control of this resource to either party and can protect that grant in a variety of ways. It can give Sturges an injunction allowing him to unilaterally determine the disposition of the air; in this case Sturges is protected by a *property right*. Alternatively, it can require Bridgman to compensate Sturges for causing damage to his medical practice; Sturges is then protected by a *liability rule*. Either of these rulings favors Sturges; there are similar options if the court wants to favor Bridgman.

But whoever controls the resource, and however his control is protected, he will find it to his private advantage to direct the resource to its most profitable use, regardless of whether that use is by him or by his neighbor. The court cannot affect the profitability of either enterprise and therefore cannot control how the resource is employed.

This startling observation about the impotence of judges was made in 1961 by Professor Ronald Coase of the University of Chicago Law School. While it is obvious once stated, it seems to have come as a revelation to economists, jurists, and legal scholars. It also marked the birth of a new academic specialty: the economic analysis of law.

In Coase's honor, his observation has come to be called the Coase Theorem. It applies whenever the parties to a dispute are able to negotiate, to strike bargains, and to be confident that their bargains are enforceable. Under these circumstances, the Coase Theorem says that the allocation of property rights, or the choice of liability rules, or more generally any distribution of *entitlements* (a formulation that includes both property rights and liability rules) has no effect on the ultimate allocation of resources. Judges' decisions don't matter.

It is easy, however, to think of circumstances in which the Coase Theorem does not apply, because negotiation is either impossible or prohibitively expensive. This can happen, for example, if the number of parties to a dispute is very large.

For example, railroads sometimes run tracks through farmland. The trains throw off sparks, which occasionally ignite the surrounding crops. Farmers suffer damage, for which they demand compensation from the railroad. What are the consequences of rulings for or against the farmers? How would various rulings affect the number of trains that are run, the quantity of crops brought to market, and the means by which the crops are produced?

If there is only one farmer involved, then the Coase Theorem answers "None" and "Not at all." Just as in the case of *Sturges* v. *Bridgman*, the court's decision is the beginning of the decision process, not the end. If the court rules that the farmer can order the trains off the land, the railroad can still offer to buy back its right-of-way. If the court rules that the trains can run but the farmer must be compensated, the railroad can either stop running trains, or run fewer, or install spark-control equipment, or go ahead and pay the damages, or offer the farmer a flat fee to move his crops so that there will be no damage. If the court rules that the farmer has no legal recourse, he can offer to pay the railroad to stop running trains, or to run fewer, or to install spark-control equipment, or he can go ahead and bear the damage, or he can move his crops. The Coase Theorem tells us that any solution that is instituted following a ruling for the railroad will also be instituted following a ruling for the farmer, and vice versa. The only thing that the court really decides is who will pay whom.

But when many farmers are affected, as opposed to just one, the situation becomes more complicated. Arranging a negotiation among a hundred individuals leads to obvious logistical problems. And more subtle difficulties crop up. Even when a contract is reached that benefits everyone, any single farmer can threaten to hold out and refuse to sign unless he is given a share of everyone else's gains. If several farmers adopt this tactic, there can be a hopeless impasse.

So in a case like this, the court's decision *does* matter. Whatever the court orders is unlikely to be undone by subsequent negotiations. If the railroad is made liable for crop damage, it might run fewer trains or install spark-control equipment, but it is unlikely to be able to strike deals with all of the farmers to remove their crops. If the railroad is freed of liability, the farmers might remove their crops but are unlikely to form a coalition to buy spark-control equipment for the railroad.

Coase considered this example in some detail and asked this question: Suppose that the court wants to encourage allocations of resources that are economically efficient. Then how should the court rule?

Prior to 1961, economists would unanimously have answered, "Make the railroad liable." The argument is this: Because the railroad creates sparks, and the sparks create damage, the railroad should be forced to take account of that damage when it decides to run a train. If running a train brings the railroad $100 worth of profit, while inflicting $200 worth of crop damage, then it is economically inefficient for the train to run. How do we convince the railroad not to run such trains? Make them pay the $200 cost.

Coase analyzed this argument and pronounced it wrong. It goes wrong exactly where it says that "the sparks create damage". In fact, what creates damage is the simultaneous presence of sparks and crops in the same place. In view of this, it makes no more sense to say that "the sparks create damage" than it does to say that "the crops create damage." If either sparks or crops are removed, the problem goes away.

Return to the train that brings the railroad $100 worth of profit, and whose sparks interact with crops to create a $200 loss. Suppose that for a cost of $10, the farmers can remove their crops to a different location or install a firebreak. When the railroad is liable, the farmers, being fully reimbursed for all fire damage, choose not to take these precautions. The railroad finds the train unprofitable and discontinues it. The owner of the railroad—and the world—is $100 poorer.

But if the railroad were *not* liable, things would turn out very differently. Trains would continue to run. Farmers, having no other recourse, would protect their crops with a $10 investment. Farmers—and the world—would be only $10 poorer.

In this instance, the economically efficient outcome—a $10 loss instead of a $100 loss—is achieved only if the railroad *is not* liable. By reversing the numbers, I could just as easily make an example in which the efficient outcome is achieved only if the railroad *is* liable.

And so we come to the flip side of the Coase Theorem. When circumstances prevent negotiations, entitlements—liability rules, property rights, and so forth—*do* matter. Moreover, the traditional economist's prescription for efficiency—making each individual fully responsible for the costs he imposes on others—is meaningless. It is meaningless because the costs in question result from conflicts between two activities, not from either activity in isolation. The traditional prescription blinds us to the fact that either party to a conflict might be in possession of the efficient solution, and that the wrong liability rule can eliminate the incentive to implement that solution.

Some factories pollute the air, damaging the health and happiness of area residents. Should the residents be allowed to sue for these damages? If we answer no, then the factory has no incentive to switch to cleaner fuels, or to install pollution control equipment, or to reduce its output, or to move. If we answer yes, then the residents have no incentive to adopt measures like pollution-resistant house paints, or to move away. Any of these solutions could be the most efficient. Economic theory does not reveal whether it is cheaper for the factory to control its emissions or for the residents to move upwind.* The court's decision matters, and the efficient decision depends on the particulars of the case.

What, then, is the court to do? Much depends on what the judges are trying to accomplish. If their goal is something other than economic efficiency—if their primary concerns involve

---

*The costs of the move need not be primarily financial. People grow fond of their neighborhoods, and this fondness is part of the cost of moving. We have to translate these costs into monetary units before making any kind of comparisons. In principle, we ask each person, How much compensation would it take to get you to move voluntarily? His answer to this question is the cost of his move.

justice, or fairness, or some abstract legal criterion—then economic analysis has relatively little to contribute. But if the goal is economic efficiency, then there is much to be learned from Coase's analysis and the body of knowledge that has grown from it. Judges often express explicit interest in the economic consequences of their actions, and economists believe that such considerations have played a major role in the evolution of the common law. For now, I will imagine a judge who shares these concerns, and ask what advice we can give him.

First, we can offer a note of reassurance: If you are trying a case in which the opposing parties are able to negotiate and enforce contracts, then your decision does not matter and you cannot be wrong. Subsequent negotiations will lead to an efficient allocation of resources that is entirely independent of what you decide.

Second, a note of caution: Do not attempt to decide a case by deciding who is at fault. Even if you think that you can make sense of this notion, there is no reason why it should lead to an efficient decision. The costs of damage should be borne by the party who can prevent the damage more cheaply, not necessarily by the one who would be labeled the "perpetrator" by misguided common sense.

Third, a note of condolence: It might be very difficult for you to tell who can prevent the damage more cheaply. Suppose you announce in court that the trains will be liable for spark damage *unless* farmers can prevent the damage at low cost, in which case the trains bear no liability. Do you then expect the farmers to reveal that they can prevent the damage at low cost? Of course they won't, and unless you are an expert in both farming and railroading, you are unlikely to know where to place the burden.

Fourth, a suggestion: Try to make it easier for the parties to negotiate. If they can, then we are back in the situation where you can't go wrong.

Let me expand a little on this suggestion by way of an example. The example does not pretend to take account of everything that might be important in the real world; it is stripped down to illustrate a point.

Coal miners suffer a lot of work-related injuries. The number and severity of these injuries can be reduced if owners install safety equipment. According to the Coase Theorem, the

decision about whether to install such equipment is independent of whether owners are liable for injuries to miners.

If a machine can be installed for $5,000 that prevents $8,000
worth of medical costs, an owner who is required to pay those
medical costs will install it. If the owner is *not* required to pay
medical costs, then he will *still* install the machine, because his
employees will offer him some amount like $7,000 to do so. (In
practice, the form of this payment is likely to be an acceptance
of lower wages.)*

Therefore, from the point of view of getting the right amount
of safety equipment installed, the judge cannot go wrong no
matter how he rules.

However, there is another way to prevent accidents: Miners
can behave more cautiously while underground. If they are liable for their own medical costs, they have an incentive to do
so. If the owner is liable for their medical costs, this incentive
is initially reduced. However, the Coase Theorem again comes
into play: The owner can offer to raise the miners' wages in
exchange for their cautious behavior. The resulting level of care
is exactly the same as when the miners themselves are liable.

But there is one more twist: Suppose that the owner is liable.
He offers each miner an additional $10 per day in exchange
for exercising extra caution in the mine. The miners accept the
money, descend into the dark earth where the owner never goes,
and continue to engage in horseplay just as if there had been
no bargain. The owner is never the wiser.

In this case, the unenforceability of the contract, brought
on by the unobservability of the miners' behavior, renders the
Coase Theorem false. Miners *do* behave differently—and more
recklessly—when somebody else is paying their medical bills.

Let us put ourselves in the judge's position. He does not know
whether the safety equipment is cost-justified, because he has no
experience in mining and no good way to estimate how many
accidents it will prevent. He does not know whether cautious
behavior by the miners is cost-justified, for the same reason (and
also because he has no way of estimating the monetary equivalent of the cost to a miner of being always on his guard). But

---

*Conversely, if the same machine prevents only $4,000 worth of injuries, then
it will *not* be installed, regardless of whether the owner is liable.

he does know this: If the miners bear their own medical costs, all things are possible. They will voluntarily choose caution if caution is efficient, and they will pay the owner to install safety equipment if the equipment is efficient.

However, if the costs fall on the owner, only half of all things are possible. It is still true that there will be safety equipment if safety equipment is efficient. But there cannot be caution, because caution requires an enforceable contract, which requires that the owner observe the miners' behavior, which is impossible.

The moral, in this simple example, is to let the miners bear the costs of accidents, so that *every* cost-justified means of preventing accidents can be adopted. The greater moral is that judges should assign liability in such a way as to maximize the opportunities for posttrial negotiations. Because judges are not omniscient, they should make rulings that can be easily reversed through bargaining among the participants. It is the participants, after all, who know the most about the costs and consequences of their own actions.

Let me close with a final example to reinforce the same point. Patients sometimes contract AIDS through blood transfusions. When this happens, should they be able to sue their doctors?

There are at least two ways to reduce the risk of AIDS. One is to be very discriminating about the source of the blood transfusion. Another is for the patient—who is at least *probably* still uninfected after the transfusion, but still faces other risk factors—to tone down his life-style.

If doctors are made liable, they will exercise caution in the choice of blood supply. Unfortunately, a patient who has just had a transfusion knows that if he contracts AIDS at a wild posttransfusion party, he can falsely blame his doctor and collect a large payment. He may therefore be more inclined to risky pleasures than otherwise. This inclination can be counterbalanced: In principle, the doctor can offer a financial incentive for the patient to live more soberly. (Fifty dollars off on blood transfusions for patients who agree to stay home on Saturday nights!) But if the doctor cannot *observe* the patient's life-style, this solution is impractical. The result is too much partying.

If on the other hand patients are made liable, they exercise efficient caution in their choice of pleasures, but doctors have no incentive to search for the best blood supplies. Here again, there is at least in principle a solution: Patients can offer to pay extra for blood that is 99% certain, rather than 98% certain, to be AIDS-free. Unfortunately, this doesn't work if the doctor is able to pocket the money, deliver 98%-blood, and express deep sympathy for the patient's rotten luck when he becomes ill.

This means that each liability rule is flawed in its own way. The court, without the luxury of endless philosophizing about pros and cons, must select one or the other. Neither I nor Professor Coase nor any economist knows what the right decision is, and nothing in economics can decide this case. But what Coase brought to the discussion was an entirely new way of balancing the issues. The court cannot know whether it is worthwhile to upgrade blood from 98% AIDS-free to 99%; it cannot know the costs involved and it cannot know how much the patient values the extra 1% security. It cannot know whether it is worthwhile for the patient, given his particular preferences, to stop having risky sexual encounters with strangers.

The suggestion here is that the court should not even attempt to estimate such costs and benefits. Instead, they are best revealed through negotiations between the patient and the doctor. The right question for the court to consider is, Which liability rule is least likely to interfere with these negotiations? We might not always know the answer, but finding the right question is progress of a sort.

III

How to Read the News

CHAPTER 10

CHOOSING SIDES IN THE DRUG WAR

How the Atlantic Monthly Got It Wrong

Richard J. Dennis is chief adviser to the Drug Policy Foundation in Washington, D.C. He is also a commodities trader, part owner of the Chicago White Sox, and president of a quarterly publication. And he is the author of a serious contender for the most poorly executed cost-benefit analysis ever to appear in print. I learned all this from the November 1990 issue of the *Atlantic Monthly*, which contains Dennis's article entitled "The Economics of Legalizing Drugs." His affiliations and career are advertised in the "Contributors" section at the front of the magazine. His championship exhibition of economic illiteracy is on display in the article itself.

Mr. Dennis concludes that the benefits of legalization would exceed the costs, and I have no doubt that his conclusion is correct. But he reaches that conclusion only by counting costs as benefits, counting benefits as costs, omitting a variety of important factors on each side of the ledger, and double counting some of those that he remembers to include.

A fiasco of this magnitude merits wider recognition. We learn from the mistakes of others, so it is a stroke of fortune to find so many mistakes gathered in a single place. What better way to master the principles of cost-benefit analysis than to analyze a single study that violates them all?

For example:

Principle 1: *Tax revenues are not a net benefit, and a reduction in tax revenues is not a net cost.* Mr. Dennis estimates that if drugs were legalized and taxed, governments could earn at least

$12.5 billion in revenue every year, and he counts that revenue as a benefit of legalization. But tax revenues are just money out of one man's pocket and into another's. From the viewpoint of the entire society—the viewpoint on which cost-benefit analysis insists—they are neither gains nor losses. There is no point in computing them, and they should neither be added nor subtracted on either side of the ledger.

If tax revenue represented a net gain to society, then it would follow that the road to riches is for government to tax every activity at the highest possible level. After the revenue was redistributed, it could be taxed again to create still more wealth. Nobody who has ever paid taxes will have difficulty finding the flaw in this scheme: Whatever the tax collector gains, the taxpayer loses.

If the government ordered everybody with an even-numbered address to pay a dollar to somebody with an odd-numbered address, nobody would argue that there had been a net increase in society's resources. If the government imposed a tax of one dollar on each of the one hundred million Americans who live at even-numbered addresses and distributed the proceeds, government revenue would increase by $100 million without any net benefit to society.

Of course, this assumes that the government *does* redistribute the income—either directly (say, through Social Security payments) or indirectly (say, by building a post office that provides valuable services). If instead the government chose to spend its $100 million in new-found revenue on some wasteful project rather than distributing it, then society would be made poorer. But this impoverishment should be attributed to the wasteful project itself, not to the taxation that financed it. The tax revenue per se is neither a net benefit nor a net cost.

Mr. Dennis rests a lot of his case on the observation that if drugs were legal we could tax them. But if the goal is to raise taxes, there is no need to legalize drugs; there are plenty of other activities available to tax. If there is a social benefit to legalization, it must lie elsewhere.

Principle 2: *A cost is a cost, no matter who bears it.* At this point, Mr. Dennis has counted $12.5 billion in nonexistent benefits of drug legalization. To this he adds another $28 billion per year that could be saved in government expenditures on the arrest, prosecution, and imprisonment of drug law violators. Having grossly overestimated the benefits of tax revenue (which, correctly measured, are $0, not $12.5 billion), he now veers off in the other direction by grossly underestimating the cost of law enforcement.

Mr. Dennis's $28 billion consists of direct cash outlays by the government. But he has forgotten to add those costs of imprisonment that are borne by the prisoners themselves. Several hundred thousand of them are deprived of opportunities to hold jobs, care for their families, or walk on the beach. Legalization would restore those opportunities. That benefit is at least of the same order of magnitude as what Mr. Dennis thinks law enforcement agencies could save.

Now some or all of these benefits might accrue to some pretty unsavory characters or to characters whom one or another of us might judge to be undeserving. But they are benefits, nonetheless, and must be counted as such. Cost-benefit analysis makes no moral distinctions; it simply totals all of the good that arises from an action and contrasts it with the bad. If a drug dealer is unhappy or unproductive when he is in jail, his losses in that dimension are as much social costs as the jailer's salary and the cost of prison construction. The prospect of abolishing those costs is a legitimate benefit of legalization.

How are we to place a monetary value on the prisoner's potential freedom? In principle, the right number to use is determined by the prisoner's willingness to pay: It is the dollar amount that he would be willing to sacrifice to avoid a prison term. In practice, we can approximate this number by the income that the prisoner could earn by virtue of his freedom. (This may be a poor approximation but the best one available.) That income, added over all drug-related prisoners, is certain to run into many billions of dollars. To this we should add the costs that drug users incur in their attempts to avoid detection, prosecution, and conviction, which Mr. Dennis also overlooks.

Principle 3: *A good is a good, no matter who owns it.* Mr. Dennis believes that drug use causes crime and in particular is responsible for $6 billion per year in theft. He views this theft as a $6 billion cost of prohibition. But stolen property does not cease to exist. When a television set is moved from one house to another, it remains as reliable a source of entertainment as it ever was.

This is true even when the new recipient of those services is a thief or a dealer in stolen property.

Theft does have social costs. One is the value of the thief's time and energy, which might otherwise have been employed in some productive capacity. (If I spend an afternoon plotting to steal your bicycle, we end up with one bicycle between us; if I spend the same afternoon building a bicycle, we end up with two.) But this cost is probably far less than the value of the property stolen.

The least efficient thief in America must expend about $100 worth of effort every time he steals $100. If his costs were below $100, others even less efficient than he would find thievery profitable; those others would enter the profession, and he would no longer be the least efficient thief in America. If his costs were more than $100, he wouldn't remain a thief for long.

But that describes only the *least* efficient thief. Because other thieves are more efficient, they must each be able to steal $100 worth of property with *less* than $100 in effort. Consequently, the value of stolen property almost always overstates the cost of stealing it.

On the other hand, we have not yet accounted for all of the social costs of theft. Other costs arise from victims' efforts to protect themselves by purchasing burglar alarms, hiring police and security guards, and avoiding walks in risky neighborhoods. When these are accounted for, the social cost of crime could be either more or less than the value of the stolen property. Therefore Dennis's $6 billion could either underestimate or overestimate the benefit of reducing crime via drug legalization; my own guess is that it is a substantial overestimate. In any event, the number $6 billion is totally irrelevant to the correct calculation.

To summarize the case so far, Mr. Dennis counts the following as annual benefits of drug legalization: $12.5 billion in tax revenue (a $12.5 billion overestimate) $28 billion in savings in law enforcement costs (a gross underestimate, because it ignores the value to prisoners of being free), and $6 billion in theft prevention (a completely random estimate that measures the value of stolen property but has nothing to do with the true cost of theft). To this he adds $3.75 billion saved on military expenditures to fight Colombian drug lords, for a total annual benefit of $50.25 billion.

Having completed his survey of the benefit side, Mr. Dennis turns his analytical powers to the calculation of costs. Here he starts right off by violating the most important principle of all:

Principle 4: *Voluntary consumption is a good thing.* Mr. Dennis recognizes that legalization would lead to lower drug prices and an increase in drug use. He counts this as a *cost* of legalization. But consumers who can increase their consumption as the result of lower prices are reaping a benefit, not bearing a cost.

Of course, this assumes that people know what's best for themselves, and one might argue that in the case of drugs, this isn't always true. But all of the theoretical machinery that has been set up to justify cost-benefit calculations relies crucially on this assumption; consequently cost-benefit analysis is impossible without it. Either we accept the assumption or we are forced to evaluate policies on something other than a cost-benefit basis.

Because Mr. Dennis wants to do cost-benefit calculations, let us accept the required assumption and estimate the benefit of legalization.

When you are hungry enough to pay $15 for a pizza and are able to buy one at the market price of $10, economists say that you have earned $5 worth of *consumer's surplus*. You earn some consumer's surplus on almost everything you buy; the maximum you are prepared to pay almost always exceeds the amount you actually do pay in the marketplace. In a competitive economy in the long run, all of the benefits created by markets tend to show up in the form of consumer's surplus. In almost any cost-benefit analysis, consumer's surplus is one of the major sources of benefit.

When the price of pizza falls from $10 to $8, your consumer's surplus increases for two reasons. First, you earn an additional $2 worth of consumer's surplus on each pizza that you buy, just because the price is lower. Second, you probably buy more pizzas and therefore have more opportunities to earn surplus. (Some people might even start eating pizzas for the first time, earning surplus where before they earned none.)

The first of these—the advantage of a lower price—is not a real social benefit. Paying $8 instead of $10 for a pizza is nice for the consumer, but the pizza maker probably has a different view of the matter. Whatever the consumer gains from lower prices is offset by an equivalent loss to the producer. The lower price in and of itself does not affect the balance of costs and benefits when the interests of both consumers and producers are accounted for.

However, the *second* source of increased surplus—the fact that people eat and enjoy more pizza than before—is a genuine social gain and must be counted as a benefit. If a change in government policy caused the price of pizza to fall by $2, one of the critical tasks in analyzing that policy would be to estimate the increase in consumers' surplus from increased pizza consumption.

Likewise with drugs. For the sake of argument, let us accept the numbers in Mr. Dennis's article: 30 million current users, spending a total of $100 billion annually, and an additional 7.5 million users after legalization causes the price to drop to one-eighth of its current level. A little arithmetic shows that those new users would spend a total of about $3 billion on drugs at the new low price. It is also reasonable to infer from these numbers that the total *value* of those drugs—the amount the new users would be willing to pay if necessary—is about $10 billion.*

Therefore legalization would create a net benefit for new users of over $7 billion per year. Even that estimate does not include gains to existing users who would increase their own consumption.

Instead of the $7 billion benefit that his own numbers imply, Mr. Dennis counts increased drug use as a $25 billion *cost*. Why $25 billion? That is his estimate of private health costs and lost personal income due to drug use by new users. (It is at least heartening to see that at this late juncture, Mr. Dennis has at last decided to start caring about lost personal income. Back when personal income was being *taxed* away, it didn't seem to bother him.)

In any event, the $7 billion increase in consumer's surplus is already net of health costs and lost income. Any such losses

---

*This number can be calculated from the numbers in this paragraph, a little economic theory, and an additional technical assumption. For initiates who are curious about the technical assumption, either a straight-line or a constant-elasticity demand curve will do.

would have been reflected in people's willingness to pay for drugs and so would have been implicitly accounted for in the original calculation. Mr. Dennis, however, would have us list these personal expenses in a separate category, thereby violating yet another principle:

Principle 5: *Don't double count.*

"The Economics of Legalizing Drugs" is one of the worst cost-benefit studies ever done. Its author (presumably in common with the editors of the *Atlantic*) has failed to master two simple superprinciples from which all of the other principles follow:

Only Individuals Matter

and

All Individuals Matter Equally

These are the rules of the cost-benefit game. You don't have to follow them, but if you don't, you're playing some other game.

If Mr. Dennis had remembered that only individuals matter, he would not have made the elementary error of counting government revenue as a good thing. The government is not an individual, so the government doesn't count. Government revenue *distributed to individuals* is a good thing but is offset by the collection of taxes *from* individuals, which is a bad thing of equal magnitude. You can count both (in which case they cancel each other) or, more simply, you can count neither.

Despite what you may have heard, economists are entirely indifferent to what's "good for the country," "good for the economy," or "good for General Motors." If General Motors's profits increase by $100 million, economists will be pleased because the individual owners of General Motors are $100 million richer. If General Motors shuts down while the owners devote themselves to meditation, achieving a state of transcendent peace that they collectively value at $100 million, economists will be equally pleased.

Should Americans work harder and invest more to increase industrial production? The economist's answer is, Only if it makes them happier. Newscasters report economic growth as if it were a benefit with no offsetting cost. Growth does benefit individuals, because it allows them to increase their consumption in the future. The conditions that create growth impose costs on individuals, who must work harder and consume less in the present. Is the trade-off worth it? The answer depends solely on the preferences of the individuals themselves. What's "good for the economy" is not one of the economist's considerations.

If Richard J. Dennis had cared about individuals, rather than abstract entities like economies or governments, he would not have made the error of counting only *government* expenses when it came to law enforcement costs. (Government expenses *are* real costs, but *only* because the bills are ultimately paid by individual taxpayers.) He would not have overlooked the costs of individuals who spend time in jail, individuals who spend resources to shield themselves from crime, and individual drug offenders who spend resources to avoid being caught.

Because all individuals matter, and because different individuals can have opposing interests, we need a rule for weighing one person's preferences against another's. If we are called upon to decide whether to expand the logging industry, and if Jack values newspapers while Jill values woodlands, we need a way to compare Jack's potential gains with Jill's potential losses. There are many philosophically defensible stands here, and the logic of cost-benefit analysis (which is another name for what I have elsewhere called "the logic of efficiency") chooses unambiguously among them.* Its position is enunciated in our second superprinciple: All individuals matter equally, with the strength of their preferences measured by their willingness to pay. If Jack values a tree in the sawmill at $100 and Jill values a tree standing in the forest at $200, then we declare the benefit of logging to be $100 and the cost to be $200. We don't inquire into the moral worthiness of Jack or Jill.

In principle, if we envision a change in policy (say, from drug prohibition to drug tolerance), we can imagine the following experiment. Line up all of the people who support the status quo and ask each of them, "How much would you be willing to pay to prevent this policy from being changed?" Add the responses, and you have measured the total cost of the policy

---

*There are people who seem to believe that cost-benefit analysis should be purely objective in the sense of incorporating no moral preconceptions, as if that were possible.

change. Now line up all of the people who support the change and ask each of them, "How much would you be willing to pay to see this policy changed?" The sum of their responses is the total benefit.

Our insistence on counting all individuals equally has some striking implications. One implication is that a change in price is never either good or bad. Whatever buyers gain, sellers lose. Price changes often result from changes in technology or in the legal environment, which can *simultaneously* affect production costs or consumption levels in ways that can be good or bad. But a price change *in and of itself* is neither a good nor a bad thing.

In 1992, many interest rates fell dramatically. The *New York Times* ran a feature article on what a fine development this was: Borrowers now found it easier to finance cars, homes, and capital equipment. As a minor caveat, the article acknowledged that the picture was not not so rosy for lenders; it referred to this problem as an unfortunate "secondary effect."

But an interest rate is like a price. For every borrower there is a lender, and every dollar borrowed is a dollar lent. *All* of the advantages of a low interest rate are exactly offset by its disadvantages. Borrowers and lenders matter equally.

When we set out to do a cost-benefit analysis, we commit ourselves to treat everybody equally. Buyers are on a par with sellers, borrowers are on a par with lenders, and drug dealers, thieves, and addicts are on a par with police officers, commodities brokers, part owners of the Chicago White Sox, and saints.

If Mr. Dennis had remembered that all individuals matter equally, he would have treated jail time for pushers as a cost and increased consumption for willing users as a benefit. He would have realized that shifting income around through taxes or through theft does not create or destroy any wealth; it only transfers wealth among individuals, all of whose preferences are equally important.

Probably Mr. Dennis does not fully approve of every philosophical or political implication of treating all individuals equally. No economist would deny his right to such a position, and many—quite possibly most—economists will have much sympathy for it. If that is his position, however, it commits him to evaluating policies on something other than a cost-benefit basis. Furthermore, it is incumbent on him to tell us just what that alternative basis *is*. Enumerating a list of things that he is willing to consider costs, and another list of things that he is willing to consider benefits, is not terribly enlightening to the reader who wants to know whether the author's philosophical preconceptions match his own. Any policy analyst ought to reveal up front what his moral criteria are—and then present an evaluation that is demonstrably consistent with those criteria.

Many economists, much of the time, adopt the cost-benefit criterion as a general guide to policy.* Sometimes its implications make us uneasy. Confronted with a policy that would enrich a Rockefeller by $1,000 at the cost of $900 to a struggling single parent, the cost-benefit criterion recommends acceptance. The same is true if Rockefeller is replaced with a murderous organized crime chieftain. In such cases, I feel sure that almost every economist would want to depart from the strict application of the cost-benefit criterion.

Nevertheless, when an economist is confronted with a policy decision, one of his first instincts is to analyze costs and benefits in accordance with the two superprinciples. There are at least two reasons for this instinct.

First, if the cost-benefit criterion is applied consistently, then most people will probably gain more than they lose over the course of many policy decisions. This is so even though any *particular* application of the criterion can hurt good people in unfair ways. When we ban logging to confer a $200 benefit on Jill at the cost of a $100 loss to Jack, Jack can at least take comfort in knowing that we will side with him in future controversies where his potential benefits are large. We who are guided by the cost-benefit criterion will be against you when you have a little to lose and for you when you have a lot to gain; on balance we will probably do you more good than harm.

Second, economists are fond of the cost-benefit criterion because they are skilled at applying it. Economic theory allows us to deduce what outcomes the criterion supports, without having to do specific calculations. For example, we know on theoretical grounds that when property rights are well defined

---

*The cost-benefit criterion is equivalent to what I have called the efficiency criterion in other chapters.

and markets are competitive, market prices maximize the excess of benefits over costs. In these circumstances, we can confidently predict that a price control must be a bad thing relative to a market outcome, even without calculating any costs or benefits explicitly.

We like the cost-benefit criterion first because we think its application makes almost everybody better off over the long haul, and second because it is easy to apply. In other words, the benefits are high and the costs are low. The reasoning may be slightly circular, but the cost-benefit criterion recommends itself highly.

CHAPTER 11

THE MYTHOLOGY OF DEFICITS

with Lauren J. Feinstone

At the rate of one dollar per second, it would take over one hundred thousand years to pay off the national debt. Such facts titillate, but they do not enlighten. Unfortunately, they have come to pervade public discourse. As a result, the public's understanding of debt and deficits is almost nonexistent. In its place is a collection of unsubstantiated beliefs—myths, if you will—that are routinely and uncritically repeated in the halls of Congress and on the nightly news. These myths have become almost as widespread as they are indefensible. Yet a few basic principles, easily mastered, suffice to clear the mind.

The myths about the deficit underlie three grand misconceptions. One is that the numbers that are officially reported and widely analyzed are actually reflective of anything approaching economic reality. Another is that government deficits clearly cause high interest rates via simplistic mechanisms that people think they understand. A third is that certain identifiable groups ("future generations," the private sector generally, the export industry in particular) are clearly and unambiguously hurt by deficits.

Each of these grand misconceptions arises from several subsidiary myths that we shall dissect individually. Before doing so, we want to present a parable that will clarify all of the important issues related to government debt. We will then return to the grand misconceptions and the myths that underlie them.

A PARABLE

Suppose that you engage a purchasing agent to do your clothes shopping for you. This agent is empowered to make certain decisions on your behalf. First, he must decide how much to spend on the various components of your wardrobe. Second, he must decide how to finance those purchases.

In order to focus on the second of these decisions, let us suppose that your agent has already resolved to spend $100 on your clothes. There are three methods of financing available to him. First, he can withdraw $100 from your bank account and use it to pay for his purchases up front. Second, he can charge the purchases to your credit card and settle the debt a year from now. In this case, the credit card bill to be paid off next year will be $110—the $100 principal and $10 interest (assuming an annual interest rate of 10%).

There is also a third option—the agent can charge the $100 to your credit card with no intention of *ever* paying off the principal. In this case, you will be billed for $10 interest every year, ad infinitum, and your agent will withdraw $10 a year from your bank account to meet these payments.

Now the question is, Which payment scheme do you prefer? To investigate this, let's consider what your financial status will be one year hence under each of the three options.

We have assumed a prevailing interest rate of 10% and will suppose that your $1,000 bank account is earning this prevailing rate. This means that in the absence of any clothes purchases, your balance would rise to $1,100 by this time next year. Any of the three plans that your agent can adopt will partially deplete this $1,100; let's see by how much.

Plan A removes $100 from your bank account today, reducing it from $1,000 to $900. A year from now that $900 will have earned $90 in interest, and your balance will be $990. This is $110 less than the $1,100 that you would expect to have if you hadn't purchased any clothes. Where did the $110 go? Exactly $100 was used to buy your clothes; the other $10 is interest forgone as a result of paying for the clothes at the time of purchase.

Under Plan B, no payments are made until next year. At that time, your bank balance will be $1,100 (just as if no purchases had been made, because nothing has been withdrawn). From this, your agent will withdraw $110 to pay the credit card bill ($100 principal plus $10 interest), leaving you with a balance of exactly $990.

In other words, Plans A and B ultimately deplete your bank balance by identical amounts. In either case, your clothes have cost you $110 by the end of the first year. Under Plan A you forgo earning $10 in interest, while under Plan B, you earn $10 in interest and then send it along to the credit card company.

There is also Plan C, under which the purchases are charged and never paid off—a policy of "eternal deficit." How does your bank balance look after a year on this plan? From a balance (one year from now) of $1,100, your agent will deduct $10 for the first annual interest payment. This leaves you with $1,090 in liquid assets—or does it? Knowing that you are committed to making payments of $10 a year forever, you will be forced to set aside a fund from which to make these payments. How large a fund will you need? The answer is exactly $100, because this will earn an interest payment of $10 a year forever, which is what you need to meet your obligations.

In other words, your bank balance is $1,090, but of this there is $100 that you dare not withdraw. This leaves you with usable assets of $990—exactly the same as you would have under Plans A and B.

Questions of finance, then, can safely be left in the hands of your purchasing agent, and you need not concern yourself with what he decides. It is true that if your agent plunges you into debt, you will incur interest obligations. It is also true that through deficit financing, he allows your assets to earn interest that would otherwise be forgone. When you assume a debt, the costs and the benefits cancel each other out exactly. The issues of whether to run a deficit—and if so, for how long—are of no consequence.

Of course, other issues are of consequence. Specifically, the decision to spend $100 on clothes—which we have been taking as given throughout this discussion—does matter to you, even if the method of financing does not. If you consider a $100 clothes budget to be either overly profligate or overly penurious, you may be very unhappy with your agent, and you may wish to fire him.

In the same way, you may be very unhappy with a government that spends either more or less on various programs than you would prefer. But once this level of spending has been chosen, there are only three ways for the keepers of the Treasury to finance it. They can tax you today. They can borrow money and pay it off (with interest) at some fixed time in the future, taxing you enough then to meet their obligations. Or they can borrow money and roll over the debt forever, periodically taxing you enough to meet the interest payments. The analogy of government as purchasing agent suggests that it doesn't make a bit of difference to you which method is selected.*

Now this parable is undoubtedly too simple, for a number of reasons. If you expect to die in six months, and if you don't care about the size of your bequest, then you can come out ahead by running up huge debts due a year from now. (On the other hand, if you view your heirs' well-being as an extension of your own, the analogy is restored.) It is also the case that individuals may have preferences between being taxed now and being taxed later if they expect their tax liabilities (e.g., their incomes) to change substantially between the two periods.

But the analogy is still a powerful one, which suggests that if deficits do "matter," then they do so for rather subtle reasons. It demonstrates that deficits, in and of themselves, are no better or worse than taxation and makes it plausible that our primary concern should be with the level and composition of government spending, rather than with how that spending is financed. These are themes to which we shall return.

MYTHS ABOUT WHAT THE NUMBERS MEAN

The official measurements of government spending (and consequently of government deficits) arise from a hodgepodge of numbers that are arbitrarily added together with no theoretical justification. These figures include actual consumption of

---

*In fact, the story becomes more realistic when we replace your clothes buyer with the government. We have been assuming that your bank account earns the same rate of interest at which you borrow from the credit card company. This may seem objectionable. But the interest payments on *government* debt are at the Treasury bill rate—which you *can* earn by the simple expedient of buying Treasury bills.

resources by the government (e.g., spending for education or the military), transfer payments (like Social Security), and interest on past debt. The result of adding together these apples, pears, and oranges (and then subtracting tax revenues to compute a deficit) has no economic significance, although it appears to be a powerful totem in our society. Government agencies attempt to estimate it, newspapers solemnly report it, and pundits agonize over it. None of them ever seems to ask what the number signifies. Here are some of the myths underlying the widespread acceptance of this meaningless calculation.

Myth 1: *Interest on past debt is a burden.* Interest payments on past debt are included in the calculation of the deficit, which implies that these payments add to the taxpayers' burden. The parable of the purchasing agent reveals this to be false. Interest payments on past debt are precisely offset by the interest we earn when we defer our tax liability. This point is crucial. Government borrowing allows us to defer paying our taxes, just as his credit card allows the clothes buyer to defer paying his clothing bill. This allows tax payers to earn interest on their own assets for a longer period of time, which exactly cancels the "burden" of eventually paying interest on the government debt.

It follows that interest on past debt should not be included in any meaningful measure of government spending or government deficits. But it always is included, and as a result all reports of the size of the deficit are grossly overestimated.*

Myth 2: *A dollar spent is a dollar spent.* That is, a dollar spent in erecting a government office building (which uses up steel, glass, labor, etc.) is the equivalent of a dollar paid out by Social Security (which makes one person richer and another poorer without actually consuming anything). Clearly this is false, and any number that results from pretending it is true must be highly suspect.

Myth 3: *Inflation doesn't count.* In fact, inflation is an enormous boon to any debtor, including the government. If the government owes a trillion dollars and inflation is at a rate of 10% per year, then in the course of a year the real value of government debt is reduced by 10% of $1 trillion (or $100 billion).

---

*Ironically, politicians often depict interest on past debt as the *most* burdensome component of the deficit!

That $100 billion is government revenue, just as surely as $100 billion raised in taxes is government revenue, and it ought to be counted as such. It isn't. After correcting for this missing revenue, Prof. Robert Barro of Harvard University found that the federal government ran a surplus as recently as 1979 and annual deficits of under $10 billion in the first two years of the Reagan administration!

Myth 4: *Promises don't count.* Suppose that a new president promises to increase government spending on highways, education, and other forms of infrastructure. Even before the program gets underway, the president's commitment to future spending is a form of debt (just as it is a form of debt if I promise today that I will deliver a $100 check to you next week) and should probably be counted in calculating the current deficit. It isn't.

The measurement problem becomes subtler when there is legitimate uncertainty about either the president's sincerity or his ability to deliver. If I promise to deliver you a $100 check next Tuesday and neither of us is sure whether you should take me seriously, have I incurred a debt or haven't I?

It is by no means clear how to solve that measurement problem; we raise it to point out that *any* potential solution is open to legitimate criticism, so that *any* single measure of the deficit can be legitimately dismissed as wildly incorrect.

The government's biggest outstanding promise is to continue the Social Security program. Whether this promise is counted as a debt makes an enormous difference in calculating the deficit. Laurence Kotlikoff, the recent author of *Generational Accounting,* puts the matter this way: According to the government's accounting, payments from workers and employers to the Social Security system count as taxes, and benefits that the system pays to retirees count as transfer payments. It would be *equally legitimate* to adopt an alternative accounting system under which payments from workers and employers count as loans to the government and benefits to retirees count as repayments of those loans.*

---

*Under this system, if benefits exceed what it would take to repay the loans at a market interest rate, only the excess would still count as a transfer payment. If benefits fall short of what it would take to repay the loan, the deficiency would count as a tax.

According to the government's accounting, the outstanding national debt is now somewhere between $3 and $4 trillion. According to the alternative accounting, the outstanding debt is closer to $10 trillion. The only reason for using one accounting system rather than the other is that somewhere in the mists of history, some accountant performed the equivalent of a coin flip. How much economic significance can underlie a number whose value depends on a perfectly arbitrary choice among equally legitimate accounting methods?

MYTHS ABOUT INTEREST RATES

In the first presidential debate of 1984, Walter Mondale made the statement that "everybody, every economist, every business-man" agrees that deficits affect interest rates. That statement, particularly as it concerns economists, is very far from true.

Do deficits affect interest rates? We don't know. Did Mr. Mondale have any good reasons for thinking that deficits affect interest rates? Almost surely not. Yet, an unwarranted faith in the power of the deficit would place him squarely in the mainstream of the electorate.

A belief in the power of deficits over interest rates seems to be indelibly ingrained in the American psyche, reinforced by two essentially fallacious arguments. The fact that these arguments break down under careful scrutiny doesn't prove that deficits *don't* affect interest rates, but it *does* mean that Mr. Mondale (like so many others) failed to prove his case. Indeed, he failed to give us any reason to suspect a connection between deficits and interest rates, other than an unjustified appeal to the authority of "every economist." Let's examine the arguments about deficits and interest rates.

Myth 5: *The "Goliath" Myth.* According to this theory, the country is populated by little "Davids," competing against the "Goliath" of the federal government, which annually consumes $200 billion that would otherwise be available to Davids seeking to finance their cars and their houses. This competition for a limited supply of money drives up interest rates to the point where David can't even afford to finance a slingshot.

The analogy is entirely without foundation. Government does not consume money by the act of borrowing it; dollars borrowed by government are immediately available to be borrowed again by individuals. Suppose that the government decides to borrow a dollar in order to purchase a paper clip for use at the Pentagon. It effects this borrowing by selling a bond to Jack, who withdraws a dollar from his bank account to make the purchase. The dollar is immediately used to buy a paper clip from Jill, who deposits it in her bank. Now it is true that Jack's bank has a dollar less in deposits, but Jill's has a dollar more. The total number of dollars that the banks have available to lend to David is exactly the same as it was before the government started borrowing. Goliath consumes no money; he just moves it around a little.

The key observation here is that governments don't just borrow without reason; they borrow to spend. The spending restores the money that the borrowing appears to "use up." The usual fallacy is to notice the borrowing but not the spending.

Myth 6: *The Myth of Dick and Jane.* The fallacious argument here runs like this: "If the government wants to increase its borrowing, it must induce people to lend to it. This means it must offer higher interest rates. Then everyone else must offer higher interest rates in order to remain competitive."

The mistaken notion underlying this argument is that if Dick wants Jane to lend him a dollar at the prevailing rate of 10%, and if she is reluctant to do so, then Dick must offer a higher interest rate to get Jane to change her mind.

Not so. There is another way to change Jane's mind. Dick can offer to lend Jane a dollar at 10% interest, in exchange for her making an identical loan to him. Indeed, Dick can convince Jane to lend him any amount at all—as long as he lends her the same amount, at the same interest rate—without producing any upward pressure on that rate.

This example is not as fanciful as it sounds. Whenever the government wants to borrow a dollar, it simultaneously lends a dollar, just as Dick does. After all, why does the government borrow? It does so to avoid raising your taxes for the time being—in effect, lending you back the taxes that it would ordinarily assess.

Unlike the borrowing of an individual, government borrowing is always accompanied by an implicit loan to the taxpayers. The government, like Dick, borrows from the public (or Jane), while simultaneously lending the same amount at the same rate. Like Dick and Jane, the government and the public can carry this on at any level without having any effect on the rate of interest.

MYTHS ABOUT THE BURDEN OF THE DEBT

The final set of myths concerns who bears the burden of government debt. Because it isn't clear that government debt is in any sense a burden, it may be unnecessary to examine these too closely. But exposing the flaws in these arguments is an instructive exercise that illustrates a number of important points.

Myth 7: *Our grandchildren will inherit our debts.* Our grandchildren will inherit not only our debts but also our savings accounts, which include the additional wealth that we save by paying lower taxes in the present. Before that day comes, both the debts and the savings will increase owing to accumulated interest. If we make a one-dollar debt payment today, we can indeed free our grandchildren from a two-dollar debt burden tomorrow, but only at a cost that undoes the favor: By removing that dollar from our savings accounts, we reduce their inheritance by two dollars as well.

Myth 8: *The Myth of Crowding Out.* It is argued that government borrowing uses resources that would be better employed by the private sector. This is similar in form to the Goliath myth, except that this one concerns physical resources rather than money. It is false because government borrowing does not consume anything. What consumes resources is government spending. If the government purchases a million tons of steel, then a million fewer tons of steel are available to the private sector. This is equally true whether the steel is purchased with tax revenues or with borrowed funds. The burden on the private sector is correctly measured by the resources government consumes, not by the way in which it acquires those resources.

Myth 9: *Deficits hurt our trade position.* Many incorrect arguments have been advanced to support the contention that deficits are bad for the domestic export industry. All of these arguments proceed in one way or another from the twin assertions that deficits affect interest rates and that these in turn affect the value of the dollar. As we have argued repeatedly, the link between deficits and interest rates is tenuous at best. It would take us too far afield to explore the relationship between interest rates and exchange rates.* We confine ourselves to the observation that a chain of reasoning is only as strong as its weakest link.

Those who would engage the attention of the public find it useful to have an instinct for the sensational. It is therefore not surprising that those myths about the deficit that find their way into public circulation all tend to exaggerate both its size and its importance. It is important to deflate such myths and to defuse the near hysteria they sometimes engender. It is equally important not to be lulled into a false sense of well-being.

Every argument we have made in this article assumes a fixed level of government spending. There is no question that high levels of spending are detrimental, in precisely the ways that large deficits are often claimed to be.

Indeed, it may very well be the case that the most harmful effect of deficits is to distract our attention from our most urgent economic priority, which is to find some mechanism for getting federal spending under control. If we fail to meet this challenge, our obsession with balanced budgets will not save us from the consequences.

*We cannot resist pointing out one common and obvious error. High interest rates on U.S. bonds increase the demand for U.S. bonds. It is not at all clear that they should make U.S. *currency* any more attractive relative to other *currencies*.

CHAPTER 12

SOUND AND FURY

Spurious Wisdom from the Op-Ed Pages

There seems to be a consensus that the Great Depression was a bad thing. It's worth asking why.

Living through a depression has two disadvantages. First, it reduces your lifetime consumption. Second, it forces you to adopt an inferior *pattern* of consumption, alternating feast with famine instead of spreading your good and bad fortunes more evenly across your life.

This second disadvantage is significant. Evidence suggests that people prefer to smooth out their consumption when they can. If you receive a $4,000 monthly paycheck, it is unlikely that you spend it in a day and eat at soup kitchens the rest of the month. By choosing to live in a hovel for your first 40 years, you might manage to afford a mansion for the second 40, but few of us make this choice if we can avoid it.

Ill fortune is easier to take in a series of small doses than in a single bitter pill. That statement is the essence of why depressions are unpopular, and I would have thought it uncontroversial until I read a letter to the *New York Times* from Felix Rohatyn, who apparently believes otherwise.

Mr. Rohatyn is a prominent financier, chairman of New York's Municipal Assistance Corporation, and a member of President Clinton's circle of advisers. His letter is worth reproducing in full.

To the Editor:

I was startled and dismayed by [an earlier *Times* editorial] supporting Government borrowing as the appropriate way to deal with the bailout of bankrupt savings and loan institutions. Borrowing may be politically expedient; it is, however, wrong, from both an economic and a moral point of view. The straightforward, and least damaging way to deal with this fiasco, is to pay off the $130 billion loss with a temporary three- to four-year surcharge on income taxes.

The economics are simple:

(1) Borrowing will turn a $130 billion loss into a $500 billion drain over 20 to 30 years. It will maintain pressure on the credit markets and lead to higher interest rates. It will add $10 billion to $15 billion annually in interest costs to the Federal budget deficit, when interest costs constitute, after defense, the largest Federal expenditure. It will require continued high inflows of foreign capital. It will squeeze out badly needed domestic programs.

(2) A three- to four-year temporary tax surcharge will eliminate $300 billion to $400 billion in interest costs and contribute to lower interest rates and capital costs. This will foster economic growth. The tax will not have negative economic impact because the bailout is basically a transfer program from taxpayers to depositors.

(3) A basic economic principle justifies borrowing only to pay for assets with a useful life. Nothing is more remote from that definition than borrowing to finance losses that have already been incurred.

The moral issue is even simpler. Borrowing burdens the next generation with the repayment of our foolishness and burdens lower-income Americans with the interest costs. The income tax puts the burden where it belongs: on the present generation and on higher-income Americans.

In the damaging legacy of the 1980's, excessive speculation and borrowing will play a prominent role. Unfortunately, your support for borrowing to bail out the savings and loans is, along with your previous support for the use of junk bonds in the private sector, consistent with that legacy. Your voice is, for many of us, the voice of reason. That, however, requires the support of reason in Government financing and private financing. Excessive borrowing is not reasonable.

—Felix G. Rohatyn
New York, June 25, 1990

I frequently scan the *New York Times* for letters that betray extraordinary economic ignorance, and I save them in a folder indecorously labeled "Sound and Fury". I use the Sound and Fury File to construct exam problems, where I reproduce a letter and require students to spot its fallacies. Although competition for the honor is stiff, Mr. Rohatyn's letter is my prize catch. Unfortunately, our exam periods are not long enough for a competent student to do justice to the wealth of material that Mr. Rohatyn provides. If I ever use his letter on an exam, I will have to abbreviate the problem by asking students to confine their analysis to, say, one major error from each paragraph.

I might ask them also to confine their analysis to the subtler errors, skipping past those that are too embarrassingly obvious to mention. This would free them, for example, from commenting on Mr. Rohatyn's point (1), where he asserts that borrowing will convert a $130 billion loss into a "$500 billion drain over 20 or 30 years." When college sophomores treat a dollar paid 20 years from now as the equivalent of a dollar paid today, we usually advise them that they have no talent for economics. If he is really committed to such accounting, Mr. Rohatyn should be pleased to lend me $200 billion today, accept a payback of $300 billion 20 years in the future, and count himself $100 billion ahead on the deal. I will be happy to oblige him.

Obeying my admonition to skip past this and several other equally elementary errors, students would be able to proceed directly to point (2) and the assertion that "the tax will not have negative economic impact because the bailout is basically a transfer program," as if a temporary income tax surcharge is no incentive to delay profitable undertakings for a few years.

This would bring them to my favorite part of the letter, point (3), where Mr. Rohatyn invents from whole cloth a "basic economic principle" that violates the basic principles of economics: *Never borrow to finance losses that have already been incurred.* I suppose this means that if your house burns down you should not take out a mortgage to buy a new one; much better to live in a cardboard box until you've saved enough to buy a new house outright.

Here is a basic principle of economics that economists have actually heard of: *Strive, within reasonable limits, to smooth your consumption.* If you spend $2,000 on a Hawaiian vacation, do not feel obliged to reduce *this month's* expenses by $2,000 to finance it; instead reduce your expenses slightly in each of many months. Do the same if you lose your wallet, or if you are called on to bail out a savings and loan institution. Bad fortune is most tolerable in many small doses. Spread the pain over time; try not to take the hit all at once.

The Rohatyn Principle, which asserts the contrary, suggests that the Great Depression was probably a great idea. Productivity fell in the 1930s, which is a "loss already incurred" and in such circumstances Mr. Rohatyn would have us endure all of the pain in a single monstrous dose. But if you talk to people who lived through the Great Depression you will find that virtually all of them would have preferred to spread the pain, taking a smaller cut in living standards over a longer period of time. If people don't like having their bad fortune concentrated into a few years by the vagaries of the business cycle, why should they like it any better when it is imposed on them by government fiat?

Fortunately, people can and would protect themselves from the Rohatyn Plan. Precisely because they prefer to smooth out their consumption, people would borrow more (or equivalently, save less) in order to get through the temporary period of high taxes that he prescribes. The result would be almost the same as if the government had done the borrowing.

Therefore if Mr. Rohatyn's point (2) were right, then his plan would have essentially no effect. The government's refusal to borrow would be offset by people borrowing on their own. But not quite. Individuals borrow at higher interest rates than the government does. Therefore Mr. Rohatyn's proposal comes down to this: Let people attempt to borrow for themselves at high interest rates, rather than let the government borrow for them at lower rates.

That's mildly bad. But unfortunately, Mr. Rohatyn's point (2) is wrong, which makes his plan not just bad but calamitous. A temporary tax increase would deter productive activity, raising interest rates and making it impossible for people to spread out the undesirable effects of "losses that have already been incurred" by borrowing as economic theory dictates that they should.

The Rohatyn Plan is a recipe for a severe recession, justified by an invented principle that implies that recessions are desirable. In that sense it is internally consistent, which doesn't seem much comfort.

Now that I have opened my Sound and Fury File, let me share another of my favorites.

To the Editor:

While spending by individuals and businesses is an important component of the United States economy, it is a mistake to underestimate the role that Government spending plays in driving the economic engine.

From my vantage point as a university-based teacher and scientist, I can see that the recession in universities, and in scientific research, is largely tied to cutbacks in Government programs. People are being laid off, new hiring is frozen, and scholarship programs are being threatened.

If Government spending in our sector were restored to former levels we could reinstitute construction and renovation programs, furnishing jobs to the construction industry and increasing our capacity for teaching and research. Students with scholarships would again have money with which to buy what they need, adding to economic activity.

We could afford to hire personnel in scientific research and to purchase supplies, which would again further not only our scientific efforts but also the economy.

I am sure that other Americans can see many examples in their own areas in which cutbacks in Government programs have directly led to our economic downturn. The Government need not sit helpless, watching the economy slide. Government is a key part of the economy, and its overfrugal policies have helped land us in this mess.

If the cutbacks we have had were quickly reversed, this might be just the pump priming needed to get us going again.

—Ronald Breslow
New York, Dec. 18, 1991

Professor Breslow is a professor of chemistry at Columbia University and a winner of the National Medal of Science. As a competent scientist, he surely understands the law of energy conservation. You can move energy from one place to another, but you can't create it out of nothing. That's why there can be no perpetual motion machines.

Economics too has its conservation laws. You can move resources from one place to another, but not even the government can create them out of nothing. As the laws of physics preclude a perpetual motion machine, so the laws of economics preclude a free lunch. The government can convert resources to laboratories and supplies at Columbia University, but those same resources are thereby diverted from alternative uses.

If the government spends a dollar to hire a graduate research assistant for Professor Breslow, the dollar comes from *somewhere*. The simplest case to understand is the one in which the dollar comes from raising somebody's taxes—say, John Doe's. As a result John buys two fewer candy bars. There are more jobs for graduate students but correspondingly fewer for confectioners.

Professor Breslow could undoubtedly offer a multitude of alternative scenarios. Maybe when John's taxes go up, he doesn't buy less candy but removes a dollar from his savings account instead. Then John's bank has a dollar less to lend to Mary Roe, who must now reduce her own spending. Mary forgoes buying an eggbeater, or delays the purchase of a car, and the manufacturers of eggbeaters or automobiles employ fewer people.

This doesn't exhaust the alternatives. I am sure that if he wanted to press his point, Professor Breslow could list a dozen other ways for the government to get a dollar and a dozen other possible reactions by private citizens. But every one of these alternatives must result in a dollar less being spent *somewhere* in the economy. It's easy to fool yourself about this, because the indirect effects of raising government revenue are sometimes subtle. It is likewise easy to fool yourself about a perpetual motion machine. All you have to do is examine selected parts of the machine while ignoring others. Viewed in isolation, the electrical outlet on your wall appears to produce energy. In reality, no more comes out than goes in at the power plant.

There is one significant difference between a perpetual motion machine and a free lunch. If I, as an economist, were to design a perpetual motion machine, the *New York Times* would probably consult an expert (such as Professor Breslow) before treating my proposal with respect. When Professor Breslow, as an eminent physical scientist, designs a free lunch, the *Times* takes it at face value. In other words, the *Times* recognizes that assertions about chemistry or physics should be disciplined by some fundamental understanding of the subject, but it fails to recognize that the same is true of economics. That failure is a symptom of a widespread economic illiteracy that makes me sad and angry.

It is certainly true that according to many economic models, government spending can stimulate aggregate output and employment. *None* of those models is consistent with Professor Breslow's simplistic analysis, which consists of blatantly ignoring the government's source of funds. The simplest models that any economist would subscribe to go something like this: The government spends wastefully on temporary projects, creating short-term economic hardship, which people attempt to overcome by borrowing. This bids up interest rates, which makes it less desirable to hold money (because money is a non-interest bearing asset), so people attempt to divest themselves of money by purchasing durable goods. This in turn drives up prices, which induces producers to expand their output, which leads to an increase in employment.*

I'm willing to bet that this isn't what Professor Breslow had in mind.

The size of my Sound and Fury File ebbs and flows with the amount of time I have for pruning outdated material and keeping up with the *Times*. Some entries are too good ever to discard, like the op-ed piece from radio commentator Ira Eisenberg, who advocates handing street beggars vouchers for services from local merchants as an alternative to cash. He explains that the vouchers "can't be exchanged for alcohol or cigarettes, let alone illegal drugs." Why not?

The *New York Times* is not the file's only source. I have in front of me a letter to the *Wall Street Journal* from Richard C. Leone of the New York and New Jersey Port Authority. Mr. Leone explains why Kennedy and La Guardia airports can't

---

*As it stands this story is still incomplete. For example, rising prices need not call forth more output if wages rise in lockstep. There has to be some subsidiary story about why wages fail to rise when prices do.

be privatized: Their value is well in excess of $2.2 billion, but no buyer would be willing to pay that much. Mr. Leone has come far in life for a man who believes that the value of an asset can differ from what somebody is willing to pay for it.

I have an Ann Landers column about pantyhose manufacturers who deliberately create products that self-destruct after a week instead of a year because "the no-run nylons, which they know how to make, would put a serious crimp in their sales." Ann concludes that she and her readers are "at the mercy of a conspiracy of self-interest." It's not clear whose self-interest Ann has in mind. It can't be the manufacturer's. With the facts as she describes them, a self-interested manufacturer would switch from selling one-week nylons for $1 to selling one-year nylons for $52, pleasing the customers (who spend $52 a year in either case but appreciate making fewer trips to the store), maintaining his revenue, and—because he produces about 98% fewer nylons—cutting his costs considerably.

I have an op-ed piece from the *Chicago Sun-Times* calling for a law that would protect artists by allowing them to collect royalties when their paintings are resold at a profit. The writer ignores the question of how his proposal would affect the price of original artwork. Let me fill in the gap for him. If the original buyer expects to pay a $100 royalty at resale time, then his willingness to pay for the original painting—and hence the price collected by the artist—is reduced by approximately $100.* What artists gain in royalties they lose on the sales of original artwork.

Actually, it's worse than that. Some artists have careers that fizzle unexpectedly. Those artists accept depressed prices for their original work but never collect enough royalties to compensate. Other artists do much better than expected; their royalties *more* than compensate for the depressed price of their originals. So the op-ed writer's plan is a prescription for making unsuccessful artists poorer and successful artists richer.

I have a letter to the editor calling for controls on crude oil prices as an indirect way to control the price of gasoline. But when crude oil prices are controlled by law, the price of gasoline

---

*"Approximately" because of an adjustment for the fact that $100 today is worth more than $100 in the future.

at the pump goes *up*, not down. The control at the wholesale level leads refiners to supply less gasoline. The fall in supply leads consumers to bid up the pump price.

A few years ago, a Florida frost caused the price of oranges to rise so high that growers earned more income than usual. One commentator earned a place in the Sound and Fury File by suggesting that the enormous price increase reveals the growers' ability to act as a monopoly. In fact it reveals just the opposite. The incident establishes that growers can raise their incomes by killing oranges. If they were able to act in concert, they wouldn't have waited for a frost.

When there is political turmoil in the Middle East, the Sound and Fury File is guaranteed to swell. An interruption in the flow of oil always elicits a burst of letters and editorials explaining how American oil companies, by exercising their monopoly power, can raise prices so high that their profits increase. Ignore the nagging question of how there can be monopoly power in an industry consisting of Exxon, Gulf, Mobil, Atlantic Richfield, Shell, Getty, Marathon, and many others. Examine instead just the internal logic. If restricting supply can increase profits, a *monopoly* oil industry doesn't wait for political turmoil before it restricts supply. You can claim that the companies profit from political crises, or you can claim that they collude to act as monopolists, but you cannot claim both and be consistent.

False monopoly is only one of the recurrent themes in the Sound and Fury File. "Low interest rates are good for the economy" is a theme sounded often by those who fail to recognize that for every happy borrower there is an unhappy lender, or that what is "good for the economy" is nothing more than what is good for the individuals it comprises.

Every Thanksgiving, I can count on finding editorials exhorting Americans to eat less meat so that what they forgo will be available to the undernourished. The truth, alas, is subtler. When people eat less meat, ranching becomes less profitable, and the ranching industry contracts. Then at least the grain formerly destined for feed troughs becomes available for human consumption, right? Wrong. Farming contracts also.

An entire genre consists of letters and editorials declaring some piece of legislation to be a "victory" for precisely that group that has the most to lose from it. "Family leave" legislation requiring employers to provide lengthy maternity leaves is hailed as a victory for female workers, but it seems odd to label as "victors" those whom the legislation comes closest to rendering unemployable.* When a court ruling made it easier for surrogate mothers to renege on contracts and keep their babies, editorialists were quick to hail a victory for potential surrogate mothers. It was a "victory" that made surrogacy contracts all but obsolete. Was the automobile a victory for the man who made buggy whips?

James K. Glassman wrote a piece in *The New Republic* to prove that stocks are better investments than real estate. He calculates that "if you bought a $200,000 home in Foggy Bottom [a neighborhood in Washington, D.C.] in 1979, it would have been worth $316,000 [ten years later]. But if you bought $200,000 worth of stock in 1979, it would be worth $556,000 [ten years later]—and you'd have another $68,000 in dividend income."

Well, yes, but if you'd bought the house you would have had a place to live for those ten years, whereas if you'd bought the stock you'd have been making rental payments to a landlord. This renders Glassman's comparison meaningless. All he shows is that if you compare *all* of the benefits of owning stock to *some* of the benefits of owning real estate, then the stock comes out ahead. Big deal.

Glassman's piece has a place of honor in my Sound and Fury File because his conclusion is so *exactly* the opposite of the truth. He explains that "stocks appreciate faster than real estate; they always have and they always will. The reason is that a share of stock is a piece of a company in which minds are producing value. Real estate just sits there." The truth is that stocks appreciate faster than houses precisely because a house does *not* just sit there; it provides shelter, warmth, and closet space every

---

*Job applicants are not permitted to opt out of the program in a voluntary bid to rise to the top of the applicant pool, or in exchange for a higher wage. Therefore the natural advantage that the bill confers on male applicants is really cemented into place. In the 1992 vice presidential debate, I loved the irony of Al Gore hammering home his point about family leave legislation ("Did you make it *mandatory*, Dan? Why didn't you make it *mandatory*, Dan?") immediately after extolling the virtues of *choice* in the abortion segment of the program.

single day that you own it. Stocks need to appreciate faster to compensate for the fact that they *don't* provide any comparable stream of services. If stocks and real estate appreciated at the same rate, nobody would own stocks.

I will close with an entry from George F. Will. Mr. Will believes that interest on the national debt represents "a transfer of wealth from labor to capital unprecedented in US history. Tax revenues are being collected from average Americans and given to the buyers of US government bonds—buyers in Beverly Hills, Lake Forest, Shaker Heights and Grosse Point, and Tokyo and Riyadh."

It boggles the mind to learn that there is an educated American who believes that interest on a loan is a form of gift. Mr. Will must be overwhelmed by the beneficence of America's bankers, who give so generously to their account holders. They are almost as generous as homeowners, who charitably donate large mortgage payments every month.

And why stop there? Before Mr. Will came along, economists thought that interest was a payment for the use of somebody else's assets. If such payments are gifts, then so is every rental payment to a landlord, every tuition payment to a college, and every admission fee at a park or a theater.

Mr. Will thinks that bondholders get rich by lending to the government. But if they didn't lend to the government, they would lend their assets elsewhere—probably to workers struggling to get through the period of high taxes that Mr. Will prescribes to reduce the national debt.

Shakespeare notwithstanding, it is not exclusively the idiot who dispenses sound and fury. My file bulges with contributions from demonstrably thoughtful individuals whose insight has failed them on at least one very public occasion. An economist might be tempted to remark that such failures are to be expected, because they are not severely punished. Most readers turn to the op-ed pages for entertainment, not enlightenment, and the writer's incentive is to supply what his readers demand.

CHAPTER 13

HOW STATISTICS LIE

Unemployment Can Be Good for You

The day I moved to Washington, D.C., I asked a cab driver where I should shop for groceries. "Magruder's!" he said emphatically. "It's *wonderful.* It seems like every time I go there, something's on sale."

This was my first encounter with the charming naïveté of Washington consumers. (Later that week we asked our baby-sitter for advice on where to shop for children's shoes and received a breathless endorsement for a local shop where "they *measure* their *feet!*") To this day, I don't believe I've ever entered a grocery store in or out of Washington where there wasn't something on sale.

I gravitate to those sale items. When bananas are cheap, I buy bananas. When apples are cheap, I buy apples instead.

Because the sale items keep changing, I can almost never hope to walk into a store and buy the same item as last week at the same low price. One week I buy a pound of apples on sale for 59 cents. The next week apples have gone up to 65 cents a pound, so instead of apples I buy a pound of bananas on sale for 39 cents. The next week bananas are up to 49 cents but apples are back down again, so I go back to buying apples.

If I wanted to talk my cab driver out of shopping at Magruder's, I might try an argument like this: "Prices at Magruder's are spiraling out of control. It seems like every time I go in there, the stuff I bought a week ago has gone up in price." If I really wanted to impress him, I could compute some percentage increases. "First I bought apples, and then apples went up about

10%. Then I bought bananas, and then bananas went up about 25%. That's a 35% price increase in two weeks!"

Of course, this little computation conveniently overlooks the fact that following a 35% price rise, I'm still buying apples on sale at the same 59 cents a pound that I was paying two weeks ago.

That computation has something in common with the way the government reports inflation statistics. The Consumer Price Index (the most commonly reported measure of inflation, often abbreviated CPI) reports price changes not for the mix of goods that people buy today but for the goods that people used to buy. That mix tends to overrepresent the goods that were bargains in the past and to underrepresent the goods that are bargains today. As a result it overemphasizes the biggest price increases and makes overall changes appear worse than they are.

A few years ago, air fares were low and laptop computers were expensive. People did a lot of flying but few carried laptops. Today air fares are higher and computer prices are far lower. An index like the CPI puts a lot of weight on the rise in air fares but almost none on the fall in computer prices. When you pay more for this year's plane ticket than you paid for last year's, the price index reflects the change. When you buy a computer that you couldn't afford last year, the price index ignores the change. You bought no computers last year, so your computer doesn't count.

Inflation has been a serious problem in this country for most of the last three decades. Correcting for measurement problems does little to diminish that seriousness. But it does matter whether inflation is 3% or 4% or 5%. Social Security payments, for example, are indexed to changes in the CPI. A person whose income goes up at the same annual rate as the CPI generally experiences an increase in buying power each year, because the CPI always makes inflation look worse than it really is.

That might sound like a criticism of the Bureau of Labor Statistics, which compiles the CPI, but it really isn't. In a world of many prices that fluctuate independently, there is no way to construct a single meaningful index that is not biased in one way or another. The United States government actually reports several different measures of inflation, each with its own built-in biases, and economists try to be careful about selecting the right index for the right purpose. The media consistently report only the CPI, perhaps because it serves *their* purpose of making things look bleak. Journalism is the dismal art.

Strictly speaking, statistics never lie, but the truths they tell are often misinterpreted. This is particularly the case with economic statistics. Let me show you some more examples.

Before and after living in Washington I've lived in Rochester, New York, where for many years Star Market and Wegman's were the two great competing grocery chains. (Star Market is now departed. Wegman's continues as the pride of Rochester and is widely considered sufficient reason to move to upstate New York, despite its recent and inexplicable decision to discontinue carrying cream cheese with chives.) Star Market used to run advertisements along these lines: "We measured what the average Star shopper bought last week, and that same basket of groceries would have cost 3% more at Wegman's prices." I believe they were telling the truth. I also believe that the average *Wegman's* shopper might easily have spent 3% more making *his* purchases at Star.

Star's computation is biased in the same way as the CPI. On a given day, Star happens to have a big sale on bananas while Wegman's has a big sale on apples. So Star shoppers buy a lot of bananas and Wegman's shoppers buy a lot of apples. Of course the Star basket would have cost more at Wegman's and the Wegman's basket would have cost more at Star. As long as prices at both stores are roughly comparable on average, and as long as there are cross-store differences in individual prices, this is exactly what one would expect. It's not a reason to prefer one chain to the other.

Journalists like to use the unemployment rate to indicate the overall state of the economy. The surrounding discussion usually overlooks the fact that unemployment is something to which people aspire. The leisure to be idle or to pursue one's fancies is generally thought of as a *good* thing; but when given the name "unemployment," it is suddenly treated as if it were bad.

Of course, unemployment can be *accompanied* by bad things, such as diminution of income, and these are the things that reporters have in mind when they suggest that unemployment is undesirable. But it is worth remembering that the benefits of unemployment help to alleviate the associated costs. When you lose your job as a $50,000-a-year assembly line worker and spend your time earning $0 a year at the beach, it is an exaggeration to suggest that you've lost a job worth $50,000 a year.

We are all grossly underemployed compared with our ancestors of 100 years ago, who toiled in sweatshops 80 hours a week. Few of us would trade places with them. This observation serves as an adequate warning that unemployment rates are no sufficient measure of our economic well-being.

We of the late twentieth century work less than our grandparents did because we are wealthier than they were. When employment falls it can mean that times are getting better. As incomes rise, families may decide that they can get by with one wage earner instead of two. Workers who cling to undesirable jobs in bad times may quit when times improve, either because of an improvement in their other income sources or because of a justified new optimism that there are better jobs to be found by those who spend time searching for them.

Economywide unemployment can be a sign that times are getting worse or a sign that times are getting better. The same is true at the level of the individual. When Peter chooses to work 80 hours a week and get rich while Paul chooses to work 3 hours a week and get comfortable in other ways, who is to say which choice is the wiser? I can find nothing in economics, morality, or for that matter my personal instincts that says we should approve more of one than of the other. Unemployment, or a low level of employment, can be a voluntary choice and a good one.

It is easy for observers to falsely convince themselves that Peter must have been wiser or more fortunate than Paul, because Peter's income is more conspicuous than Paul's leisure. A very naive observer might argue that fairness requires us to remedy the income discrepancy by transferring some of Peter's income to Paul. But the same argument would require us to remedy the leisure discrepancy by transferring some of Paul's leisure to Peter. If fairness dictates taxing Peter to pay Paul, does it also dictate conscripting Paul to mow Peter's lawn?

Because they forget that it is the *fruits* of labor rather than labor itself that is desirable, reporters seem eternally doomed to making the hilarious error of suggesting that natural disasters can be welcome developments because they put people to work. When Hurricane Andrew devastated South Florida in 1992, this suggestion was rampant. According to newscasters, there were mysterious hidden benefits to massive destruction followed by feverish activity to restore the *status quo ante.* I wonder whether they applied this observation to their own lives, say, by periodically gouging holes in their living room walls so that they could employ themselves as plasterers.

It is not a good thing to build a house. It is a good thing to *have* a house. The having can make it worth the building, but the less building you have to do, the better off you are. A community that ends up with the same physical resources it started with after months of unanticipated effort cannot possibly be collectively wealthier than it was before.

It is easy to be fooled by the fact that we observe some things and not others. When I go into a restaurant and ask for a non-smoking table, I am often told that I can be seated more quickly in the smoking section. For a while, this led me to believe that smoking sections are generally less crowded, which seemed like an interesting economic riddle. When I raised my riddle at lunch, my more clear-thinking friend Mark Bils pointed out that restaurants don't have any reason to tell me about the times when the wait is shorter for *non*smoking. Presumably there are a lot of smokers who think that nonsmoking is always less crowded than smoking.*

You and your doctor probably have different opinions about the average size of his waiting room crowd. Perhaps it's because you are just more aware of people when they are coughing on you and there are no empty chairs. More likely it's because you and your doctor are measuring different things.

---

*It's not terribly relevant, but I can't resist telling you about the time when my wife and I asked for a non-smoking table at the Hamburger Hamlet in Washington, D.C., and were seated between two tables of smokers. When we called this to the waitress's attention she was quick to reassure us, "Oh, it's perfectly all right. This section is for *both.*"

Your doctor measures the size of the crowd all day long. You measure it only when you are a patient. And when are you a patient? Probably at the most crowded times. How do I know? Because there are more people there at the most crowded times—that's what makes them crowded. If the doctor tells me that there were 3 people in the waiting room this morning and 25 in the afternoon, and if I have to guess what time *you* were there, I'd say that the odds are 25 to 3 that it was afternoon.

There are always plenty of people around to observe a crowd. There is nobody around to observe a vacuum. The doctor knows that he had 28 patients today, or 14 per half-day on average. Of those 28, only 3 believe that the typical crowd size is 3, but 25 believe that it is 25. The average patient's waiting time estimate is guaranteed to be biased upward.

Unemployment statistics measure not just the number of people unemployed but the average *length* of unemployment spells. Often these data are collected by surveying the people who are unemployed on a given day, asking them how long they've been out of work, and averaging the responses. The resulting number is guaranteed to be biased upward for fundamentally the same reason that most patients overestimate waiting room crowds.

People who are unemployed for long periods are very likely to be unemployed on the day when the pollster arrives. Those who are unemployed for short periods are very *un*likely to be unemployed on that day. So in a sample confined to a single day or a single week, you are sure to encounter a deceptively large number of long-term unemployed.

Statistics seem to indicate that the general prosperity of the 1980s was accompanied by a substantial widening in the gap between the rich and the poor. It appears that as the rich got richer, the poor stayed put. I do not know whether these statistics reflect any underlying economic reality. But there are several reasons why they might not.

First, income tax rates were cut dramatically in the 1980s. Those tax cuts had important real effects, but they had important illusory effects also. When tax rates fall, people devote less effort to hiding their incomes. For that reason alone, *reported* incomes go up. People at the low end of the income scale typically report most of their income in any event, both because they are in low tax brackets and because their income is primarily from highly visible sources such as wages. Therefore we don't see much change in reported incomes at the low end. People at the high end have more in the way of both motives and opportunities to be devious, but they become less devious when their tax rates go down. High-end incomes appear to rise, and the income gap appears to widen.

Second, family breakups create a statistical illusion of poverty. A household with two wage earners each earning $25,000 per year is counted as a middle-class household with a $50,000 income. When the family breaks up, that middle-class household disappears and two $25,000-a-year households arise to take its place.

Third, and I think most interestingly, increased disparity among *annual* incomes need not be associated with increased disparity in *lifetime* incomes. This is because people tend to move around a lot in the income distribution. (In the United States, if you are in either the top or the bottom fifth of the distribution, chances are better than even that you won't be there eight years from now.) A big increase in high incomes accompanied by a small decrease in low incomes can be good for *everybody* if we all spend some time near both ends of the income scale.

Suppose that initially we all have incomes of $50,000, with no inequality whatsoever. Now a change in the economic environment causes half of all incomes to fall to $40,000 while the other half rise to $100,000. You might think that half of all households are worse off and the other half are better off. But if we all take turns, so that half of us earn $40,000 in the even-numbered years and $100,000 in the odd-numbered years while the rest of us do the reverse, then we all average $70,000 a year and we all win.

That vision of extreme income mobility is, of course, quite unrealistic. The usual stereotype of "the rich and the poor" entrenched in their positions for life is quite unrealistic in the opposite direction. Most people have good years and bad years. In any given year, people with high current incomes are likely to be having one of the best years of their lives and people with low current incomes are likely to be having one of the worst. The gap between the highest and the lowest annual income is the gap between one man's best year and another man's worst year. But it's hard to see who—other than a journalist hard up for a sensational story—would want to make that comparison. The right comparison is between two men's incomes, each averaged over many years. I do not know how the changes of the 1980s affected that comparison. I do know that nothing in the annual income statistics can tell us the answer.

One way to create a false impression of widening income gaps is to point out that a lot of people with high incomes have recently gained and a lot of people with low incomes have recently lost. All this shows is that people have good years and bad years. *Of course*, people near the top have recently gained: For the most part they are having unusually good years and are therefore doing better than last year. They are also probably doing better than *next* year, when things will be closer to normal again.

Imagine a colony of nomads who wander randomly up and down the slope of a mountain. Take a snapshot of this colony. Those nomads who are near the summit at the moment when the snapshot was taken are likely to have traveled upward in the recent past. Those near the bottom have probably been traveling downward recently. From this we may infer absolutely nothing about whether the altitude gap between high and low nomads is increasing over time.

There is a general lesson here, which is that it is a mistake to judge a person's overall well-being on the basis of his current well-being. To argue, for example, that the elderly are worse off than the rest of us—say, because they have more health problems—is to overlook that we each take a turn at being young and a turn at being old. My wife and I trade baby-sitting with some of our neighbors. There are nights when our friends are out on the town while we entertain a group of five-year-olds. Our friends don't feel that they are more fortunate than we, because they know what future weekends hold in store for *them*.

This makes it quite impossible to have a general policy of transferring income from the young to the old. If such a policy is in place over your lifetime, you lose when you are young and gain when you are old, which is no net benefit. It *is* possible to transfer income from one *generation* to another. But a clear-eyed observer will note that income is being shifted from the *currently* young to the *currently* old, and that in view of the life cycle that we all share, the first group does not start with an inequitable endowment of youth.

Actually, we don't quite all share a life cycle, because accidents and disease intervene to deprive a few of us of our old age. This means that the young are actually *under*privileged with respect to the old. Young people have only a probability of living a full life; old people are assured of it. Transfers from the young to the old tend to *exaggerate* the underlying inequity.*

A similar observation applies to the current ban on mandatory retirement. Firms seem to believe that they can increase efficiency with mandatory retirement (if they did not believe this, then there would be no need to outlaw the practice); if they are right, then a permanent ban on mandatory retirement lowers average lifetime incomes. (After all, the efficiency loss must be felt by *someone*; probably it means that the wages of young people fall.)* The ban on mandatory retirement is touted as a boon to old people; more plausibly, it benefits only those who are old without first being young—the newborn 67-year-olds I occasionally read about in the supermarket tabloids.

The gross national product is the most frequently reported measure of general economic well-being. As such, it has some obvious deficiencies. It counts the value of all goods and services produced in the economy, but not the value of time spent relaxing on the beach.

It also has some less obvious deficiencies. First, it really *doesn't* count the value of all goods and services produced in the economy. Many goods and services are produced within the household. Whether you wash your own dishes or pay a maid to wash them, the net benefit is a cabinet full of clean dishes. If you pay the maid, the GNP reflects this benefit; if you wash them yourself, it doesn't.

*My colleague Mark Bils argues that we should subsidize tobacco for fairness' sake, because smokers don't get their fair share of Social Security benefits.

*Only one group shares in the gains but not in the losses, namely, those who are already old at the time when the ban goes into effect.

In less liberated times, the standard textbook example to illustrate this point was that of the man who marries his housekeeper. As a housekeeper, she earns $25,000 a year scrubbing floors, washing dishes, and doing laundry. When she becomes a wife, she earns $0 a year doing exactly the same things. Although nothing has changed, the GNP appears to have fallen by $25,000.

This observation is particularly important when GNP is compared across countries. In less developed countries, there is usually more household production and consequently a greater discrepancy between reported GNP and actual output. When you read that GNP in the United States is over 100 times as great as it is in Mali, remember that people in Mali grow their own food and make their own clothes and get no credit for it in the national income accounts. They are much poorer than we are but not as much poorer as the statistics seem to indicate.

Another deficiency is that increased output of goods and services can be either a good or a bad thing. A construction boom that creates thousands of desirable new houses is a good thing; a construction boom that replaces thousands of old houses destroyed by a hurricane consists of running as fast as possible just to stay in one place. The GNP counts them equally.

It is said that figures don't lie, but liars figure. Perhaps a more serious problem is that honest people figure carelessly. The antidote is careful attention to exactly what is being measured, and how it differs from what you would really like to measure if you could.

The Consumer Price Index measures the price of a particular basket of goods; that is not the same thing as the income necessary to maintain a particular level of happiness. The unemployment rate measures the number of people not working; that is not the same thing as the number of people who are unhappy. Annual income statistics measure the distribution of current incomes; that is not the same thing as the distribution of lifetime incomes. The GNP measures the value of all goods and services that are traded in the marketplace; that is not the same thing as the value of all goods and services that are produced, or of those that are desirable.

Some of these discrepancies are simple problems of measurement, as when the GNP omits household production. Others are more subtle, as when the income gap appears exaggerated because those with unusually high or low current incomes are unlikely to remain at those extremes.

By training, economists are sensitive to problems of measurement and statistical fallacies. By cultivated instinct, we correct for them as best we can.

CHAPTER 14

THE POLICY VICE

Do We Need More Illiterates?

The economist's greatest passion is not to change the world but to understand it. Yet every human heart conceals a secret desire to improve its surroundings. Scratch an economist and you'll find a reformer.

For economists, policy is a vice, but a delicious one, and we indulge in it as you might indulge in a hot fudge sundae or an ill-advised affair, succumbing to its seductive and unhealthy pleasures while nurturing our disdain for colleagues who fall prey to the same temptation. We are passionate in our insistence that policy is unworthy of our attention, and in the attention that we give to it.

While economists take up positions on nearly every side of every issue, we share certain perspectives. The economic way of thinking emphasizes the importance of incentives, the gains from trade, and the power of enforceable property rights as forces for good. It embraces the confidence that perfect markets generally yield desirable outcomes and an instinct to make outcomes more desirable by making markets more nearly perfect.

When we are told that we should subsidize defense-related industries so that they will be available in times of war, economists are immediately skeptical. In ordinary circumstances, entrepreneurs can foresee the probability of war as accurately as government officials can. If there is a $\frac{1}{3}$ chance of a major land war in five years, then there is a $\frac{1}{3}$ chance that a factory capable of producing tanks will be a very profitable thing to own. Why doesn't that prospect provide sufficient incentive to keep the factory in business?

Of course, there will be fewer such factories when the chance of war is $\frac{1}{3}$ than when it is $\frac{1}{2}$, but that is presumably the outcome that would also be chosen by a wise government. It makes good sense to invest fewer resources to defend against a less probable event.

The proper incentive is missing only if investors expect that the government will follow historical precedent and impose price controls in time of war.* If we are concerned about our defense preparedness, the problem arises not from too *little* interference with the market (in the form of subsidies) but from too *much* interference (in the form of controls). The best prescription for military preparedness might be a constitutional amendment guaranteeing freedom from price controls.†

When pundits decry the quality of American-made automobiles, economists wonder what all the fuss is about. *Somebody* has to specialize in the manufacture of low-quality automobiles. Why shouldn't it be Americans?

There are markets for automobiles at every point along the price/quality spectrum. There is no special glory in success at the high end of that spectrum and no shame in success at the low end. I would far prefer to have founded the Kmart chain than a high-quality apparel store with a single retail outlet.

Quality need not be correlated with profit. Quality is costly to produce. Some consumers prefer to pay more for better—and expensively manufactured—products; others prefer to pay less for inferior—and cheaply manufactured—alternatives. There is honor in serving either market well.

---

*In World War II, price controls were administered by the Office of Price Administration (OPA). I have been present at discussions where serious attempts were made to assess the OPA's damage to the Allied cause, measured in terms of the equivalent number of German panzer divisions. The estimates tended to be large.

†For the record, I would not want to defend the view that this is a complete analysis of the problem. For example, it might be possible to argue that investors' attitudes toward risk do not coincide with the attitudes that are in some sense socially appropriate regarding an event such as a major war. I am not sure whether there is a convincing case along these lines or not. But the argument in the text certainly represents the sort of first pass at this issue that a typical economist might attempt.

If in fact American cars are of lower quality than their Japanese counterparts, there are a lot of candidates for a good reason why. One candidate is that there are gains from having each type of production concentrated in a single place, that it doesn't matter which is done where, and that historical accident has located the lower-quality plants in the United States. A second candidate is that Americans build low-quality cars because high-quality American workers are most productively employed in other industries; better American cars would entail poorer American banking services. A third candidate is that American workers, being wealthier than their Japanese counterparts, are quite sensibly unwilling to exert as great an effort for a given wage. It is neither unusual nor dishonorable to adjust your priorities to reflect your income bracket.

A common response to these observations is that it would be all very good to sacrifice quality in exchange for keeping costs down, but American manufacturers sacrifice quality *without* keeping costs down: It takes as many hours to build an American luxury car as to build a Japanese equivalent with a better maintenance record. To this there are two counter-responses. First, worker-hours are a poor measure of overall costs. If one hour of a Detroit worker's time produces less than one hour of a Tokyo worker's time, it might be because Detroit wisely spends less on worker training or on devising methods to coordinate various aspects of its operations. Second, *measured* worker-hours are a poor measure of *actual* worker-hours. If the Detroit worker spends 15 minutes out of every hour drinking coffee, then it takes only three-fourths as much time to build an American car as naive statistics might suggest.*

Economists exempt themselves from the common chorus of despair because they recognize the gains from trade. One product is made in Detroit; another is made in Tokyo. Whether you buy a Ford Escort or a Lexus, it doesn't matter where it comes from. Trade separates our consumption choices from

---

*An economist would have little sympathy for the counter-counterresponse that time spent drinking coffee is wasted. We drink a lot of coffee ourselves. I can imagine no reasonable basis for a blanket assumption that better cars are more important than better working conditions.

our production choices. We can build cheap cars and drive expensive ones, if we build the cheap ones profitably.

When "The David Brinkley Show" devotes an hour to platitudes about the "problem" of illiteracy, the economist's first question is, What problem? Of course, literacy is a good thing, but that doesn't mean we have too little of it. Literacy is costly to produce and becomes costlier as it is extended to successively less receptive segments of the population. There is a right time to decide that additional resources devoted to reading programs would be better spent elsewhere.

You would think—or at least *I* would think—that a journalist who bemoans having the *wrong* amount of something would feel some obligation to divulge what he means by the *right* amount. None of Mr. Brinkley's guests, and none of his regulars, felt that obligation. If they *had* told us what they meant by the right amount of literacy, they could have gone on to tell us what leads them to suspect that we have too little, rather than too much.

An economist might incline to apply an efficiency criterion: We should encourage further literacy until the additional costs begin to exceed the additional benefits. A journalist who objects to that criterion is well within his rights but is not thereby relieved of the obligation to reveal his alternative. If efficiency is our guide, we might expect that markets already provide approximately the right literacy rate. The adult who learns to read captures most of the benefits, via higher wages and the satisfaction of being able to educate himself beyond the level of George F. Will and Sam Donaldson. Those benefits provide ample incentive to undertake any cost-justified self-improvement program.

Now, that argument could easily be contradicted in several ways. It is fashionable to argue that educated citizens vote more wisely (though I am not aware of any study that establishes this) and thereby confer benefits on their neighbors beyond those that they capture for themselves. Or maybe the illiterate, by virtue of their illiteracy, are unaware of life's possibilities and therefore make unwise choices that a well-crafted literacy program could efficiently alter. Or maybe people choose too much illiteracy because social welfare programs protect them from the consequences.

To investigate whether there is a literacy problem, Mr. Brinkley ought to have begun by asking whether there is any evidence that these or other considerations significantly distort the market's natural tendency to find the efficient outcome. If so, there is a case for nonmarket remedies. Now comes the crux of the entire matter: *How will we know when those remedies have gone too far?* How do we measure the benefits of literacy, how do we measure the costs of providing it, and how do we determine whether we currently have too much or too little? That is the central question, and Brinkley's crew ducked it completely. If these guys are literate, what is the point of literacy?

Responding to the quadrennial editorials demanding free network television time for presidential candidates, economists recognize that two quite separate propositions are being deceptively packaged as one. The first proposition is that more network television time should be devoted to political messages and less to the alternatives. The second is that television networks should be taxed more heavily.

Network time can be purchased with income tax dollars, or for that matter with a special tax on carrots, as well as it can be confiscated from the networks. If a presidential candidate preempts an episode of "Married With Children," the social cost is a forgone episode of "Married With Children." That cost is the same whether it is borne by the general public, by carrot eaters, or by the owners of television networks. "What should we buy with our tax money?" is not at all the same question as "Who should pay taxes?"

Let me put this another way. Suppose that we agree to make the networks provide $1 million worth of free air time, effectively taxing them $1 million and using the revenue to purchase campaign ads. Now we change our minds and decide we'd rather see "Married With Children" after all, either because we've learned that the candidates are planning to run completely uninformative ads or because we learn that this was the week of the much-awaited episode where Al abandons Peg for the family dog. The reasoning that led us to prefer campaign ads over Al and Peg has changed, but whatever reasoning led us to want to tax the networks $1 million is presumably still intact. Why would we want that decision to depend on something as irrelevant as which programming we prefer to see?

When columnists suggest that the federal government, in possession of large parcels of real estate after the savings and loan crisis, should sell only limited quantities to maintain a high price, economists are bemused. A high price transfers income from citizens to the government. But the government has never lacked for mechanisms to accomplish such transfers. Why adopt a new mechanism with the primary effect of idling valuable resources?

Economists are sensitive to the effects of incentives. When a new Civil Rights Bill imposes costs on businesses with 25 or more employees, we expect to see a lot of businesses contract to 24 employees. We are sensitive to questions of symmetry. Why does that same Civil Rights Bill forbid me to apply racial criteria when I choose an employ*ee* but allow me to apply racial criteria when I choose an employ*er*? If I turn down a job offer, should I be required to prove that my motives were not discriminatory? We are sensitive to analogies. Why am I permitted to apply racial criteria when I select a wife but not when I select a secretary?*

Economists are sensitive to the importance of enforceable contracts. It was an economist who told me that he'd much rather live in a world where power flows from the barrel of a gun than a world where power flows from the muscles of the arm. We can agree to turn in our guns, but we cannot agree to turn in our fists.

Economists are sensitive to the problems that arise when people are unable to collect the fruits of their own labor. You can work for years to develop a major technological innovation, then watch the demand for your product fall to zero when a competitor makes a slight improvement on your design. Consequently, you might not be willing to put in those years of effort to begin with, and neither your design nor the improvement ever gets developed. Ironically, the solution might be either to subsidize inventors, so that you are compensated for the risk

---

*Of course, to raise a question does not imply that there can be no satisfactory answer. It *does* imply that the issue is worth thinking about.

of being scooped, or to tax inventors, so that you have fewer rivals breathing down your neck.

There are many ways to be deprived of the rewards due your efforts. I am intrigued by the market for movie endings. Moviegoers want two things in an ending: They want it to be happy and they want it to be unpredictable. There is some optimal frequency of sad endings that maintains the right level of suspense. Yet the market might fail to provide enough sad endings.

An individual director who films a sad ending risks short-term losses, as word gets around that the movie is "unsatisfying." It is true that there are long-term gains, as viewers are kept off their guard for future movies. Unfortunately, most of those gains may be captured by other directors, because moviegoers remember only that the murderer *does* sometimes catch up with the heroine in the basement, and do not remember that it happens only in movies with particular directors. Under these circumstances, no individual director may be willing to incur costs for his rivals' benefit.

A solution is for directors to display their names prominently, so that viewers know when a movie was made by someone unpredictable. Viewers, however, may find it in their interests to retaliate by covering their eyes when the director's name is shown.

I have a colleague who believes that it is particularly expensive for trash hauling companies to dispose of those Styrofoam peanuts that are often used as packing material. If this were the case in a world of private trash haulers (such as we have in our community), it appears that there would be no social problem. The collection company could charge extra for taking Styrofoam peanuts, and people would discard them only when it was worth the extra cost. (They would also put appropriate pressure on shipping companies to find some other packing material.) But, my colleague argues, that solution is impractical because it is easy to hide Styrofoam peanuts in your trash and expensive for the collection company to check up on your behavior. Therefore, he believes that there *is* a problem and that it might best be solved by a tax on Styrofoam peanuts.

I am not sure he's right, for a couple of reasons. First, it seems that the collection company could enforce honesty by checking your trash for Styrofoam peanuts once a year and levying a $100,000 fine for violations. The monitoring would be cheap and the violations few. Second, under my colleague's proposal people would effectively pay twice for the cost of trash removal—once via the peanut tax and once via the trash collector's bill—which could result in people deciding to discard *less* than the optimal amount of trash. This second objection can be overcome, however, with a government subsidy to trash collectors, partly financed if you wish with the peanut tax.

This particular colleague and I reach different conclusions about Styrofoam peanuts, as we have reached different conclusions on every other subject we have ever discussed. Yet we have much in common. We agree that there is such a thing as too many Styrofoam peanuts and such a thing as too few, and that either error can be costly. We agree that a perfectly functioning market would yield the best possible outcome, and we define "best possible" by the criterion of efficiency. We agree that markets can fail when information is hidden from one party, or when contracts cannot be enforced. My colleague and I have never voted for the same candidate, but I am sure that in the most important senses, my views are closer to his than to those of 99% of the people who always vote as I do.

We both approach the world as economists, and as economists resigned to—and sometimes even reveling in—the character deficiency that diverts us from pure science to policy analysis. An economist who has abandoned his resistance to policy *analysis* is liable to fall prey to the even more seductive and dangerous vice of policy *formulation*. Each day over lunch, my colleagues and I design a better world. We are a merciless crew, and most of our ideas are thoroughly discredited before dessert is ever served. A few survive. In the next chapter, I will share a few of those modest proposals.

CHAPTER 15

SOME MODEST PROPOSALS

The End of Bipartisanship

Driving through northwest Washington, D.C., I remarked on the opulence that is so conspicuous in that quarter of the city. My friend Jim Kahn, in the passenger seat, wondered how such great wealth could have accumulated in a city that is notorious for producing almost nothing of value. I was too quick with the obvious cynical response: Most of it is the moral equivalent of stolen, partly through direct taxation and largely through political contributions that constitute the collection arm of a vast protection racket.

But Jim was quicker than I and saw that according to economic theory, my explanation was not cynical enough. In the presence of competition between the parties, *all* of those ill-gotten gains should be used to buy votes. If the Republicans are in power, pocketing $100 billion per year, then the Democrats can offer to duplicate Republican policies exactly *plus* give away another billion per year to key constituents. Unchallenged, this strategy would enable them to buy the next election, pocketing a net $99 billion. But the Republicans would counter by offering to give away an extra $2 billion and settle for $98 billion for themselves. Our experience with competitive markets tells us that there is no end to this bidding war until all excessive profits are competed out of existence.

When an industry is dominated by two highly profitable firms, theory tells us that if there is no price war then there is probably collusion. In the case of the Republicans and Democrats, the requisite collusion is on display for all to see. It is called bipartisanship.

When Republican and Democratic legislators meet to "hammer out a compromise," they are engaging in an activity that could land any of their private-sector counterparts in jail. We do not allow the presidents of United and American Airlines to hammer out compromises regarding airfares. Why do we allow the majority and minority leaders of the Congress to hammer out compromises regarding tax policy?

Adam Smith observed that "people of the same trade seldom meet together, even for merriment and diversion, but the conversation ends in a conspiracy against the public, or in some contrivance to raise prices." That truth is the basis for the antitrust legislation that attempts to prevent such conspiracies and contrivances from getting off the ground. When the president of United runs into the president of American at a picnic, he is forbidden by law to say "I will not undercut you on the Chicago-to-Los Angeles route provided that you do not undercut me on New York-to-Denver." Yet we allow Republican leaders to greet Democrats with offers like, "I will support housing aid to your urban constituents if you will support agricultural programs for the farmers in my district."

When people get rich running airlines, I can surmise that it is because they have an extraordinary talent for delivering good air service. When people get rich in the political establishment, I am reluctant to surmise that it is because they have an extraordinary talent for delivering good government. Economics provides an alternative explanation: the absence of political antitrust legislation.

I propose that all political compromise—indeed, all discussion between candidates, officeholders, or officials of competing parties—be fully subject to the same provisions of the Clayton and Sherman Antitrust acts that regulate the activities of every private business in America. I predict that political antitrust legislation will confer on voters the same benefits that economic antitrust legislation confers on consumers. Once the wealth of northwest Washington is depleted by the resulting political price wars, politicians might be forced to compete by offering more efficient government.

You are engaged to be married. Acting on your fiancé's promise of eternal love, you turn away other suitors. In the event, you are left waiting at the altar. The law provides recourse in the form of a suit for breach of promise.

You cast your vote in a presidential election. Acting on the candidate's declaration, "Read my lips; no new taxes," you pass up the opportunity to vote for other candidates. In the event, your candidate wins and signs one of the largest tax increases in history. What is your recourse?

You can, of course, vow never to vote for your candidate again, just as you can vow never to reunite with your ex-fiance. But why is the promise itself not redeemable in a court of law? Why can't betrayed voters file a class action suit against the candidate who betrayed them?

Our experience outside the realm of politics indicates that candidates might welcome the opportunity to offer enforceable guarantees. The ability to make legally binding promises is frequently more an opportunity than a burden. Because you can make a legally binding promise to repay your loans, you are able to obtain a mortgage on a house. If the courts refused to enforce your promise, you wouldn't be able to acquire a mortgage in the first place.

Economists know that there are many circumstances in which governments could benefit if their promises were enforceable. Theory and evidence suggest that when an expected inflation fails to materialize, aggregate output can fall. A government that could credibly promise not to follow inflationary policies could prevent costly expectations from forming in the first place.

What is true in private affairs and in government is true in politics as well. A candidate whose no-tax pledge is met with skepticism gains no votes; a candidate who accepts personal liability for his no-tax pledge acquires valuable credibility.

My colleague Alan Stockman proposes that candidates be permitted to issue legally enforceable promises. It would be rash to hold politicians liable for every pledge they make in response to unexpected questions on the campaign trail, so let us restrict the program to those promises that the candidate explicitly declares to be legally binding.

You might argue that it is a bad thing to bind candidates to policies that may prove unwise under unforeseen circumstances. I reply that we already do that. There might be unforeseen circumstances in which freedom of speech or the right to trial by jury or the separation of powers proves unwise, but we are prepared to accept that eventuality in return for the guarantee of certain liberties. Allowing politicians to make real commitments would foster public debate regarding which additional guarantees are sufficiently important to justify a further sacrifice of flexibility.

A politician's binding promise would be akin to a provisional constitutional amendment, in effect for the politician's term of office. It would be binding only on the candidate himself, so that, for example, a president who had promised to veto any tax increase might still have his vetoes overridden. The resulting limitations on policy options would be far less restrictive than the provisions of the United States Constitution, many of which seem to be generally regarded as desirable.

There are details to sort out. If a president reneged on a pledge to veto any tax increase, would we ignore his refusal and honor the original pledge, treating each new tax bill as automatically vetoed? Or would we allow him to violate his promise and then hold him legally responsible via a class action suit or an impeachment proceeding? Should we construct an escape clause, under which an officeholder, convinced that he had erred, could escape liability by resigning his office?

I support the Stockman proposal in any of these forms. The Constitution itself, in Section 10 of Article I, protects the right of individuals to enter into enforceable contracts. Why should politicians, uniquely among American citizens, be denied that fundamental freedom?

It is a recurring American nightmare: The accused criminal out on bail who commits a grisly murder while awaiting trial. The judge who signed the release order is second-guessed in the press and sometimes at the voting booth. Politicians decry the leniency of the justice system and call for stricter standards in the granting of bail.

There are two separate problems here. The first is to decide where we stand regarding the trade-off between public safety and the rights of the accused. How much certainty about a prisoner's character do we require before we are willing to accept the risk of freeing him prior to trial? Reasonable people will disagree about their answers to this question. Ordinarily in our system, we consider such difficult trade-offs to be properly in the domain of the legislature.

The second problem, once the legislature has agreed on a standard, is to induce judges to abide by it. We can appoint watchdog agencies, but the watchdogs are likely to have far less information than the judge about the character of various defendants. They can therefore never be certain that the judge is really using all of his information to the best of his ability.

Economic theory tells us that when we cannot monitor a decision maker, we should at least endeavor to present him with the right incentives. Judges will begin to have the right incentives when we make them personally liable for criminal damage done by the defendants they release.

Personal liability would at least give the right incentive in one direction: Judges would be loath to release those defendants whom they believe to be the most dangerous. Unfortunately, they would be loath to release *any* defendants. So I propose a simultaneous countervailing incentive in the form of a cash bounty to the judge for each defendant he releases.

Whether judges would release more or fewer defendants than they do today would depend on the size of the cash bounty, which could be adjusted to reflect the wishes of the legislature. The advantage of my proposal is not its effect on the *number* of defendants who are granted bail but its effect on *which* defendants are granted bail. Whether we favor releasing 1% or 99%, we can agree that those 1% or 99% ought not be chosen randomly. We want judges to focus their full attention on the potential costs of their decisions, and personal liability has a way of concentrating the mind.

I make no plea for greater strictness or for greater leniency. I plead only that we recognize the nature of the trade-off. My proposal's second advantage is that it would encourage clarity. Through ongoing debate about adjustments to the cash bounty, legislators would be forced to take unambiguous stands on fundamental issues of safety versus freedom. Rather than being able to hide their views in complex and mutually contradictory legislation, they would have to face the voters and defend an unambiguous position, which the voters could then accept or reject.

You might object that we should not trivialize a complex issue by asking legislators to commit themselves to a single number. I respond that they commit themselves to a single number already. The current network of laws does select some specific point on the scale between strictness and leniency. We just aren't told exactly what it is. Why should the complexity of an issue be an excuse for being coy about the choices that have been made?

My proposal would force judges to be more diligent and legislators to be more straightforward. Those are its two advantages. I see no offsetting disadvantages, and therefore move that it be adopted forthwith.

You purchase a videotape that is unsavory but perfectly legal. Six months later, a new law prohibits the purchase of such videotapes. A zealous prosecutor attempts to indict you.

The Constitution takes a dim view of such proceedings. You have a fundamental right to know the consequences of your actions at the time when you undertake them. Therefore Article I grants you absolute immunity from ex post facto proceedings such as this. Any court would instantly dismiss the prosecutor's case.

You purchase an asset that produces a stream of dividends that are taxed at 25%. Six months later, a new law raises the tax rate to 35%. A zealous Internal Revenue agent attempts to collect from you.

You go to tax court, arguing that you have a fundamental right to know the consequences of your actions at the time when you undertake them. Because you bought your asset under the reasonable expectation that the dividends would be taxed at 25%, that is all you should be required to pay. The judge finds your argument ludicrous and attaches your wages.

I'd like to understand what differentiates these cases. One argument is that you bought the asset with full awareness that tax laws sometimes change. On the other hand, you bought the videotape with full awareness that criminal laws sometimes change. So I'm not sure there is any meaningful distinction here.

A subtler distinction is that an unexpected tax increase serves the purpose of collecting government revenue, whereas an ex post facto criminal prosecution serves no purpose whatsoever.

The new law is able to deter future videotape purchases by promising to punish those who disobey it in the future. The strength of that deterrence is independent of whether we punish those who disobeyed it in the past.

But ex post facto prosecutions *do* serve the purpose of deterring behavior that is likely to become the subject of criminal legislation in the near future, and presumably governments do want to deter such behavior. Those who would legislate against certain videos would presumably be happy to see their sales volume plummet even in advance of the legislation.

I asked my friend the law professor whether he could articulate the deep philosophical principle that proscribes ex post facto prosecution but allows tax rates to rise. He told me that my question presupposed a falsehood: "You want a distinction based in legal theory—but there is no such thing as legal theory." He told me not to waste my time scrutinizing the law for consistency.

As is my habit with lawyers, I ignored him. I admit to a gut feeling that the proscriptions of the Constitution are wise and that at the same time there should be flexibility in the tax laws. But I propose that serious thought be given to the source of that gut feeling and the question of whether it is really justifiable. Whatever justification we find will probably have significant policy implications. If we find none, the policy implications are even greater.

Every now and then I read a magazine article suggesting that the justice system turn criminals over to their victims for punishment. I suspect that such a system would have a bias toward leniency. Victims are often aware that their losses are irreparable and feel uncomfortable extracting revenge for its own sake. Their discomfort might even be great enough to preclude punishments that are not purely vengeful, such as putting your prisoner to work on the equivalent of a chain gang and attaching his wages.

If I am right, then deterrence would be hampered and criminal activity would increase. But there is a market solution to this imperfection.

I predict that if markets were permitted to function, people would sell their punishment rights in advance to firms with show-no-mercy reputations and advertise that they had done so. The contract with the firm could be made irrevocable, so that criminals would know that there was no possibility of a reprieve from the victim.

One advantage would be that punishment firms would have every incentive to put prisoners to work as productively as possible—after all, the firm gets to collect what the prisoners produce. The present system puts investment bankers to work in the prison laundry.

I am not sure whether this justice system would be better than the present one, though my promarket bias leads me to view it favorably. I *am* quite sure that *if* we adopt the more common proposal of allowing victims to mete out justice, then we should also allow the right of punishment to be bought and sold.

When Jonathan Swift advocated using babies as a food source, he titled his essay "A Modest Proposal" and did not intend it to be taken seriously. Although the proposals in this section may seem as offbeat as Swift's, I *do* intend them to be taken seriously. Enhanced competition, enforceable contracts, appropriate incentives, attention to consistency, and market forces generally serve us well, and I believe we should be ever on the lookout for new settings where we can employ them.

There is nothing in economic theory to suggest that existing political institutions are even close to optimal, in any sense of the word. If the best policy proposal seems bizarre, it might be only because we are unused to seeing anything like the best policy proposal in action.

Each of these proposals has serious flaws. That is no argument against them. Some standard is required for determining how their flaws compare with those of the status quo. Initially, much analysis is called for. But eventually, there is no substitute for the daring experiment.

IV

How Markets Work

CHAPTER 16

WHY POPCORN COSTS MORE AT THE MOVIES AND WHY THE OBVIOUS ANSWER IS WRONG

"They *pay* you to think about things like that?" My airline seat-mate didn't come right out with the question, but despite his best efforts, his expression revealed all. "Are you really," he wanted to continue, "the only person in America who doesn't know the answer to that question? Or are all economists equally dense?"

I'd been thinking idly about one of the recurring problems of modern economics, one that has occupied great minds and boosted great careers. My seatmate had expressed some mild curiosity about the equations and diagrams I was scribbling. I had a feeling I'd be best off muttering something about the magnetodynamics of the solar system, but I opted for the truth instead. I was working on the mystery of why popcorn is so expensive at the movie theater.

Actually, I'm not 100% certain that popcorn *is* so expensive at the movie theater. My guess is that when a quart of popcorn sells for $3 or so, the theater owner is earning back substantially more than his expenses. Perhaps I'm wrong about this; there may be a lot of hidden costs to running those concession stands that are not so obvious to the casual moviegoer. Still, there is no evident reason why costs should be so much higher in the theater than they are at the candy store, where you can buy the same size popcorn at one-third the price. So it seems a worthwhile exercise to assume that the theater's markup really is enormous and to look for an explanation.

My seatmate, of course, already had an explanation. Popcorn is expensive because, once you have entered the movie theater, the theater owner has a monopoly. If there were only one candy store in town, and if that were the only place to buy popcorn, it would cost $3 a quart at the candy store. When you are trapped in the theater, the concession stand might as well be the only candy store in town.

As my seatmate wanted so badly to tell me, you don't have to know any economics to see the logic of that simple story. As I wanted so badly to tell him—he wasn't the only one restraining himself for politeness' sake—you actually *do* need to *not* know any economics to see the logic. Because the story makes no sense.

Once you enter the theater, the owner has a monopoly on a lot of things. He is the only supplier of rest rooms, for example. Why doesn't he charge you a monopoly price to use the rest room? Why isn't there a monopoly price for the right to proceed from the box office to the outer lobby, another to proceed from the outer lobby to the inner lobby, another to pass through the double doors so that you can see the screen, and another to take a seat?

The answer, of course, is that a rest room fee would make the theater less attractive to moviegoers. To maintain his clientele, the owner would be forced to sell tickets at a lower price. What he collected at the rest room door would be lost at the box office.

As with rest rooms, so with popcorn. When I go to watch a movie and buy a quart of popcorn, I am quite indifferent between paying $1 for the popcorn and $7 for the ticket or paying $3 for the popcorn and $5 for the ticket. By the end of the evening, the owner collects $8 from me under either strategy.

This calculation makes it look like a matter of indifference how the popcorn is priced. But it leaves out one thing, and that one thing argues for making the popcorn cheap and the tickets expensive: *If popcorn is cheap, I might buy two quarts instead of one.* That's good for the owner, because if I am willing to pay $8 for a movie plus a quart of popcorn, I might be willing to pay $10 for a movie plus *two* quarts of popcorn. He can extract the additional $2 by raising the ticket price.

Shall I run through that again? The cheaper the popcorn, the more I eat. The more I eat, the more I enjoy going to the theater. The more I enjoy going to the theater, the more I am willing to pay for an evening there (counting the ticket price plus popcorn). The more I am willing to pay for an evening at the theater, the more coins end up in the owner's pocket.

With a little more argument along lines like these, it is not difficult to establish that the owner's best strategy is to sell me popcorn at a price equal to the cost of production, earning *no profit whatsoever* at the concession stand. This leads me to buy a lot of popcorn, which makes me happy and willing to pay a very high price at the box office.

Which returns me to my question. Why is popcorn so expensive at the movie theater?

Of course, a possible answer is that the owner doesn't know enough economics to realize that his pricing strategy is suboptimal. But it is probably a safe bet that theater owners know more about running theaters profitably than economists do. So the right question is, What does the owner know that my analysis ignores?

I believe he knows this: *some moviegoers like popcorn more than others.* Cheap popcorn attracts popcorn lovers and makes them willing to pay a high price at the door. But to take advantage of that willingness, the owner must raise ticket prices so high that he drives away those who come only to see the movie. If there are enough nonsnackers, the strategy of cheap popcorn can backfire.

My seatmate's clear intuition to the contrary, the purpose of expensive popcorn is *not* to extract a lot of money from customers. *That* purpose would be better served by cheap popcorn and expensive movie tickets. Instead, the purpose of expensive popcorn is to extract *different* sums from *different* customers. Popcorn lovers, who have more fun at the movies, pay more for their additional pleasure.

In fact, expensive popcorn makes sense *only* if popcorn lovers are really willing to pay more than other people for their evenings at the theater. If things were otherwise, and nonsnackers were all cinemaphiles happy to pay $15 a ticket, then the owner would be best advised to mark the popcorn down and the tickets up. Then every moviegoer would have some incentive to buy those expensive tickets—in some cases to see the movie, and in others to gain access to the concession stand. In fact, it would be even better to sell popcorn *below* cost. To exploit the cinemaphiles, the admission fee should be $15; at this price popcorn lovers need a special inducement to get them into the theater.

The owner's objective is not to set a uniformly high price but to match the price to the customer. When you go to buy a car, the salesman is likely to ask a question like "How much do you want to pay?" (Personally, I always answer "zero.") What he really means to ask is "What is the *most* you are *willing* to pay?" or in economists' jargon, "What is your reservation price?" If he could get an honest answer to that question, he would charge each customer accordingly. In practice, he connives to estimate your reservation price by engaging you in conversation about what other cars you have been looking at, what you do for a living, and the size of your family. Then he does the best he can.

In a seller's paradise, each customer would be charged exactly his reservation price and not a penny less. In the worldly realm we inhabit, sellers concoct mechanisms for charging a little more on average to those who are willing to pay a little more and a little less on average to those who would otherwise walk away.

I recently bought a new car myself and was offered the opportunity to add a decorative rear spoiler bar at a price that I believe was much greater than the cost of production. If everybody took the spoiler bars, there would be no point in this. It is a matter of indifference whether you pay $20,000 for the car and $3,000 for the spoiler or $22,000 for the car and $1,000 for the spoiler. But if the manufacturer believes that people who like spoilers are willing to pay $23,000 for a car that most people think is worth no more than $20,000, then the pricing strategy begins to make sense.

Fads and tastes evolve over time, and there may come a year in which low-income people are generally fond of spoiler bars and high-income people are generally not. If that year arrives, I expect to see spoiler bars selling for a *negative* price: $20,000 for a bare car, $18,000 if you take it with the spoiler. Like popcorn at the theater, the spoiler helps the seller match the customer to the appropriate price.

A movie theater is in the business of selling neither movies nor popcorn but evenings at the theater that, at the customer's option, include both. Like any seller, the owner seeks to charge the highest price to those most willing to pay it. Cheap tickets and expensive popcorn effectively charge a higher price to those who eat a lot of popcorn. This works—but only because those who are willing to pay high prices and those who eat a lot of popcorn are, on average, the same people. If popcorn lovers were generally from low income groups who needed special inducements to come to the theater, popcorn would be free and you'd get a discount at the box office for agreeing to eat at least a quart of it.

When you buy a Polaroid camera or a ticket to Disneyland, your expenses have only just begun. To get any use out of your purchase, you must also buy Polaroid film or Disneyland ride tickets.* If all customers were identical, the seller would provide film or ride tickets at cost to maximize the value of the camera or the park admission. The only reason why Polaroid film is expensive is because some people are willing to pay more for the ability to take pictures than others are. Expensive film extracts more from the heavy users, and Polaroid sensibly believes that the heaviest users are willing to pay the most.

Why do supermarkets print discount coupons in the newspaper? No doubt my seatmate on the airplane could have explained it to me in a sentence: To lure customers with the prospect of a bargain. But why should a coupon for 50 cents off a bottle of detergent be a more effective lure than an ad announcing that the price of detergent had been slashed by 50 cents? The "obvious" explanation is wrong.

Discount coupons are intended *not* to lure customers in general but to lure a certain *class* of customers—namely, those who would shop elsewhere in the absence of a bargain. The device works only if the discounts end up in the right hands: It must be the case that coupon clippers, on average, are more sensitive to price. Most economists believe that the connection is established by the fact that some people have more free time than others. Those with a lot of free time are both more likely to be clipping coupons *and* more likely to be shopping around for

*This statement was true when I wrote it but is false today because Disneyland has changed its pricing policy. The right question for an economist to be asking now is, Why did they change it?

bargains. The correlation is imperfect, but it probably means that the average coupon clipper is more likely than the average non clipper to leave the store if the price isn't right.

It is worth stressing that if everybody clipped coupons, they would serve no purpose. They make sense only as a device to charge more to those who are willing to pay more.

Sometimes an easily identifiable group, such as students or senior citizens, is particularly sensitive to price. In such cases, sellers give discounts to those groups directly. It has been remarked that senior citizen discounts are an odd convention in a country where the elderly, despite stereotypes, are on average quite well-to-do. The remark overlooks the fact that price sensitivity is not a function of income alone. Most senior citizens are retired and have time to shop for bargains. Their sons and daughters, though far less financially secure, are often strapped for time and willing to pay a higher price to avoid a time-consuming search.

Did you buy this book in hardcover or in paperback? It might interest you to know that the production costs for the two kinds of binding are very close to equal. By pricing the hardback several dollars higher, the publisher effectively charges different prices to different classes of customers. As in all these examples, the scheme works only if those who choose the paperback are those who were initially more frugal in what they were willing to spend for the book. Perhaps the connection is that real booklovers insist on hardcovers because they expect to keep their books a long time.

I have known economists who made hobbies of collecting examples of price discrimination. (*Price discrimination* is economic jargon for selling the same product at more than one price.) Airlines charge different prices depending on whether you stay over a Saturday, hotels charge different prices depending on whether you make reservations in advance, car rental agencies charge different prices depending on whether you belong to a frequent flyer program, doctors charge different prices depending on your income and your insurance status, and universities charge different prices depending on your grades and your family's income. Any giveaway that is claimed by only some buyers (such as trading stamps or free delivery) can be a form of price discrimination, as is a policy of "ten cents apiece, three for a quarter." Leaded gasoline sells for less than unleaded gasoline despite comparable production costs, free coffee refills mean that some people pay more per cup than others, and two prices at the salad bar depend on whether you order a complete meal or just the salad. Price discrimination, in short, appears ubiquitous.

Yet there is a good theoretical reason to believe that price discrimination should be relatively rare, and therein lies a puzzle. To see the problem, let's return to the movies.

I have argued that $3 popcorn makes sense only as a form of price discrimination. Popcorn lovers have more fun at the movies and are therefore asked to pay more. But if this is the whole story, then why don't popcorn lovers simply patronize a different theater?

Presumably my airline seatmate would have had no trouble with this one; he could have told me that shopping elsewhere is not an option because the situation is the same all over town. But it is extremely difficult to see how such an outcome could persist. According to my seatmate's model, each theater makes huge profits selling popcorn. The theater that sold a quart for $2.50 instead of $3 could attract all of the big popcorn eaters and under most circumstances would more than make up in volume what was lost by cutting the price. Other theaters, having lost the bulk of their popcorn business, would be forced to cut prices. Why don't we see popcorn price wars?

Even if for some reason existing theaters were insufficiently competitive to bring down the price, the lure of high popcorn profits should suffice to spur new theater construction. Newcomers would offer discounts and the price wars would be underway.

So one more ingredient must be added to the price discrimination story. Price discrimination can work only when the seller has a monopoly of the appropriate kind. (The theater owner needs a monopoly in the *theater* market, not just the popcorn market, to make price discrimination work.) If Wegman's grocery store can profitably sell detergent at 50 cents off to coupon clippers, then it can profitably sell detergent at 50 cents off to anyone. If Wegman's archrival, Tops, advertises "no coupons but all prices 10 cents lower than Wegman's," it can strip away

all of Wegman's nonclipping customers and earn 40 cents more
on each sale than Wegman's (now catering to clippers only)
earns. To retrieve the high-profit business of the nonclippers,
Wegman's cuts prices 20 cents. Tops responds with further cuts.
If there is real competition, this process must continue until all
customers are paying the same price.

The standard textbook example of a perfectly competitive industry is wheat farming. No wheat farmer has any control over
market conditions, and no wheat farmer represents a significant
share of the market. That is precisely the reason why wheat
farmers do not give senior citizen discounts. If all wheat farmers charged $1 a bushel to senior citizens and $2 a bushel to
everyone else, I would start a wheat farm and charge $1.90 a
bushel to everybody. Let others have the senior citizen business;
I'll take all the rest.

Senior citizens don't get wheat discounts because there are
too many opportunists like me around. Price discrimination can
succeed only where it cannot be competed away.

If price discrimination is viable only for a monopolist, and if
price discrimination is as common as our many examples seem
to indicate, we are forced to conclude that monopolies are everywhere. But many economists—including most of those whom I
know well—are quite skeptical of that conclusion.

From this skepticism, there arises a parlor game. The game is
to take examples of apparent price discrimination and debunk
them. The goal is to argue convincingly that the single product
being sold at two different prices is not a single product at all
but two quite different products. One product at two prices
requires monopoly power, but two products at two prices is the
normal order of things.

Some cases are easy. The salad bar costs more if you don't
order dinner. But people who don't order dinner generally take
more from the salad bar. There are two prices for the salad bar,
but they probably work out, on average, to about the same price
per chick-pea or carrot slice. No price discrimination here.

Others are slightly harder. Doctors charge wealthy patients
more than they charge poor patients. Is this price discrimination? Perhaps. But perhaps wealthy patients are in general more
demanding of the doctor's time, more likely to phone in the
middle of the night, and more likely to sue for malpractice when

things go wrong. If so, then wealthy patients really purchase a different level of service than poor patients do, and it is not surprising that better service carries a higher price tag.

What about those supermarket coupons? The usual price discrimination story is that clippers get a price break because they have a lot of free time and therefore shop for bargains. When I wrote a college textbook on economic theory, I included this standard example. One reviewer suggested an intriguing alternative: Coupon clippers, because they have more free time, tend to shop in the middle of the day, when the store is not crowded and the checkout clerks are idle. Nonclippers shop on their way home from work when lines are long and tempers are short. Thus nonclippers are actually more expensive to serve than clippers. They pay extra not because of price discrimination, but because they have purchased the right to shop at times that the grocery store finds inconvenient.

I applaud the spirit that concocted this story, though I don't believe it is correct. If grocery stores really wanted to charge extra for shopping between 5 and 7 P.M., it seems to me that the most straightforward way to do it would be to impose a surcharge on all groceries sold between those hours. On the other hand, I am equally uncomfortable with the price discrimination story because it implies a level of monopoly power for which I see no other evidence. More ideas are needed.

Leaded and unleaded gasoline are more or less the same good from the producer's viewpoint in the sense that their production costs are comparable. Yet they sell for substantially different prices. How can this be price discrimination, which requires monopoly power, when there are sometimes three gas stations at a single intersection?

The economists John Lott and Russell Roberts recently gave an ingenious answer when they observed that leaded gasoline is used primarily by older vehicles with larger gas tanks. To sell 30 gallons of leaded gas, the station manager needs to record one sale, write up one credit card slip, and watch other customers shop across the street because his pumps are busy for the length of time that it takes to fill one gas tank. To sell 30 gallons of unleaded, he needs to record two or three sales, with the consequent doubling or tripling of all these related costs. Different prices that result from different retailing costs do not constitute price discrimination and can survive perfectly well in competition.

On a recent trip to New Mexico, I visited the Taos Pueblo, an Indian community that welcomes tourists. The entrance fee is five dollars per car plus five dollars per camera. The more cameras you carry, the more you pay. Is this price discrimination? Maybe, because those who carry many cameras might be most eager not to miss a major tourist attraction. On the other hand, tourists with cameras are likely to be more intrusive in any number of ways that are all too easy to imagine. Less gracious guests can be thought of as consuming more hospitality and paying more for their additional consumption.

Taxis sometimes charge one rate for a couple traveling together and a higher rate for two strangers going to the same destination. To support a diagnosis of price discrimination, one must argue that the couple is more likely to consider alternative transportation than the strangers are. Perhaps people traveling in pairs are more adventurous, or more likely to be from in town and aware of their options. To reject a diagnosis of price discrimination, one must argue that it is genuinely more expensive to serve two strangers than to serve a couple. Here I have no argument that makes me comfortable, but I am looking.

And finally and once again, why is popcorn so expensive at the movie theater? If this be price discrimination, whence the monopoly power? Theaters might have a small amount of monopoly power, at least when they are the exclusive local outlets for popular first-run movies. But this can hardly account for the exorbitant popcorn prices that seem to be the norm.*

Economists Luis Locay and Alvaro Rodriguez recently gave an ingenious answer to this age-old question, and to me it has the ring of truth. People go to movies in groups. Popcorn lovers often travel with companions who eat no popcorn. The usual argument says that you cannot price discriminate against popcorn eaters without losing them to another theater. The Locay/Rodriguez response is that popcorn eaters cannot go to

---

*My insightful student Jeff Spielberg suggests that the high price you pay for popcorn is not price discrimination at all but a fee for cleaning up after you. He might be right.

another theater without splitting up their social groups. If another theater offers cheap popcorn and high ticket prices, the nonsnackers in the group will vote to stay put. Locay and Rodriguez have constructed a complete argument demonstrating that under plausible hypotheses about the way groups make decisions, theater owners have a degree of monopoly power over popcorn lovers who travel with popcorn nonlovers, and can plausibly exploit this power by pricing popcorn high.

I like that story, but it does leave a thread hanging. It doesn't tell me why the popcorn lover fails to offer his friends a deal: Let's stick to theaters with low-priced popcorn, and I'll occasionally pay for your tickets.

Other cases baffle me even more. Canadian restaurants near the border sometimes accept U.S. currency at above-market exchange rates. This appears to be price discrimination in favor of Americans. Is it? If so, why are Americans more price-sensitive than Canadians? And if not, then what is the alternative explanation? Do Americans demand less service than Canadians?

Disneyland offers discount tickets to its stockholders. Are Disneyland stockholders more price-sensitive than the general public?

In the United States, hotels typically set a price per room that is independent of the number of occupants. In Great Britain, hotels typically set a price per guest that is independent of how many rooms they occupy. Which if either of these is price discrimination? In either case, what is the source of the monopoly power and what makes one group of travelers more price-sensitive than another? If neither is price discrimination, what does account for the differential pricing? And why does the outcome differ so radically across countries?

It might have been fun to discuss these questions with my neighbor on the airplane. But I decided to let him sleep.

CHAPTER 17

COURTSHIP AND COLLUSION

The Mating Game

In the tenth century B.C., the Queen of Sheba (near what is now Yemen) had monopolized the shipment of spices, myrrh, and frankincense to the Mediterranean. When King Solomon of Israel threatened to invade her market, the book of Kings tells us that "she came to Jerusalem, with a very great train, with camels that bear spices, and very much gold, and precious stones" as a prelude to striking a deal. Twenty-eight centuries later, the first modern economist, Adam Smith, observed that "people of the same trade seldom meet together, even for merriment and diversion, but the conversation ends in a conspiracy against the public, or in some contrivance to raise prices."

Collusion, like sex, is ancient and ubiquitous. It should come as no surprise that two such popular enterprises have been pursued in tandem.

In the markets for sex and marriage, men compete among themselves for women and women compete among themselves for men. But men compete differently than women do, in part because men are more inclined to seek multiple partners. The reasons for this inclination are rooted perhaps partly in biology (it can be good reproductive strategy to scatter your seed widely if your seed is regenerated every day, and equally good reproductive strategy to focus your attention on a single partner if you can give birth little more than once a year), and perhaps partly in social conditioning. There are, of course, many people of both genders who fail to fit the pattern, but more often than not, there is a germ of truth in the observation that "a woman seeks one man to fill her every need, while a man seeks every woman to fill his one need."*

In societies that allow polygamy, it is almost invariably men who take multiple wives, rather than the reverse. Males drunk on testosterone might imagine that their lives would be better in such societies, but if the fantasy were realized most of the fantasizers would be disappointed. For each man with four wives, there must be three with no wives at all. You can change the laws of marriage, but you cannot repeal the laws of arithmetic.

In a world where each man sought four women, the competition for women would be intense. Even those men who came out victorious would pay dearly for their victories. Women would be doubly fortunate: They would have more suitors, and their suitors, each trying to stand out from the crowd, would be more attentive and deferential. On dinner dates, the woman would be more likely to pick the restaurant and the man more likely to pick up the tab. Married men, sensitive to their wives' continuing opportunities, would do more housework.†

Perhaps if polygamy were legal, most or even all women would still insist on monogamous marriages and we would pair up in pretty much the same combinations as we do today. Even so, it would be a very different world. Today, when my wife and I argue about who should do the dishes, we start from positions of roughly equal strength. If polygamy were legal, my wife could hint that she's thought about leaving me to marry Alan and Cindy down the block—and I might end up with dishpan hands. Wives would have more power in deciding all of the big and little conflicts that arise in marriage: how many children to have, what city to live in, who cooks dinner, and, on quiet evenings in front of the television, who operates the remote control.‡

*I wish I knew who first observed this.

†I am envisioning how polygamy would work in modern America. In some primitive polygamous societies, women have no say in their choice of marriage partners and therefore do not necessarily reap the benefits of competition.

‡The same phenomenon occurs in nonpolygamous situations and regardless of gender. An increase in the population of single women might seem to be a matter of indifference to those married men who do not engage in extramarital affairs. On the contrary, it allows those men to issue more credible threats about dissolving one marriage for another and therefore gives them more power within their families. *All* men benefit when more single women are available.

Men in a polygamous society are like spice merchants perpetually resisting encroachments from competitors. Merchants respond by agreeing to divide the territory. Somewhere back in history, the masculine gender did the same. By custom and by law, men have managed to enforce a collusive agreement to limit their attentions to one woman apiece. There is a lot of cheating on that agreement, but that is just what economic theory predicts.

In fact, the antipolygamy laws are a textbook example of the theory of cartels. Producers, initially competitive, gather together in a conspiracy against the public or, more specifically, against their customers. They agree that each firm will restrict its output in an attempt to keep prices high. But a high price invites cheating, in the sense that each firm seeks to expand its own output beyond what is allowable under the agreement. Eventually, the cartel crumbles unless it is enforced by legal sanctions, and even then violations are legion.

That story, told in every economics textbook, is also the story of male producers in the romance industry. Initially fiercely competitive, they gather together in a conspiracy against their "customers"—the women to whom they offer their hands in marriage. The conspiracy consists of an agreement under which each man restricts his romantic endeavors in an attempt to increase the bargaining position of men in general. But the improved position of men invites cheating, in the sense that each man tries to court more women than allowed under the agreement. The cartel survives only because it is enforced by legal sanctions, and even so violations are legion.

Cartels have changed very little in the last three thousand years, but they've gotten slicker about public relations. In 1991, it was discovered that the Overlap Group, consisting of MIT and the Ivy League universities, had conspired to keep tuition rates high and financial aid offers low. Overlap's defense was at least creative, suggesting that its goal was to prevent financial considerations from unduly influencing students when they choose a college. If the three major auto manufacturers had been caught colluding to keep prices high, they might not have thought to argue that they served a noble purpose by preventing financial considerations from unduly influencing consumers when they choose a car.

With the same effrontery that led Overlap to maintain that it exists solely as a favor to its victims, men have maintained that antipolygamy laws are designed to somehow protect women. But a law that prohibits any man from marrying more than one woman is not different in principle from a law that prohibits any firm from hiring more than one worker. I suppose that if such a law were enacted, firms would argue that it was designed to protect workers. Who would believe them?

Theory suggests that when an enforcement mechanism is available, any group of competitors will attempt to collude. The observation is not limited to competitors of a particular gender. As men conspire against women, so women conspire against men.

When firms discover an innovative but costly way to improve their products, they might profitably conspire to withhold the innovation from the marketplace. Such conspiracies usually founder on the ambitions of maverick firms that see huge profit opportunities in being the market's only innovator. The cartel's best hope for survival is a law that bans the innovation, and substantial resources are devoted to lobbying for such laws.

Modern technology offers women a variety of innovative but costly ways to attract men. These innovations include everything from new methods of birth control to silicone breast implants. The costs to women include not only out-of-pocket expenses but a variety of health risks.

It can be advantageous for women to withhold such products from the marketplace. In doing so, they act like Ford, General Motors, and Chrysler agreeing to stifle a new automotive technology that would serve their customers well. In ordinary circumstances, each of the Big Three would be left wondering who was going to violate the agreement first. But if they can arrange to have the innovation outlawed, auto executives can sleep more soundly at night.

Likewise, women cannot simply agree among themselves to avoid dangerous methods of birth control or cosmetic surgery. Aside from the logistical problems of arranging a contract among a hundred million parties, cheating would be uncontrollable. The only hope is to ban the products, and feminist organizations have exerted substantial effort in this direction.

At first blush it seems inexplicable that a political lobby committed to a woman's absolute right to choose an abortion could seek to deny that same woman the right to choose her bra size. If women are rational, intelligent creatures capable of weighing the health risks (not to mention other weighty issues) of terminating a pregnancy, then one might expect that they are capable of weighing the health risks of a silicone implant or a hormonal birth control device.

The theory of cartels suggests that the feminists are right and the plausible objections I have just voiced are wrong. Producers *can* be made better off by laws that limit innovation. General Motors is capable of deciding for itself whether to adopt a new automotive technology but might still want the technology banned—not to protect it from *itself* but to protect it from its competitors. If GM could be the only innovator on the block, it would be happy; given the realities of competition, it would prefer to see the innovation disappear.

And likewise for women. Any woman who wanted silicone breast implants and could be assured of having the only implants in America would be happy. Given the reality—that if implants are legal her competitors will acquire them too—she might prefer an absolute ban.*

The best argument for keeping new technologies legal is not that they benefit manufacturers but that they benefit their customers. Analogously, the best argument for keeping cosmetic breast implants legal is not that they guarantee freedom for women but that they gratify men. The economically correct argument is the most politically *in*correct argument imaginable.

A careful cost-benefit analysis would probably conclude that breast implants should be legal, because the benefits to men exceed the costs to women.† It *might* even conclude that the benefits to women alone (in terms, for example, of self-esteem and employment opportunities) *already* exceed the costs to women. But a plausible alternative is that a ban on breast implants

---

*The same argument could explain why men choose to limit the availability of steroids that could make their bodies more attractive to women. I chose to talk about breast implants instead of steroids because they've been in the news lately.

†I infer this not from any direct estimates of the costs or benefits but from the fact that some women willingly bear the costs of implants in exchange for capturing part of the benefits in the form of increased attention from men.

protects women from harmful competition and does so at men's expense.

When Chicago area butchers wanted to spend evenings at home with their families, they convinced the city council to outlaw meat sales after 6:00 P.M. (The law has since been repealed.) A simple agreement among the butchers to close early would have invited cheating by creating an irresistible temptation to be the only evening butcher in town.

A naive observer might think that butchers could not possibly benefit from a law restricting their freedom to choose their own hours—just as that same observer might think that men could not possibly benefit from a law restricting their freedom to pursue multiple marriage partners, or women from a law restricting their freedom to pursue cosmetic surgery. But an agreement, even when it is mutually beneficial, needs to be enforced.

In early twentieth-century China, goods were transported by barges pulled by teams of six men who were rewarded heavily if they arrived at their destination on time. Because each man calculated that success depended largely on the efforts of the other five, teams were plagued by chronic shirking. If everyone else is pulling hard, the team will make it anyway, so why pull hard? If *nobody* else is pulling hard, the team *won't* make it anyway, so why pull hard? Everyone makes the same rational calculation, everyone shirks, the goods arrive late, and nobody gets paid.

Barge teams quickly evolved a mechanism for averting such unfortunate outcomes. The six team members collectively hired a seventh man to whip them.

Pressing the government into service as an enforcer is not so different from hiring an enforcer with a whip. (There is, however, a significant difference between the bargemen and the butchers: When bargemen conspire to work harder, they form a victimless conspiracy. When butchers conspire to offer less service, they conspire against the public.)

The mating game is a game that everyone can win. Even so, there is room for conflict about how to divide the spoils. With so much at stake, it is not surprising that coalitions form, break apart, and call on governments to resurrect them. Games breed strategic behavior. That includes the game where some believe that every strategy is fair.

CHAPTER 18

CURSED WINNERS
AND GLUM LOSERS

Why Life Is Full of Disappointments

Economic theory predicts that you are not enjoying this book as much as you thought you would. This is a special case of a more general proposition: *Most* things in life don't turn out as well as you thought they would. While psychologists, poets, and philosophers have often remarked on this phenomenon, few have recognized that it is a necessary consequence of informed, rational decision making.

Choosing a book is a process fraught with risk and uncertainty. Fortunately, your lifetime of experience as a reader is a valuable guide. It enables you to form some expectation of each book's quality. Your expectations are sometimes very wrong, but on average they are far better than random guesses.

Some books are better than you expect them to be and others are worse, but it is unlikely that you err in one direction much more often than the other. If you consistently either overestimated or underestimated quality, you would eventually discover your own bias and correct for it. So it is reasonable to assume that your expectations are too low about as often as they are too high.

This means that if you chose this book randomly off the shelf, it would be as likely to exceed your expectations as to fall short of them. But you didn't choose it randomly off the shelf. Rational consumer that you are, you chose it because it was one of the few available books that you expected to be among the very best. Unfortunately, that makes it one of the few available books whose quality you are most likely to have overestimated. Under the circumstances, to read it is to court disappointment.

174

The logic of probable disappointment haunts every aspect of life in which we choose among alternatives. Even when your judgments *in general* are free of bias, your judgments about *those activities that you choose to engage in* are usually too optimistic. Your assessments of potential marriage partners might be exactly right on average, but the one who seems the perfect match is the one whose flaws you are most likely to have overlooked.

Things are even worse when you buy a good at auction. When you are the high bidder, you can be certain of one thing: Nobody else in the room thought the item was worth as much as you did. That observation alone implies that you've probably overestimated its true worth. Economists, ever dismal, call this phenomenon the *winner's curse.*

Imagine that you are a knowledgeable real estate developer submitting a sealed bid on a parcel of land. Your expert judgment tells you that if you could acquire this land for $50,000, you would make a handsome profit. You might think that under the circumstances you'd be happy to win that land at auction for $50,000. But if you *do* win the auction at that price, you learn that your competitors' expert judgments led all of them to less optimistic assessments than your own. Unless you are quite sure that your own information is better than anybody else's, you are likely to wonder if $50,000 is such a bargain after all.

When you are deciding how much to bid for a piece of land, the right question is not, "Given what I know now, would I be happy to buy this land for $50,000?" Instead, the right question is, "Given what I know now, and assuming also that no other developer was willing to bid $50,000, would I *still* be happy to buy it for $50,000?" These are very different questions. Those who frequently buy goods at auction must learn to appreciate that difference and to adjust their bids accordingly.

On the other hand, there are circumstances where the winner's curse is not an issue. Some auction goers are quite certain of how much they are willing to pay for an item, without any regard for what others may know or think. If you are bidding on an antique brass candelabrum, and you have examined it closely, and you know exactly how you plan to use it, and you don't care whether it is attractive to others, and you are certain that you will never want to resell it, then buying the candelabrum for $1,000 is an equally good bargain regardless of what the other bidders may think. In such cases there is no winner's curse. There is still the possibility of disappointment— the candelabrum might not look as good on your mantelpiece as you thought it would—but there is not the *probability* of disappointment that constitutes a true winner's curse. After all, it's equally possible that the candelabrum will look *better* than you imagined, and the fact that you have won the auction does nothing to diminish this possibility.

The presence or absence of a winner's curse is of immediate concern to the buyer, who must account for it in his bidding strategy. It is therefore of indirect concern to the seller, who cares very much how buyers behave. But the seller's role is not limited to hoping that buyers will bid high. The seller is also a strategic player in the auction game. He gets only one move, but it is the most important: He sets the rules.

There are many types of auction. The most familiar is the common English auction, where bidders offer successively higher prices and drop out until only one remains. There is the Dutch auction, where an auctioneer calls out a very high price and successively lowers it until he receives an offer to buy. There is the first-price sealed bid auction, where each buyer submits a bid in an envelope, all are opened simultaneously, and the high bidder gets the item for the amount of his bid. There is the second-price sealed bid auction, where the high bidder gets the item but pays only the amount of the *second*-highest bid. There are third-, fourth-, and fifth-price sealed bid auctions. And there are more exotic possibilities. In the Glum Losers auction, the high bidder gets the item for free and everybody else pays the amount of his own bid.

The seller can choose among these or any other rules that he manages to dream up. Ideally, his goal is to maximize the selling price. In practice, he rarely has enough information to achieve that goal. If two bidders are both willing to go very high, an English auction can force them to compete with each other, pushing the price up as high as possible. If only one bidder is willing to go very high, an English auction is disastrous for the seller: Everyone else drops out early and the potential high bidder gets a fabulous bargain.

Is an English auction good for the seller? The answer is yes if there happen to be two high bidders in the audience and no if there happens to be just one. Because bidders are unlikely to reveal their bidding strategies in advance of the auction, the seller can never know for certain on any given night whether an English auction is preferable to, say, a Dutch auction.

Even to decide between a first-price and a second-price sealed bid auction can be difficult for the seller. On the one hand, in a first-price auction he collects the high bid, while in a second-price auction he collects only the amount of the second-highest bid. On the other hand, bidders generally submit higher bids in a second-price auction. They submit even higher bids in a third-price auction. Which is best for the seller? Again the answer depends on who shows up to bid, and what the bidders' strategies are.

Given his limited information, the seller is in no position to choose the rule that will maximize the selling price at any one auction. But he *can* hope to choose the rule that will maximize the *average* selling price over *many* auctions. At some auctions, English rules yield the highest prices, while at others Dutch rules yield the highest prices. Which rules yield the highest prices on average?

At this point, economic theory makes its entrance, to announce an astonishing truth. Under certain reasonable assumptions (about which I will soon say more), and as a matter of mathematical fact, all of the auction rules I've mentioned yield the same revenue to the seller on average over many auctions. If I regularly sell merchandise at English auctions, while you sell at Dutch auctions, your brother sells at first-price sealed bid auctions, your sister sells at second-price sealed bid auctions, and your crazy Uncle Fester sells at Glum Losers auctions, and if we all sell merchandise of comparable quality, then in the long run we must all do equally well.

This result applies as well to a vast number of other auction rules—in fact, to any rule you can imagine that does not involve some entrance fee to the auction hall or its equivalent.

I haven't told you how I know that sellers using vastly different rules all do equally well on average, because the argument is technical and I haven't yet figured out how to translate it into simple English. (Probably this means that I don't yet understand it well enough.) But there is no doubt that the argument is correct.

A result like this is a great joy to a theorist. It is surprising, elegant, and emphatic. There is no need to mince words or to introduce qualifications. We need not make long and ugly catalogues ("The English auction is superior under any of the following seven conditions, while the Dutch auction is superior under any of the following six other conditions . . . "). We can state our conclusion in no more than five words ("All rules are equally good") and we can prove it incontrovertibly to anyone with an undergraduate's knowledge of advanced calculus. The best thing about it is that almost nobody would have guessed it. If theory never did more than confirm what we already know, there would be no need for it.

And yet . . . It remains disturbingly the case that real-world auctioneers show marked preferences for some rules over others. Cattle and slaves have always been sold in English auctions, tulips in Dutch auctions, and oil drilling rights in sealed bid auctions. If all rules are equally good for the seller, why do sellers insist on one rule rather than another?

An economist might feel some temptation to respond that auctioneers are not economists and so are likely to live in ignorance of the latest breakthroughs. Not only do many auctioneers fail to subscribe to the *Journal of Economic Theory*, but all too often their advanced calculus has grown sufficiently rusty that it would be difficult for them to stay abreast of the field even if they made an honest effort. But the economist's temptation is best resisted. It is a fair assumption that people who run auctions for a living know what they are doing, and that if there is some discrepancy between their behavior and the prescriptions of the economic theorist, then it is the theorist who is missing something. Our job as economists is not to tell auctioneers how to run their business. It is to assume that they *know* how to run their business and to figure out why their strategies are the right ones.

On the one hand we have an argument that under certain assumptions, the choice of auction rule is a matter of indifference. On the other hand, we have the behavior of auctioneers, from which we infer that the choice of auction rule is a matter of considerable concern. The inescapable conclusion is that those "certain assumptions" do not always apply. So it is time to be explicit about what they are.

The most important assumption is that there is no winner's curse. More precisely, the argument assumes that a bidder does not change his mind about the item's value when he learns that another bidder disagrees with him. If you are bidding on a van Gogh to hang on your wall, you might be willing to pay $50 million regardless of what anyone else thinks; if you are bidding on the same painting in anticipation of a large profit at resale, you are likely to be chagrined when you learn that none of the other dealers in the room bid more than $10 million. The equivalence of auction rules holds in the first case but not in the second.

In fact, when bidders care about one anothers' opinions, the seller is well advised to choose the English auction. Going into the auction, there may be only one bidder willing to pay above $10 million. When others observe his willingness to go high, they may reason that he knows something and decide to compete with him. A sealed bid auction precludes this outcome. So does a Dutch auction—by the time the high bidder reveals his enthusiasm, the auction is over.

English auctions are by far the most common and appear to be the form most favored by auctioneers. The theory suggests that the only reason why auctioneers would have such a preference is that bidders respond to information about one anothers' assessments. This means in particular that bidders are subject to the winner's curse. So while the curse is initially no more than a theoretical possibility, the prevalence of English auctions suggests that it is a pervasive phenomenon.

Although the argument for the equivalence of auction rules assumes away the winner's curse, this is not the only direction in which it may depart from reality. Another key assumption is that buyers do not have large fractions of their wealth riding on the outcome of the auction. This assumption is important, because in its absence, buyers bid more conservatively, which affects the entire analysis. In that case, the seller should prefer a first-price sealed bid auction to an English auction. Because buyers are loath to risk losing, and because a sealed bid gives them only one chance to win, they tend to shade their bids upward, profiting the seller.

Another questionable assumption in the standard theory is that the population of bidders does not change when the rules change. In reality, a Dutch auction might draw an entirely different class of bidders than an English auction. Some future theorist will earn fame by figuring out how to incorporate this effect into the analysis.

Rather than venture into such uncharted territory, let me take a side path to explore another issue that confronts the seller. Sellers frequently know more about their merchandise than buyers do and can acquire reputations for honesty by always revealing everything they know, good or bad. Does honesty pay?

Honest John holds used-car auctions on a regular basis. He makes it a point always to announce everything that he knows about the cars he sells. If a car burns oil, or if it's been in an accident, Honest John will tell you. People bid lower when John announces that the car on the block is a lemon, but they bid higher at other times because they know that if John were aware of any problems, he would tell them.

John earns less on the lemons than he would if he were secretive, but he earns more on the good cars. These effects can cancel, leaving John no better or worse off than his counterpart, Silent Sam, in the next town, who reveals nothing. So far, we have found no good argument for Honest John's honesty. But John has one additional advantage over Sam: His policy partly alleviates the threat of the winner's curse and so gives buyers an *additional* reason to bid high. In the long run, John is sure to do better than Sam.

To put this another way, the winner's curse is initially the buyer's problem but becomes the seller's problem also because buyers defend against it by shading their bids downward. It is therefore a good idea for the seller to help buyers ward off the curse. A history of honest dealings can be an effective talisman.

The news that honesty is the best policy would not surprise your grandmother, any more than the news that life is full of disappointments. Like auctioneers, grandmothers have a lot of instinctual knowledge that economists work hard to acquire.

CHAPTER 19

IDEAS OF INTEREST

Armchair Forecasting

Each profession has its drawbacks. Doctors get emergency calls in the middle of the night. Mathematicians spend months stuck in blind alleys. Poets worry about where their next check is coming from. And economists get asked to predict interest rates.

I have a colleague who deals with this most onerous of questions by adopting the deliberative demeanor of a very wise man, pausing for effect, and then pronouncing "I think they'll probably fluctuate."

If I could forecast future interest rates, I wouldn't share it in this book. But I do know something about how future interest rates will be determined, and I am willing to share what I know.

I should first clarify an ambiguity in the term *interest rate*. When economists talk about interest rates, they automatically make an adjustment for inflation. If you lend at 8% in a time of 3% inflation, your buying power grows not by 8% each year but by 5%; the first three cents that you earn on every dollar goes just to maintaining the real value of your principal. The quoted rate of 8% is the *nominal* interest rate; the inflation-corrected rate of 5% is the *real* interest rate. The real interest rate is the nominal interest rate minus the rate of inflation. George Bush, the most economically illiterate of modern presidents, proudly proclaimed his inability to grasp this distinction in his 1980 debate against Walter Mondale.

Bowing to the inevitability of the pun, I pronounce that only the *real* interest rate is of real interest. An investment that earns 10% in a time of 7% inflation is neither more nor less desirable than one that earns 3% in a time of 0% inflation. In each case the real rate is 3%. People who fail to focus on the real rate make the mistake of saving too much. I once knew a woman who had dramatically increased her savings when she calculated that a dollar saved at a nominal rate of 10% would grow to $20 in 30 years. She didn't realize that at a realistic 3% real rate, that $20 would be worth only about two and a half of today's dollars. The trade-off between current and future consumption is a matter of personal taste, but it pays to understand the terms of trade.

When I say interest rate, I mean the *real* interest rate. That said, I can return to the question of how the interest rate is determined.

Let me begin by disposing of a confusing falsehood. Whatever you might have heard, the interest rate is *not* the price of money. Almost nobody ever borrows in order to hold money. People borrow to buy cars, houses, college educations, and extravagant life-styles. Bank loans might initially be disbursed in the form of dollars, but those dollars are typically spent and deposited back into the banking system within hours. The car that you purchase with your bank loan is with you for years.

The interest rate is the price of *consumption,* and consumption refers to real tangible goods and services, not some abstract entity like money. More precisely, the interest rate is the price of *current* consumption as opposed to future consumption. If you expect to come into an inheritance next year, you can wait until then to buy a new $20,000 car, or you can borrow at 10% to buy the car today and pay off $22,000 a year from now. The extra $2,000 is the price of having your car now instead of later.

That analysis probably does not surprise you, but it has a surprising consequence. Because the interest rate is the price of tangible consumption goods, it is—at least to a first approximation—determined by the supply and demand for tangible consumption goods. From reading the financial pages, you might think that interest rates are determined by the central bankers who control the money supply. But central bankers don't build cars or houses, and they can't control people's desire for cars or houses. It would take a power beyond all human understanding to change a market price without being able to change either supply or demand.*

The only thing we are sure the money supply can influence is inflation. When the money supply grows rapidly, prices grow rapidly in response. If fast money growth increases inflation, then it must also increase the *nominal* interest rate, because the nominal interest rate is nothing but the real interest rate (which is unchanged) and the inflation rate (which is up) added together. So money growth affects nominal interest rates, but it affects them in quite the opposite direction from what the financial pages typically suggest. Flood the economy with money and the nominal interest rate goes *up* in lockstep with inflation to keep the real rate constant, not *down*, as the typical *Wall Street Journal* reporter seems to expect.

Great events are linked to interest rate movements through the choices of ordinary consumers. The good news in this is that if you are anything like an ordinary consumer yourself, you have most of the insight necessary to develop a good feel for how interest rates respond to great events.

Suppose, for example, that the president and Congress agree to spend $20 billion this year on a new attack helicopter that

*A caveat is in order here. If you believe, as economic theory suggests, that all prices are determined by supply and demand (or in economic lingo, that markets *equilibrate*), then the interest rate is determined by the supply and demand for current consumption goods and so is quite independent of changes in the money supply. A generation of macroeconomists—spanning a range of time and ideology from John Maynard Keynes to Milton Friedman—postulated that there are important markets that do *not* equilibrate as in the textbooks, and pursued the consequences of that postulate. One consequence is that money *does* affect interest rates, though for reasons far subtler than the unambiguously false notion that "the interest rate is the price of money." More recently, beginning in the early 1970s, many economists have returned to the view that macroeconomic phenomena can be modeled perfectly adequately without resorting to the radical abandonment of theory that characterized the thought of both Keynes and Friedman. (A substantial inspiration for this modern revolution came from some prophetic remarks by Friedman himself.) Others (sometimes called neo-Keynesians) have sought new theoretical justifications for the assumption that markets do not always equilibrate, with the goal of making it no longer an assumption but the consequence of a richer basic theory. Their work provides some justification for the conclusion that money can affect interest rates (at least over short time periods), but again the effect is through subtle channels. It is in deference to these ideas that I have inserted the qualification "to a first approximation" in this paragraph.

does not fly. The $20 billion worth of steel, labor, engineering talent, and other resources that go into making that helicopter have to come from somewhere, so we can be sure that there will be fewer cars or kitchen appliances or personal computers. In fact, $20 billion worth of resources can produce $20 billion worth of output, because the potential output is what gives the resources their value. So when resources are diverted to building the helicopter, the total value of all available consumer goods must fall by $20 billion.

When there are fewer goods available, the average American ends up with fewer goods; this is a law not of economics but of simple arithmetic. When the value of available goods falls by $20 billion in a country of 250 million people, the average citizen must consume $80 less than planned.

In general, if the supply of a good falls, its price rises until consumers demand no more than is available. In this case, the "good" is current consumption and the price is the interest rate. As the interest rate rises, savers choose to save more and borrowers choose to borrow less. Both groups reduce their current spending accordingly. The interest rate continues rising until the average American has decided to spend $80 less this year than his original plans had called for.

When I want to know how a new weapons system will affect the interest rate, I start from the observation that I live in a fairly typical three-person household, and that households like mine are going to be spending, on average, $240 less this year than we thought we were. I ask myself how high the interest rate will have to rise to elicit that response, and I put this in highly personal terms: How high will the interest rate have to go to get *my family* to cut back our spending by $240? If I answer honestly, and if my household is really typical, then I can make a fairly good prediction.*

---

*Actually total consumption by Americans need not fall by the full $20 billion for two reasons. First, rising interest rates can discourage investment projects and free up resources for immediate consumption; steel that would have been used to produce industrial machinery is used instead to make cars. Second, Americans can borrow resources from abroad. For both reasons, the typical family of three is actually able to reduce its consumption by something less than $240.

A $20 billion crop failure or a $20 billion natural disaster would generate exactly the same analysis and exactly the same answer.

That's really all there is to understanding interest rates. The interest rate has to be whatever is necessary to convince the average family to consume its average share of the goods that are available for consumption. If the supply of goods falls, as when the government wastes resources, the interest rate must rise. If the supply of goods rises, as when there is an unusually good harvest, the interest rate must fall.

Let me offer an example to illustrate that demand can change instead of supply. Suppose that the average household finds a reason to become more optimistic about the future. Maybe new developments in technology herald increased productivity, or climatic changes herald better harvests, or a new administration takes office promising policies that are widely perceived to assure an era of prosperity.

Generally speaking, people who expect their incomes to rise in the future respond by wanting to consume more in the present. It makes sense to scrimp and save when you expect to be poor all your life, but not when you think you are on the verge of a financial breakthrough. If you win the lottery today, with the first $200,000 payment due in a year, chances are that your spending habits will change long before the check arrives.

So when the future looks brighter, everybody decides to consume more in the present. But here's the rub: There's nothing more in the present to consume. In the short run, there are a certain number of cars, a certain number of houses, a certain number of ice cream cones, and a certain number of seats at the theater. It is simply not possible for everybody to consume more, and in fact the *average* family must end up consuming the *average* allotment, just as before.

So what convinces people to abandon their new spending plans? The answer is that the interest rate must rise. By rising, the interest rate convinces people to spend less, and it continues to rise until the average family's original spending plans are restored.

When a new generation of computers is announced, I expect productivity to increase, the future to be brighter, and the interest rate to rise. How much will it rise? As always, I try to answer this by thinking about my own family. First, I wonder how much our future incomes will go up. Then I ask how much I am likely to increase my current spending as a result. If the answer is $100, I ask how high the interest rate must rise to convince me to *cut* my spending by $100, restoring the status quo ante.*

Now the answers to all of these questions are, of course, highly speculative, and their relevance depends very much on how typical I really am. My speculation is sure to be inexact. But there is great comfort in taking a question that seems to concern forces both mysterious and invisible ("how does technology affect interest rates?") and converting it to a question about the behavior of people like me.

Of course, there are economists who are unsatisfied with that kind of introspection and want to go further, by making careful statistical measurements of how people have responded to similar developments in the past, and finding sophisticated techniques for converting observations of the past into predictions for the future. Those economists surely make considerably more accurate estimates than whatever I come up with from my armchair, trying to imagine how I would act in various hypothetical circumstances. More power to them, but I like my armchair.

A famous professor of finance once lectured a group of successful investors on how markets behave. His talk painted a profound vision of how the world works but offered little in the way of practical investment advice. The audience, which had come seeking not wisdom but wealth, grew restless. When the professor invited questions, the first was overtly hostile and entirely predictable: "If you're so smart, how come you're not rich?" The professor (who was in fact the richest man in the room, but that's another story) responded, "If you're so rich, how come you're not smart?"

---

*As in the previous footnote, these calculations should be tempered by considerations involving investment decisions. If firms building the new computers divert resources away from the production of consumption goods, the average family's consumption may be forced to go *below* what was originally planned.

Economists study interest rates because interest rates are a pervasive social phenomenon and economists aspire to understand everything about human society. I hope that here and there in this book I have conveyed something of the sheer joy of understanding. Still, it must have occurred to some readers to wonder whether this kind of analysis can be a road to both wisdom *and* wealth. Let me try to address that question.

Harry Truman used to say his administration needed a one-armed economist, because the economists around him were incapable of completing a sentence without adding the phrase "On the other hand." Harry Truman wouldn't like where this discussion is headed. On the other hand, Harry did appreciate honesty, and I will be as honest as I can.

With no more theory than I've presented here, you really *can* begin to estimate how interest rates are likely to respond to a bumper crop or a natural disaster, to a wasteful or enlightened government policy, or to good or bad news about what the future holds.

On the other hand, that knowledge alone won't make you rich. The consensus among economists is that interest rates adjust to news in effectively no time at all. When the president announces the new missile project, you can begin to reason, "Now let's see; this means that there will be fewer consumption goods, so . . . " but by the time you've gotten up to the semicolon, the interest rate has completed its upward adjustment. Once the news arrives, it's too late to take advantage of it.

But there is a third hand. Just possibly, you have some knowledge or some talent or some instinct that makes you smarter than the average bear when it comes to predicting what the president is going to announce at tomorrow's news conference, or whether the hurricane raging toward the coast is going to dissipate before it hits land, or when IBM is going to develop a technology for attaching a laptop computer directly to your brain. If you are so blessed, and if you have a basic understanding of how interest rates behave, then you can really make predictions and you probably *can* get rich.

If you do get rich, it will please me to hear about it. Send me a note. I'll be in my well-worn armchair, thinking about things.

CHAPTER 20

RANDOM WALKS AND STOCK MARKET PRICES

A Primer for Investors

When I was young and first heard that stock market prices follow random walks, I was incredulous. Did this mean that IBM might as well replace its corporate officers with underprivileged eight-year-olds? My question was born of naïveté, and of considerable ignorance. I've learned a lot in the interim. One thing I've learned is that a random walk is not a theory of prices; it is a theory of price *changes*. In that distinction lies a world of difference.

My original (entirely wrong) conception invoked a roulette wheel as its central image. One day the little ball lands on 10, and the stock price is $10; the next day it lands on 8, and the price falls to $8, or it lands on 20 and the stockholders get rich. Blinded by that false vision, I could not see why it mattered if IBM appointed a president who cared more about paper dolls than balance sheets. If fate dictated a $20 stock price, then fate would have its way.

The *right* image also invokes a roulette wheel, but in a very different way. The wheel is marked with both positive and negative numbers. Each day the wheel spins, and the little ball's destination determines not today's price, but the *difference* between yesterday's price and today's. If the current price is $10 and the ball lands on −2, then the price falls to $8; if instead it lands on 5, then the price rises to $15.*

---

*An even more accurate image is that the roulette wheel determines not the actual price change but the *percentage* price change; when the ball lands on −2 the stock price falls 2%, and when the ball lands on 5 the stock price rises 5%. The image I've adopted in the text is slightly easier to think about and close enough to true that nothing interesting will be lost in the discussion.

With a random walk *every change is permanent*. Today's price is the sum of all the (positive and negative) changes that have come before, and each of those changes is determined by a separate spin of the wheel. If today's spin yields −15, then all future prices will be $15 lower than if today's spin had yielded 0. The effect is entirely undiminished by the passage of time.

When IBM brings in Mrs. Grundy's third-grade class to serve as its board of directors, the wheel comes up −20 and the stock price falls from $25 to $5. But future price *changes* continue according to their original destiny. If one-fourth of the spots on the wheel are +.25, then the stock price goes up by 25 cents on one-fourth of all future days; if three-eighths of the spots are marked −.20, then the stock price goes down by 20 cents three-eighths of the time. *Those* numbers don't change. The only change is that the stock price itself is permanently $20 lower than it might have been.

You might object that the $20 drop is itself unprecedented and clearly not from the usual roulette wheel. I reply that the roulette wheel is large, with many spots, and only one of those spots is labeled −20; that is why it doesn't come up very often. But the spot always existed, because there always was the same small probability that IBM would do something very foolish.

Which brings me to another of my early misconceptions. I had misinterpreted the word *random* to mean "unrelated to anything else in the world," which is why I thought that the random walk theory denied that IBM's behavior could affect its stock price. But one random event can be perfectly correlated with another. Great corporate blunders arrive randomly, and the corresponding stock price changes arrive along with them.

Economists believe that stock market prices behave a lot like random walks most of the time. That is, we believe that price *changes* (not *prices*) usually have the same statistical characteristics as the series of numbers generated by a roulette wheel. If *prices* were random, as I once erroneously believed, then today's price would be useless as a predictor of tomorrow's. Because price *changes* are random, the opposite is true. Today's price is the *best possible* predictor of tomorrow's. Tomorrow's price is today's price, plus a (usually small) random adjustment.

Imagine a simple game of chance. Start with $100 and spin the roulette wheel—the one with both positive and negative numbers—repeatedly. If you spin 5, collect $5; if you spin −2, pay $2 to the house. Your balance follows a random walk. As with any random walk, the present is an excellent predictor of the future. If your balance is low after 10 spins of the wheel, it is likely to remain low after 11.

But while the present value of a random walk foretells a lot about the future, its *past* values are of no additional use. Once I've had a look at the wheel and your current balance, I know all that a mortal can know about your probable destiny. You might have a gripping story to tell about how rich (or poor) you were five minutes ago, but hearing it adds nothing to the accuracy of my forecast.

So it is with stock market prices. IBM's current share price is an excellent predictor of its future price. But the history that led to the current price is quite irrelevant.

Commentators report that because a particular stock, or the market as a whole, has recently fallen, it is likely to undergo a "correction" upward in the near future. Or that because it has recently fallen, it is likely to continue downward in the near future. Or that because it has recently risen, it is likely to fall soon or to rise further. But if stock prices are like random walks, as economists believe they usually are, then future price changes are quite independent of past history. The current price predicts the future price. The commentators notwithstanding, past price changes predict nothing.

Those who play the market like to believe that they are more sophisticated than those who play casino games. Yet only the most naive roulette player would suggest that because his cash balance has fallen over the last several plays, it is now due for a "correction" upward. Experienced gamblers know what to expect from a random walk.

When I was young, I harbored many misconceptions (not all of them related to finance). Another was that in the presence of a random walk, there can be no role for investment strategy. I don't know where I got this idea, except perhaps that I knew there is no role for strategy in a random *lottery* and I came to attribute that to some mystical property of the word *random*. In any event, I was wrong.

First, different stocks are attached to different roulette wheels. Some grow predictably (their wheels have the same number in nearly every spot where the ball might land), while others fluctuate wildly (their wheels have many different numbers, some quite large in both the positive and negative directions). Choosing the right wheel is a matter of taste and of judgment.

Second, and more interesting, the same wheel can control more than one stock. The daily weather is like the spin of a roulette wheel. Sometimes the ball lands on a spot marked "rainier," whereupon Consolidated Umbrellas goes up 5 points and General Picnic Baskets goes down 5. Other times the ball lands on a spot marked "sunnier," whereupon Consolidated goes down 10 and General goes up 10. A savvy investor who buys stock in *both* Consolidated Umbrellas *and* General Picnic Baskets can shield himself from fluctuations, as one asset's losses are offset by the other's gains. Careful diversification can create a low-risk portfolio that earns more on average than any single low-risk asset.

Typically, even the best diversification is imperfect. The wheel has a spot marked "earthquake," and when the ball lands there Consolidated Umbrellas and General Picnic Baskets *both* fall. On the other hand, those are precisely the occasions when the stock of American Home Maintenance Services rises, and the strategic investor might want to add a few shares of American to his portfolio as a form of earthquake insurance.

If asset prices behave as economists believe they do, most investors should focus not on picking the right assets but on constructing the right portfolios. The question "Is Consolidated Umbrella a good buy?" is meaningless except in the context of an existing portfolio. In conjunction with General Picnic Baskets, Consolidated can compose a well-diversified portfolio. In conjunction with International Raincoats, Consolidated composes a portfolio with a lot of unnecessary risk, courting disaster if the sun comes out.

To earn large rewards, you must accept risk. (This is a moral that runs at large, extending beyond the world of high finance.) The trick is to accept no more risk than is necessary. The method

is to diversify, by recognizing assets that tend to move in opposition and by using this information judiciously. That is very
different from the traditional prescription to "pick winners,"
which economists believe is rarely possible. But it requires no
less savvy. With or without random walks, financial markets
continue to reward hard work, talent, and occasionally luck.

Strategy matters. Unfortunately, financial counselors don't always distinguish between strategy and superstition. They engage, for example, in a bizarre ritual called dollar-cost averaging, which will make as much sense to your great-grandchildren
as the Salem witch trials make to you.

The "idea" of dollar-cost averaging is to purchase an asset
in fixed dollar amounts at regular intervals—say, $1,000 worth
of General Motors stock each month for a year. That way, it
is argued, you buy less when the price is high (only 50 shares
when the price is $20) and more when the price is low (100
shares when the price falls to $10).

"Buy more when the price is low" sounds deceptively appealing, but it also suggests that we pause to consider the question
"low compared with what?" A price is attractive not when it is
low compared with the past, but when it is low compared with
the expected future. Unfortunately, a random walk is *never* unusually low compared with the expected future. The price is as
likely to go down $1 when it starts at $10 as when it starts at
$100. Would a wise roulette player ever believe that he could
improve his fortunes by betting more when his balance is low?

A low current stock price forecasts a low future price. If today's price is low, there is a good reason to buy *more* (it's cheap)
and also a good reason to buy *less* (it's likely to *stay* cheap). The
two reasons cancel out and make "buying more when the price
is low" no more attractive than "buying more when the price
is high."

Dollar-cost averaging is a very bad strategy against a random
walk. Imagine walking into a casino where ten identical roulette
wheels are to be spun simultaneously. You have $55,000 to bet.
You can, if you choose to, bet $1,000 on the first wheel, $2,000
on the second, $3,000 on the third, and so on. (These numbers
add up to $55,000.) But that is an unnecessarily risky way to
play roulette; over a third of your wager is riding on the ninth

and tenth wheels. The low-risk strategy is to bet $5,500 on each wheel, so that no spin is more important than any other.

Having money in the stock market for ten months is like betting on the spins of ten roulette wheels. If you dollar-cost average, adding $1,000 to your investment each month, then you have $1,000 riding on the first spin, $2,000 on the second, $3,000 on the third, and so on.* But we've just agreed that this is a great mistake. The wise gambler bets $5,500 on each wheel. In terms of investment strategy, this means that you should invest $5,500 the first month; then adjust your holdings up or down as necessary so that your stock is always worth $5,500. (If the value falls to $5,000, invest another $500; if it rises to $6,000, sell $500 worth of stock.)

Under either strategy, you have $5,500 at risk in the average month. Either strategy yields the same expected return. But dollar-cost averaging introduces an extra element of unnecessary risk. If the stock goes up in six out of ten months and down the same amount in the other four, the investor with a constant $5,500 holding is a guaranteed winner. The dollar-cost averager, who has less invested in the early months than in the late ones, has to worry about *which* six months are good and which are bad. If the good months are the early ones, the dollar-cost averager is a loser.[†]

Anxiety about whether your stocks will rise is part of being an investor. By contrast, anxiety about *when* they will rise is easily avoidable. Dollar-cost averaging is a good way to lose more sleep than necessary.

Until now, my case against dollar-cost averaging has been based on the random walk hypothesis. But even when stock prices *fail* to follow random walks, I cannot imagine *any* belief about price behavior that would justify dollar-cost averaging. Suppose, for

---

*This is an approximation to the truth; you won't have exactly $2,000 riding on the second spin because by the second month your initial investment will be worth something other than exactly $1,000.

[†]This discussion ignores a few incidentals like tax consequences and broker's fees, which tend to discourage a lot of buying and selling. In real life, it might be best to invest $5,500 at the beginning and make adjustments less often than I've suggested. But the perfect strategy is surely much closer to keeping a constant investment than it is to dollar-cost averaging.

example, that your belief is the naive one I held when I was young, that stock *prices* (as opposed to price *changes*) fluctuate randomly according to the spins of a mythical roulette wheel. In that case, your goal should not be to buy a lot of stock when the price is low and somewhat less when the price is high—it should be to buy a lot of stock when the price is low and *none at all* when the price is high.

The next time somebody advises you to dollar-cost average, ask him what he believes about the behavior of stock prices. Don't accept a meaningless answer like "they fluctuate"; pin him down on exactly *how* they fluctuate. Are they random walks, with price changes drawn randomly each day? Are the prices themselves drawn randomly each day? Do they follow a trend, with deviations from the trend drawn randomly? Are they chosen randomly from different roulette wheels on different days, and if so what is the procedure by which the day's wheel is chosen? Chances are, the question will be new to him. In that case, it is better to pour boiling oil in your nostrils than to take this person's investment advice. If he *does* have an answer, it is almost surely inconsistent with his advice to dollar-cost average.

The current high priest of dollar-cost averaging seems to be Bob Brinker of radio's "Moneytalk," an inexhaustible source of unexamined platitudes. Call Mr. Brinker for advice, and he'll tell you to dollar-cost average. I tend to view this apocalyptically, as a sure sign that Western civilization has decayed beyond resurrection. The advice you get from "Moneytalk" would not survive five minutes of critical examination, yet it is dispensed as from an oracle weekly without fail and without objection. If Mr. Brinker had ever taken a moment to test his advice against some simple numerical examples, he would know it was wrong. Presumably, he has too little respect for his listeners to bother.

Random walk theory implies that you can never improve your prospects via a strategy that relies on examining past price behavior. It is, however, silent on the issue of what can be gained by examining other variables.

In principle, one "roulette wheel" could determine both the weather and the price of Consolidated Umbrellas, with a time lag between them. First the sky darkens; then 24 hours later

Consolidated's share price responds. A savvy investor who noticed this pattern could make a fortune. By observing variables other than past price history, you might beat a random walk.

Having raised the hope that investors can achieve unlimited wealth by observing simple correlations, I am sorry to report that economists consider such a prospect most unlikely. It is reasonable to expect that more than one investor will notice the relationship between the weather and Consolidated's share price. As soon as the weather turns, those investors rush to buy stock, and, in competing with one another, they drive the price up almost instantly. The predicted future price rise takes place in the present instead of the future, and the typical investor is unable to purchase any shares while there is still time to realize a profit.

Nothing in this story requires that all or even most investors are on to the secret. It requires only that a small number of investors be alert enough to spot a profit opportunity and to exploit it fully.

The hypothesis that markets behave in this way is called the *efficient markets* hypothesis. According to the efficient markets hypothesis, no investment strategy based on the use of publicly available information can successfully beat the market.

The efficient markets hypothesis and the random walk hypothesis are closely related, and they are often confused with each other. But the hypotheses are quite distinct. The random walk hypothesis says only that you can't get rich by observing price histories; the efficient markets hypothesis says that you can't get rich by observing anything that is publicly available.

There is good empirical evidence for the random walk hypothesis as a description of most stock price behavior most of the time. For over 25 years, the economics and finance journals have overflowed with articles reporting unsuccessful attempts to reject the random walk hypothesis. The vast majority of economists find this evidence overwhelming, and among this vast majority there are some who are smart, skeptical, and not easily bamboozled.

By contrast, the efficient markets hypothesis, because it makes an assertion about *all* publicly available information, is much harder to test. However, various limited tests have been successful. For example, there is a substantial literature in support of the hypothesis that information about past trading volumes has no value for predicting future prices. For another example, Lauren Feinstone (the economist whom I married) has examined the statistical patterns of changes in asset prices; from these she infers (in the *Journal of Applied Econometrics*) that all new information about an asset is fully incorporated into the price within 30 seconds of its arrival.

Surprisingly little of this has penetrated the reporting of financial news. When a stock price begins to fall after having recently risen, the radio commentators report that the fall is due to "profit taking." When the Dow-Jones average begins to approach a previous high, we hear about its efforts to break through a "resistance area" and hear predictions that if it succeeds in breaking through, then it will continue to rise through a period of "clear sailing"—unless, of course, there is profit taking.

The "Abreast of the Market" column in the *Wall Street Journal* is the purest source for this kind of analysis. Economists have the same feelings about "Abreast of the Market" that many people have about horoscope columns. They find it entertaining, and they tell themselves that it is intended only for amusement. But deep down, they wonder how many readers take it seriously, and they shudder.

CHAPTER 21

THE IOWA CAR CROP

A thing of beauty is a joy forever, and nothing is more beautiful than a succinct and flawless argument. A few lines of reasoning can change the way we see the world.

I found one of the most beautiful arguments I know while I was browsing through a textbook written by my friend David Friedman. While the argument might not be original, David's version is so clear, so concise, so incontrovertible, and so delightfully surprising, that I have been unable to resist sharing it with students, relatives, and cocktail party acquaintances at every opportunity. The argument concerns international trade, but its appeal is less in its subject matter than in its irresistible force.

David's observation is that there are two technologies for producing automobiles in America. One is to manufacture them in Detroit, and the other is to grow them in Iowa. Everybody knows about the first technology; let me tell you about the second. First you plant seeds, which are the raw material from which automobiles are constructed. You wait a few months until wheat appears. Then you harvest the wheat, load it onto ships, and sail the ships eastward into the Pacific Ocean. After a few months, the ships reappear with Toyotas on them.

International trade is nothing but a form of technology. The fact that there is a place called Japan, with people and factories, is quite irrelevant to Americans' well-being. To analyze trade policies, we might as well assume that Japan is a giant machine with mysterious inner workings that convert wheat into cars.

Any policy designed to favor the first American technology over the second is a policy designed to favor American auto producers in Detroit over American auto producers in Iowa. A tax or a ban on "imported" automobiles is a tax or a ban on *Iowa-grown* automobiles. If you protect Detroit carmakers from competition, then you must damage Iowa farmers, because Iowa farmers *are the* competition.

The task of producing a given fleet of cars can be allocated between Detroit and Iowa in a variety of ways. A competitive price system selects that allocation that minimizes the total production cost.* It would be unnecessarily expensive to manufacture all cars in Detroit, unnecessarily expensive to grow all cars in Iowa, and unnecessarily expensive to use the two production processes in anything other than the natural ratio that emerges as a result of competition.

That means that protection for Detroit does more than just transfer income from farmers to autoworkers. It also raises the total cost of providing Americans with a given number of automobiles. The efficiency loss comes with no offsetting gain; it impoverishes the nation as a whole.

There is much talk about improving the efficiency of American car manufacturing. When you have two ways to make a car, the road to efficiency is to use both in optimal proportions. The last thing you should want to do is to artificially hobble one of your production technologies. It is sheer superstition to think that an Iowa-grown Camry is any less "American" than a Detroit-built Taurus. Policies rooted in superstition do not frequently bear efficient fruit.

In 1817, David Ricardo—the first economist to think with the precision, though not the language, of pure mathematics—laid the foundation for all future thought about international trade. In the intervening 150 years his theory has been much elaborated but its foundations remain as firmly established as anything in economics. Trade theory predicts first that *if you protect American producers in one industry from foreign competition, then you must damage American producers in other industries.* It predicts second that *if you protect American producers in one industry from*

---

*This assertion is true, but not obvious. Individual producers care about their individual profits, not about economywide costs. It is something of a miracle that individual selfish decisions must lead to a collectively efficient outcome. In my chapter on Why Prices Are Good, I have indicated how economists know that this miracle occurs. In the present chapter I will pursue its consequences.

foreign competition, there must be a net loss in economic efficiency. Ordinarily, textbooks establish these propositions through graphs, equations, and intricate reasoning. The little story that I learned from David Friedman makes the same propositions blindingly obvious with a single compelling metaphor. That is economics at its best.

V

The Pitfalls
of Science

CHAPTER 22

WAS EINSTEIN CREDIBLE?

The Economics of Scientific Method

In 1915, Albert Einstein announced his general theory of relativity and some of its remarkable implications. The theory "predicted" an aberration in the orbit of Mercury that had been long observed but never explained. It also predicted something new and unexpected, concerning the way light is bent by the sun's gravitational field. In 1919, an expedition led by Sir Arthur Eddington confirmed the light-bending prediction and made Einstein an international celebrity.

Both the explanation of Mercury's orbit and the successful prediction of light bending were spectacular confirmations of Einstein's theory. But only the light bending—because it was unexpected—made headlines.

Imagine for the moment that Eddington had undertaken his expedition in 1900 instead of 1919. The facts of light bending would have been as well established—and as mysterious—as the orbit of Mercury, long in advance of Einstein's work. Einstein would have lost the psychological impact that comes from predicting the unexpected. He might never have established his remarkable hold on the public imagination and on the grooming habits of a generation of physicists. But putting aside the issue of Einstein's personal glory, we can ask, What would have been the fate of relativity theory itself? Would the scientific community have been slower to embrace it? And if so, would that response have been justifiable?

Conversely, we can imagine that the aberration in Mercury's orbit had gone unnoticed until Einstein predicted it, and that subsequent observations had confirmed the prediction. Would the psychological impact of a second unexpected prediction have established relativity theory even more securely? And should it have?

For at least four hundred years, scientists and philosophers have argued about the relative merits of explaining known facts (like Mercury's orbit) and making unexpected predictions (like the bending of light rays). René Descartes and Francis Bacon addressed the issue, and it is hotly debated in academic journals today.

Certainly a new explanation for an old fact, and a successful prediction of a new fact, should both count in a theory's favor. The more psychologically spectacular case, the successful new prediction, is sometimes called *novel* evidence for the theory. The question is, Should novel evidence count more heavily in a theory's favor than nonnovel evidence? Or, more succinctly, Does novelty matter?

The "novelty doesn't matter" camp argues that a theory should be judged on its own merits, independent of how it was discovered. Here we have Theory A, which conforms to Facts X, Y, and Z. Let us judge it accordingly. Why should it matter whether the researcher knew X, Y, and Z before he invented Theory A? Why should the researcher's state of mind have any more relevance than how his hair was combed?

Consider a simple analogy. Of the socks in your left-hand drawer, one-half are black. Of the socks in your right-hand drawer, none is black. If you choose a sock from the left-hand drawer, what is the probability it is black? Surely one-half. Now suppose that while blindfolded, you reach into a randomly chosen drawer and remove a sock. Your spouse, who has been watching, then informs you that you chose from the left-hand drawer. What is the probability that the sock is black? Still one half. All that matters is where the sock came from, not what you knew when you were choosing it.

The scientist choosing among possible theories bears some resemblance to a man choosing a sock. In his left-hand drawer are theories that conform to a particular set of facts, and one-half of these theories are true. In his right-hand drawer are theories that are refuted by the facts, and none of these theories is true. Professor Smith begins by learning all of the facts and then constructs a theory that conforms to them; Professor Smith takes care to choose a theory from his left-hand drawer. That theory is true with probability one-half. Professor Jones theorizes in advance of the facts, making a novel prediction. He chooses blindfolded from a randomly chosen drawer. On learning that his theory fits the facts, Professor Jones discovers that he chose from the left-hand drawer. His theory is true with probability one-half, just like Professor Smith's.

Of course, socks and theories are very different sorts of things, but both are subject to the same basic laws of probability. If choosing scientific theories does not differ in any significant way from choosing socks, this argument is definitive and proves that novelty does not matter.

Although the case against novelty appears simple and airtight, it is greeted with great skepticism by many working scientists. They argue that anybody can take existing facts and concoct some sort of theory to "explain" them, so that a novel prediction is the one true hallmark of genuine scientific accomplishment. They have a powerful intuition that novelty *does* matter, and the intellectual challenge is to explain why.

If novelty actually matters, it must be because constructing scientific theories differs in some relevant way from choosing socks while blindfolded. Of course, anyone can list obvious differences between the two activities—one takes place in a laboratory and the other in a bedroom; one is supported by government grants and the other is not—but it is surprisingly difficult to put one's finger on the *key* difference that makes novelty matter.

In recent decades, the novelty debate has been confined almost exclusively to philosophy journals. But the most obvious issue involved is, How should we draw inferences in the face of incomplete information? This is an issue that economists know something about.

Even in the simplest context, novel prediction makes sense as a mechanism for revealing information. Suppose that some scientists are naturally more talented than others, and that it is impossible to know a priori who is who. Talented scientists are *both* more likely to construct true theories *and* more likely to be successful in their novel predictions. When Professor Jones makes a novel prediction, he reveals something—at least in a probabilistic sense—about his talents. The successful novel predictor is more likely to be talented, hence more likely to produce a true theory. We give Jones's theory more credence than Smith's not because of the *direct* influence of the novel prediction, but because the success of his novel prediction tells us something about Professor Jones.

Our story is still very far from complete. We haven't yet said anything about why Professor Jones *attempted* a novel prediction in the first place, while Professor Smith did not. Has Professor Jones revealed something about his confidence in his own abilities—and has Professor Smith revealed some telltale self-doubt? If so, this may be an additional reason to have more confidence in Professor Jones than in Professor Smith. In other words, we are entitled to draw inferences not just from Professor Jones's *success* at novel prediction but also from his initial willingness to *risk* novel prediction.

To take a concrete example, suppose that scientists who successfully make novel predictions routinely earn $100,000 per year, those who unsuccessfully make novel predictions earn $20,000, and those who never attempt novel predictions earn $50,000. The novel predictor puts his income on the line. Because he is willing to gamble on his own talents, it might well be rational for others to gamble along with him by believing his theory. By the same token, the scientist who chooses to take the $50,000 and run leaves us wondering whether we are being asked to have more confidence in him than he has in himself.

Exactly what inferences we can draw depends on the precise incentives that Jones and Smith are responding to. Now we are really on the economist's turf. We need a theory that predicts the structure of rewards to different kinds of scientists, the reactions of individual scientists to this reward structure, and the inferences that an observer can draw from these reactions.

A fully satisfactory theory of incentives would take account of competition among scientists, among research institutions, and among the patrons and beneficiaries of science. That clash of interests gives rise to a salary structure that offers a variety of rewards for different research strategies and different levels of success. Unfortunately, understanding the implications of such a theory appears to be a formidable task.

So we retreat to an easier problem. Imagine a national science czar, charged with designing a system that induces scientists to behave efficiently. We can hope that the system he would concoct is not too different from the one that actually arises under competition. We do, after all, know many other examples in economics where competitive forces yield efficient outcomes. Therefore, let us think about what the czar should do, in hopes that our investigation will yield some approximation to what we actually observe in the world. Even if those hopes are dashed, our effort won't be entirely wasted; we can always seek employment advising future science czars.

The czar can order scientists either to "look first," examining all of the data before they theorize, or to "theorize first," attempting novel predictions and then discarding their theories if those predictions are wrong.

Theorizing first is wasteful, because scientists devote resources to constructing theories that are—at least some of the time—ultimately rejected by the facts. By gathering facts in advance, scientists can avoid such mistakes and have more time to produce good theories. Thus an economical czar might be expected to order everybody to look first. But there is also a downside to looking first: A lot of (possibly conflicting) theories get constructed, and there is no way to distinguish the most promising among them. When the czar wants to build a bridge, he is confronted with a deluge of mutually contradictory theories of bridge building and has no idea which one to follow.

When scientists theorize first, many theories are ultimately rejected by the evidence, and those that survive have passed a test that indicates their proponents may be smarter than average. The czar can justifiably have extra confidence in those theories, and when he builds a bridge he can have extra confidence that the bridge will not fall down.

The trade-off, then, is this: If scientists theorize first, their work is expensive, too few theories survive, and not enough good bridges get built. If scientists look first, there is no way to tell the good theories from the bad ones and too many bad bridges get built and then fall down.

An enlightened czar might seek a middle way between the wastefulness of theorizing first and the alternative wastefulness of looking first. It might be best to designate some scientists as theorizers and others as lookers. But what is a reasonable basis for deciding who should be assigned to which group?

A potential answer emerges if we assume that scientists have private information about their own abilities, preparation, and motivation for the project at hand. Some scientists are more confident of producing good theories than others are, and their confidence is grounded, at least some of the time, in good judgment.

To simplify as much as possible, assume that scientists are either *good* or *bad*, where "good" simply means "more likely than average to produce a true theory" and "bad" means the opposite. Assume also (again, just for simplicity) that all scientists know their own types. (This is a first approximation to the more realistic assumption that *some* scientists have *some* information about their own types.)

In these circumstances, one of the czar's chief goals must be to distinguish between good and bad scientists. This information is valuable to him for two quite distinct reasons. First, if he can identify the good scientists, he will know whose theories to use when it comes time to build a bridge. Second, if he can identify the good scientists, he can pay them more on average than he pays the bad ones; this encourages more talented people to become scientists in the first place, while discouraging those whose talents lie elsewhere.

How is the czar to determine who is good and who is bad? The simplest method is to ask. Unfortunately, because he plans to offer higher salaries to good scientists than to bad ones, the czar might not be confident that everybody will respond honestly to such a straightforward question. Instead, he must find a way to reward people for telling the truth.

Here is a solution, along lines I've already hinted at. The czar sets up two separate research institutions: the Look-First Institute and the Theorize-First Institute. At Look-First, all scientists always look first and all are paid $50,000 per year. At Theorize-First, all scientists always theorize first. Those whose theories are subsequently confirmed get paid $100,000 per year; those whose theories are subsequently rejected get paid $20,000.

If these salaries are chosen correctly, then good scientists— those who are confident of their ability to make successful novel

predictions—will take jobs at Theorize-First, where they antic-
ipate high rewards. Bad scientists, who know that their novel
predictions often fail, accept the guaranteed $50,000 at the Look-
First Institute. The remarkable thing about this solution is that
scientists *voluntarily* reveal information that is useful to the czar,
even though they initially have no reason to do so.

Of course, some good scientists get unlucky in this scheme
and end up earning only $20,000 per year. But good scientists
earn more on average than bad scientists do, and relatively more
of them are attracted into scientific careers. Moreover, the czar
knows where to go for advice when he wants to build a bridge.
The scientists at Look-First make contributions that are politely
acknowledged but never acted upon.

This scheme, then, has some pretty desirable features. It also
has some that are disconcerting. For one thing, good scientists
waste time and effort by theorizing first. If they looked first
they could avoid some blind alleys. Unfortunately, looking first
would make their careers less risky, and bad scientists would
start to infiltrate their ranks. Only the possibility of a rejected
theory scares bad scientists away from the Theorize-First Institute. By forcing good scientists to be wasteful, the czar can
induce bad scientists to reveal themselves. The information is
worth the waste.

Another odd feature is that bad scientists are paid $50,000
per year even when their theories are known in advance to
have no social value. This too is necessary to prevent bad scientists from infiltrating the prestigious Theorize-First Institute.
Unless conditions for bad scientists are kept pretty pleasant, bad
scientists begin to masquerade as good scientists, much to the
consternation of the czar.

It is worth noting that if scientific research were left to the
private sector, no firm would choose to hire bad scientists who
produce useless theories. Yet it can be socially important to have
such firms in order to keep bad scientists from passing themselves off as good. So the theory suggests that the government
ought to play a significant role in organizing scientific activity—
because only a government would be willing to fund research
that has no social value whatsoever!

How realistic is this model? It certainly has a number of characteristics that are recognizable from the real world of scientific

research. In the real world, there are "high-powered" research institutions where salaries are highly dependent on research outcomes, and "low-powered" research institutions where everybody is treated pretty much equally. Scientists do, to a large extent, make decisions about what kind of institution to enter based on their expectations about their own abilities. The theory also implies that a lot of bad scientists are reasonably well paid for producing entirely useless research, and that there are probably more bad scientists than a benevolent czar would prefer; to those familiar with the structure of modern science, these implications have the ring of plausibility.

The good scientist/bad scientist model is not the only possible argument for justifying novel prediction. I suspect, however, that it is the only argument that has ever been spelled out in such detail. It would be a good thing for alternative theories to be spelled out in equal detail so that we could seriously discuss their merits. Somehow the debate about novelty has gone on for over four hundred years without any of the participants feeling obliged to specify his model of scientific behavior. Beware of great thinkers who advertise their conclusions without revealing their assumptions. I like economics because it insists on a higher standard.

CHAPTER 23

NEW, IMPROVED FOOTBALL

How Economists Go Wrong

Once there was an economist who wanted to understand football. He knew the rules but had no feeling for the game. So he decided to observe the great coaches and to learn from them.

Each time he watched a game, the economist painstakingly recorded all of the plays that were called and all of the surrounding circumstances that might have been relevant. Each night he performed sophisticated statistical tests to reveal hidden patterns in the data. Eventually his research began to pay off. He discovered that quarterbacks often throw the ball in the direction of a receiver, that the ball carrier usually runs in the direction of the opposing team's goalpost, and that field goals in the final minute are most often attempted by teams that are one or two points behind.

One day the commissioner of the National Football League became concerned about punting. He had come to believe that teams punt far too often, and that their behavior is detrimental to the game. (Exactly why he thought this has never been determined, but he was quite sure of himself.) The commissioner became obsessed with the need to discourage punting and called in his assistants for advice on how to cope with the problem.

One of those assistants, a fresh M.B.A., breathlessly announced that he had taken courses from an economist who was a great expert on all aspects of the game and who had developed detailed statistical models to predict how teams behave. He proposed retaining the economist to study what makes teams punt.

The commissioner summoned the economist, who went home with a large retainer check and a mandate to discover the causes of punting. Many hours later (he billed by the hour) the answer was at hand. Volumes of computer printouts left no doubt: Punting nearly always takes place on the fourth down.

But the economist was trained in the scientific method and knew that describing the past is less impressive than predicting the future. So before contacting the commissioner, he put his model to the acid test. He attended several football games and predicted in advance that all punting would take place on fourth down. When his predictions proved accurate, he knew he had made a genuine scientific discovery.

The commissioner, however, was not paying for pure science. Knowledge for its own sake might satisfy a philosopher, but the commissioner had a practical problem to solve. His goal was not to understand punting but to eradicate it.

So the commissioner sent the economist back to his computers to formulate a concrete policy proposal. After a few false starts, the economist had a brainstorm. What if teams were allowed only three downs?

To test his idea, the economist wrote a computer program to simulate the behavior of teams in a game with three downs. The program was written to fully incorporate everything the economist knew about when teams punt. Simulation after simulation confirmed his expectation: Because punting takes place on fourth down only, nobody punts in a game without fourth downs.

The commissioner was impressed by the weight of the evidence and held a press conference to announce a change in the rules of football. From now on, only three downs would be permitted. The commissioner announced his confidence that the days of excessive punting were behind us. But the reality was otherwise. Teams began punting on third down, and the commissioner stopped listening to economists.

Our hero was well within the mainstream of twentieth-century policy analysis. In the years following World War II, economists learned statistics. The new subject of econometrics made it possible to detect deep patterns in economic data and to test whether those patterns were likely to be repeated. Economists scrutinized consumption behavior, investment decisions, farm output, labor supply, sales of financial assets, and everything else they could think of. And the enterprise succeeded beyond their dreams. The data revealed striking consistencies that were used to predict the future with remarkable accuracy.

A contemporary American might find it difficult to imagine a time when macroeconomic predictions were frequently correct. But that brief golden era did exist. The natural question is, What went wrong?

What went wrong appears to be that governments started taking economists seriously, and that this development undermined everything. Let us follow the trail of one particular economist, formerly a consultant to the National Football League, and now employed by the U.S. government to help formulate economic policy.

The goal was to stimulate agricultural production. Our hero was assigned to analyze the cereal market and design a policy that would put more corn flakes on the average American breakfast table.

The first task was to determine the facts about corn flake consumption. After many months of poring over data, the economist found the statistical regularity he was looking for. The average family buys two boxes of corn flakes every month. This behavior is remarkably consistent. For example, small changes in after-tax income have almost no effect on corn flake sales.

Ever the skeptical scientist, the economist was unwilling to rely exclusively on historical data. Instead, he put his theory to the acid test of prediction. He forecast that over the next several months, families would continue buying about two boxes of corn flakes every month regardless of small fluctuations in income. His forecasts were repeatedly confirmed. His sense of triumph recalled that glorious day in his youth when he had first detected the fourth down/punting connection.

The economist's superiors were pleased with his finding, and even more pleased when he made it the basis of a policy proposal: Let the government provide each American family with two boxes of corn flakes every month. Financing the program will require a small tax increase, but we know that small tax increases don't affect corn flake sales. Therefore families will continue buying two boxes a month at the grocery store. To-gether with the two boxes that the government gives them, they will consume a total of four boxes, or twice as much as they used to.

But a strange thing happened. When the government started giving away corn flakes, shoppers reacted like football players given only three downs to gain ten yards: They changed their strategies. As soon as people realized that the government was delivering corn flakes to their doorsteps, they stopped buying corn flakes at the grocery stores.

Our economist-hero is no exaggerated fiction but a true rep-resentative of his generation. In the 1950s and 60s, his path was the path to fame and glory. Only 20 years ago, Robert E. Lucas, Jr. (now of the University of Chicago), issued the first widely recognized warning that human beings respond to pol-icy changes, and that this simple observation renders traditional policy analysis completely invalid. Even today, college students taking their first economics course are taught to assume that when the government provides corn flakes, people go on buy-ing corn flakes just as before. (Of course, the textbooks express this assumption in terms of algebra rather than corn flakes, to insure that students will not understand what it means.)

Unfortunately for policy analysts, people are not simple au-tomatons. They are strategic players in a complicated game where government policies set some of the rules. The behav-iors that economists can observe—the decision to buy a car or a house, to quit one job or to take a new one, to hire additional workers or to build a new factory—are bits of strategy. As long as the rules stay fixed, we can reasonably expect the strategies not to change very much, and we can accurately extrapolate from past observations. When the rules change, all bets are off.

Our economist/hero would have been well advised to devote less effort to his statistics and more to pure theory. Guided by the right theory of football—which is that each team attempts to score more points than the other—he could have accurately pre-dicted how players would respond to a new set of rules. Guided by the right theory of corn flakes—which is that families decide how much to eat on the basis of taste, convenience, price, and available alternatives—he could have accurately predicted that letting the government do people's shopping would not make them any hungrier.

Of course, some theories are wrong, and economists who subscribe to those theories do not predict accurately. But an economist with a theory has at least a *chance* that his theory is the right one. An economist who relies on nothing but statistical extrapolations has no chance at all.

The area where macroeconomists have failed most spectacularly is in the relationship between employment and inflation. For many years, good evidence indicated a powerful correlation: Times of high inflation are times of high employment, and vice versa. By the late 1960s, this observation had survived rigorous statistical testing and was generally accepted as a scientific truth. Accepting that truth as a basis for policy, politicians attempted to manipulate the inflation rate as a means of controlling unemployment. The result was contrary to all expectations: a decade of stagflation—high inflation and low employment combined.* Then in the 1980's, inflation fell dramatically, and, after an initial severe recession, employment opportunities expanded at unprecedented rates. The old statistical regularities seemed to have been turned on their heads.

What had changed? It is impossible to answer that question without a theory of how the inflation rate affects individual employment decisions. In 1971, Robert Lucas offered the first example of such a theory.

Imagine Willie Worker, currently unemployed not because he has literally *no* job opportunities, but because his opportunities are so unattractive that he prefers unemployment. Willie's best wage offer is $10,000 a year, which would barely cover the cost of getting to work. If the wage were $15,000, Willie would take the job.

One night, while Willie sleeps, there is a massive inflation, causing all prices and all wages to double. The employer who offered $10,000 yesterday offers $20,000 today. That's still not good enough, though. In a world of doubled prices,

*Milton Friedman, almost uniquely among economists, forecast the possibility of stagflation in advance, for essentially the right reasons. The work of Lucas described in the remainder of this chapter was largely inspired by Friedman's observations.

Willie doesn't want to work for less than $30,000. He remains unemployed.

Now let me change the story only slightly. The morning after the night of the great inflation, Willie is awakened by a phone call from an employer offering $20,000. At this point, Willie has not yet read the morning papers and is unaware that prices have changed. He happily reports for work. Only on his way home, stopping at the supermarket to spend his first paycheck, does Willie discover the cruel truth and begin composing a letter of resignation.

This highly stylized fable captures a potentially important aspect of reality. One way that inflation can increase employment is by fooling people. It makes job opportunities look more attractive than they really are and entices workers to accept jobs they would reject if they knew more about the economic environment.

We can tell pretty much the same story from the employer's viewpoint. Suppose you own an ice cream parlor, selling ice cream cones at one dollar apiece. If you could sell them for two dollars apiece, you would expand your operation, but you've learned by experimenting that two dollars is more than the traffic will bear.

If all prices and wages—including all of your costs—were to double, then you'd be able to sell cones for two dollars, but that two dollars would be worth no more than one dollar was worth yesterday. You would continue as before.

But suppose that prices and wages double without your noticing. You notice only that your customers suddenly seem willing to pay more for their ice cream cones. (Probably you first discover this when traffic picks up, because your one-dollar cones have begun to seem like quite a bargain to customers whose wages have doubled.) You expand your operation and hire a lot of new workers. Even after you discover your mistake, part of the expansion is irrevocable: The new freezers are in place, the new parking spaces are under construction, and you might want to keep at least some of those new employees.

The Lucas story implies not that *inflation* puts people to work but that *unanticipated inflation* puts people to work. In his story, fully anticipated inflations do not affect anyone's behavior. A (highly stylized) history of modern macroeconomics would go something like this: Inflations fool workers into accepting more jobs and employers into hiring more workers. Governments notice that inflation is consistently accompanied by high employment and decide to take advantage of this relationship by systematically manipulating the inflation rate. Workers and employers quickly notice what the government is up to and cease to be fooled. The correlation between inflation and unemployment breaks down precisely *because* the government attempts to exploit it.

Let me be entirely explicit about the analogy. Throughout the history of football, there has been no distinction between *fourth* downs and *last* downs. If economist A asserts that "teams punt only on *fourth* down" and economist B asserts that "teams punt only on *last* down," then nothing in the historical data can distinguish between their hypotheses. Anything that goes to confirm economist A's theory will go to confirm economist B's theory, and vice versa. Both theories will predict equally accurately *until the rules change*. But *after* the rules change, when the last down becomes the third down instead of the fourth, one theory will continue to be correct while the other goes drastically wrong.

Throughout the history of corn flakes, there has been no distinction between corn flakes *purchased* and corn flakes *eaten*. If economist A asserts that "families *purchase* two boxes of corn flakes per month" and economist B asserts that "families *eat* two boxes of corn flakes per month," then nothing in the historical data can distinguish between their hypotheses. Anything that goes to confirm economist A's theory will go to confirm economist B's theory, and vice versa. Both theories will predict equally accurately *until the rules change*. But *after* the rules change, when the government provides each family with two boxes of corn flakes over and above what they purchase for themselves, one theory will continue to be correct while the other goes drastically wrong.

Throughout the two decades following World War II, fluctuations in the inflation rate were largely unanticipated. There was no distinction between *inflation* and *unanticipated inflation*. If economist A asserts that *inflation* puts people to work and economist B asserts that *unanticipated inflation* puts people to work, then nothing in the historical data can distinguish between their hypotheses. Anything that goes to confirm economist A's theory will go to confirm economist B's theory, and vice versa. Both theories will predict equally accurately *until the rules change.* But *after* the rules change, when the government starts systematically manipulating the inflation rate in foreseeable ways, one theory will continue to be correct while the other goes drastically wrong.

With nothing but history as a guide, predicting human behavior in a fixed enviroment is easy; predicting human behavior in a changing environment is impossible. In New York in the summertime, I carry an umbrella to work if the morning sky is mostly gray. If you watched me for a while, you would probably notice this pattern and get good at predicting when I was going to carry an umbrella. But in Colorado in the summertime, I *never* carry an umbrella to work, because it is virtually certain that the regular afternoon thunderstorm will be over before I leave the office at 5:00. Move me to Colorado and your predictions will go completely haywire.*

An economist who understands *why* teams punt *knows* what will happen if you change the rules; an economist who understands *why* people buy cereal *knows* what will happen if you give out free corn flakes; an economist who understands *why* people accept certain job offers *knows* what will happen if you manipulate the inflation rate; and an economist who understands *why* I carry an umbrella *knows* what will happen if I relocate to a desert. To understand behavior, economists must tell stories—stories like the tale of the unemployed worker or the saga of the ice cream parlor—and spend a lot of time worrying about whether their stories are plausible, and how they can tell better ones.

Many economists are deeply unsatisfied with the Lucas stories and ask embarrassing questions like "Why can't the ice

*William F. Buckley fell into this pitfall when he criticized calls for federal aid to Los Angeles following the 1992 riots. Buckley argued that Californians send $1.20 to Washington for every dollar they get back; hence a billion dollars in federal aid to California would end up *costing* Californians $200 million. Buckley assumed that the 1.20 to 1 ratio was not susceptible to change, which is akin to assuming that my umbrella behavior is not susceptible to change. This is similar to arguing that because Buckley has always voted in the morning, he would not vote if polling places opened at noon. It is more likely that he would change his voting habits.

cream store owner learn the inflation rate from the *Wall Street Journal* before he embarks on a massive expansion program?" In response, Lucas and others have constructed increasingly elaborate versions of the original story, and also a host of competing stories.

But whatever the fate of any *particular* story, Lucas permanently changed macroeconomics by his insistence that a macroeconomist must have *some* story to tell and must tell it in sufficient detail so that its flaws are readily apparent. In 1971, Lucas began his paper on "Expectations and the Neutrality of Money" by describing all of the minutiae of an artificial society, including the life spans of its citizens, the age at which they retire, and exactly how much they can observe of each others' private affairs. Given those precise specifications, he was able to trace every consequence of an increase in the money supply. In the Lucas world, a random fluctuation in the money supply increases both inflation and employment. That same fluctuation, when it occurs not randomly but as a component of government policy, increases inflation but leaves employment unchanged.

According to legend, when Lucas submitted his paper to one of the premier economics journals, the rejection letter suggested that the paper was interesting but bore no relation to macroeconomics. Today, that paper is the archetype that defines what macroeconomics is about. Some economists like the story and others hate it, but there is a widespread consensus that our best hope is tell and dissect explicit stories about worlds that are simple enough to understand, but complicated enough to bear some relation to the world we inhabit. That is a radical departure from the old macroeconomics, and a necessary one.

As a predictive science, modern macroeconomics has yet to succeed. But modern macroeconomics is only 20 years old, determined not to repeat the mistakes of its elders, and eyeing the future with the impatient confidence of youth.

CHAPTER 24

WHY I AM NOT AN ENVIRONMENTALIST

The Science of Economics Versus the Religion of Ecology

At the age of four, my daughter earned her second diploma. When she was two, she graduated with the highest possible honors from the Toddler Room at her nursery school in Colorado. Two years later she graduated from the preschool of the Jewish Community Center, where she matriculated on our return to New York State.

At the graduation ceremony, titled Friends of the Earth, I was lectured by four- and five-year-olds on the importance of safe energy sources, mass transportation, and recycling. The recurring mantra was "With privilege comes responsibility" as in "With the privilege of living on this planet comes the responsibility to care for it." Of course, Thomas Jefferson thought that life on this planet was more an inalienable right than a privilege, but then he had never been to preschool.

I'd heard some of this from my daughter before and had gotten used to the idea that she needed a little deprogramming from time to time. But as I listened to the rote repetition of a political agenda from children not old enough to read, I decided it was time for a word with the teacher. She wanted to know which specific points in the catechism I found objectionable. I declined to answer. As environmentalism becomes increasingly like an intrusive state religion, we dissenters become increasingly prickly about suggestions that we suffer from some kind of aberration.

The naive environmentalism of my daughter's preschool is a force-fed potpourri of myth, superstition, and ritual that has much in common with the least reputable varieties of religious Fundamentalism. The antidote to bad religion is good science. The antidote to astrology is the scientific method, the antidote to naive creationism is evolutionary biology, and the antidote to naive environmentalism is economics.

Economics is the science of competing preferences. Environmentalism goes beyond science when it elevates matters of *preference* to matters of *morality*. A proposal to pave a wilderness and put up a parking lot is an occasion for conflict between those who prefer wilderness and those who prefer convenient parking. In the ensuing struggle, each side attempts to impose its preferences by manipulating the political and economic systems. Because one side must win and one side must lose, the battle is hard-fought and sometimes bitter. All of this is to be expected.

But in the 25 years since the first Earth Day, a new and ugly element has emerged in the form of one side's conviction that its preferences are Right and the other side's are Wrong. The science of economics shuns such moral posturing; the religion of environmentalism embraces it.

Economics forces us to confront a fundamental symmetry. The conflict arises because each side wants to allocate the same resource in a different way. Jack wants his woodland at the expense of Jill's parking space and Jill wants her parking space at the expense of Jack's woodland. That formulation is morally neutral and should serve as a warning against assigning exalted moral status to either Jack or Jill.

The symmetries run deeper. Environmentalists claim that wilderness should take precedence over parking because a decision to pave is "irrevocable." Of course they are right, but they overlook the fact that a decision *not* to pave is *equally* irrevocable. Unless we pave today, my opportunity to park tomorrow is lost as irretrievably as tomorrow itself will be lost. The ability to park in a more distant future might be a quite inadequate substitute for that lost opportunity.

A variation on the environmentalist theme is that we owe the wilderness option not to ourselves but to future generations. But do we have any reason to think that future generations will prefer inheriting the wilderness to inheriting the profits from the parking lot? That is one of the first questions that would be raised in any honest scientific inquiry.*

Another variation is that the parking lot's developer is motivated by profits, not preferences. To this there are two replies. First, the developer's profits are generated by his customers' preferences; the ultimate conflict is not with the developer but with those who prefer to park. Second, the implication of the argument is that a preference for a profit is somehow morally inferior to a preference for a wilderness, which is just the sort of posturing that the argument was designed to avoid.

It seems to me that the "irrevocability" argument, the "future generations" argument, and the "preferences not profits" argument all rely on false distinctions that wither before honest scrutiny. Why, then, do some environmentalists repeat these arguments? Perhaps honest scrutiny is simply not a part of their agenda. In many cases, they *begin* with the postulate that they hold the moral high ground, and conclude that they are thereby licensed to disseminate intellectually dishonest propaganda as long as it serves the higher purpose of winning converts to the cause.

The hallmark of science is a commitment to follow arguments to their logical conclusions; the hallmark of certain kinds of religion is a slick appeal to logic followed by a hasty retreat if it points in an unexpected direction. Environmentalists can quote reams of statistics on the importance of trees and then jump to the conclusion that recycling paper is a good idea. But the opposite conclusion makes equal sense. I am sure that if we found a way to recycle beef, the population of cattle would go down, not up. If you want ranchers to keep a lot of cattle, you should eat a lot of beef. Recycling paper eliminates the incentive for paper companies to plant more trees and can cause forests to shrink. If you want large forests, your best strategy might be to use paper as wastefully as possible—or lobby for subsidies to the logging

*My friend Alan Stockman has made a related point. There seems to be general agreement that it is better to transfer income from the relatively rich to the relatively poor than vice versa. It seems odd then to ask present-day Americans to make sacrifices for the benefit of future generations who will almost surely be richer than we are.

industry. Mention this to an environmentalist. My own experience is that you will be met with some equivalent of the beatific smile of a door-to-door evangelist stumped by an unexpected challenge, but secure in his grasp of Divine Revelation.

This suggests that environmentalists—at least the ones I have met—have no real interest in maintaining the tree population. If they did, they would seriously inquire into the long-term effects of recycling. I suspect that they don't want to do that because their real concern is with the ritual of recycling itself, not with its consequences. The underlying need to sacrifice, and to compel others to sacrifice, is a fundamentally religious impulse.

Environmentalists call on us to ban carcinogenic pesticides. They choose to overlook the consequence that when pesticides are banned, fruits and vegetables become more expensive, people eat fewer of them, and cancer rates consequently rise.* If they really wanted to reduce cancer rates, they would weigh this effect in the balance.

Environmentalism has its apocalyptic side. Species extinctions, we are told, have consequences that are entirely unpredictable, making them too dangerous to risk. But unpredictability cuts both ways. One lesson of economics is that the less we know, the more useful it is to experiment. If we are completely ignorant about the effects of extinction, we can pick up a lot of valuable knowledge by wiping out a few species to see what happens. I doubt that scientists really *are* completely ignorant in this area; what interests me is the environmentalists' willingness to *plead* complete ignorance when it suits their purposes and to retreat when confronted with an unexpected consequence of their own position.

In October 1992 an entirely new species of monkey was discovered in the Amazon rain forest and touted in the news media as a case study in why the rain forests must be preserved. My own response was rather in the opposite direction. I lived a long time without knowing about this monkey and never missed it. Its discovery didn't enrich my life, and if it had gone extinct without ever being discovered, I doubt that I would have missed very much.

*I owe this observation to the prominent biologist Bruce Ames.

There are other species I care more about, maybe because I have fond memories of them from the zoo or from childhood storybooks. Lions, for example. I would be sorry to see lions disappear, to the point where I might be willing to pay up to about $50 a year to preserve them. I don't think I'd pay much more than that. If lions mean less to you than they do to me, I accept our difference and will not condemn you as a sinner. If they mean more to you than to me, I hope you will extend the same courtesy.

In the current political climate, it is frequently taken as an axiom that the U.S. government should concern itself with the welfare of Americans first; it is also frequently taken as an axiom that air pollution is always and everywhere a bad thing. You might, then, have expected a general chorus of approval when the chief economist of the World Bank suggested that it might be a good thing to relocate high-pollution industries to Third World countries. To most economists, this is a self-evident opportunity to make not just Americans but *everybody* better off. People in wealthy countries can afford to sacrifice some income for the luxury of cleaner air; people in poorer countries are happy to breathe inferior air in exchange for the opportunity to improve their incomes. But when the bank economist's observation was leaked to the media, parts of the environmental community went ballistic. To them, pollution is a form of sin. They seek not to improve our welfare, but to save our souls.

There is a pattern here. Suggesting an actual *solution* to an environmental problem is a poor way to impress an environmentalist, unless your solution happens to feed his sense of moral superiority. Subsidies to logging, the use of pesticides, planned extinctions, and exporting pollution to Mexico are outside the catechism; subsidies to mass transportation, the use of catalytic converters, planned fuel economy standards, and exporting industry from the Pacific Northwest are part of the infallible doctrine. Solutions seem to fall into one category or the other not according to their actual utility but according to their consistency with environmentalist dogma.

In the last weeks of the 1992 presidential campaign, George Bush, running as the candidate of less intrusive government,

signed with great fanfare a bill dictating the kind of showerhead you will be permitted to buy. The American Civil Liberties
Union took no position on the issue. I conjecture that if the
bill had specified allowable prayerbooks instead of allowable
showerheads, then even the malleable Mr. Bush might have
balked—and if he hadn't, we would have heard something from
the ACLU. But nothing in the science of economics suggests any
fundamental difference between a preference for the Book of
Common Prayer and a preference for a powerful shower spray.
Quite the contrary; the economic way of thinking forces us to
recognize that there *is* no fundamental difference.

The proponents of showerhead legislation argued that a law
against extravagant showers is more like a law against littering
than like a law against practicing a minority religion—it is designed to prevent selfish individuals from imposing real costs
on others. If that was the argument that motivated Mr. Bush,
then—not for the first time in his life—he had fallen prey to bad
economics.

There are good economic reasons to outlaw littering and other
impositions (though even this can be overdone—walking into
a crowded supermarket is an imposition on all the other shoppers, but few of us believe it should be outlawed). But in most
parts of the United States, water use is *not* an imposition for
the simple reason that you *pay* for water. It is true that your
luxuriant shower hurts other buyers by driving up the price
of water but equally true that your shower helps *sellers* by exactly the same amount that it hurts buyers. You would want
to limit water usage only if you cared more about buyers than
sellers—in which case there are equally good arguments for lim-
iting the consumption of *everything*—including energy-efficient
showerheads.

Like other coercive ideologies, environmentalism targets children specifically. After my daughter progressed from preschool
to kindergarten, her teachers taught her to conserve resources by
rinsing out her paper cup instead of discarding it. I explained
to her that time is also a valuable resource, and it might be
worth sacrificing some cups to save some time. Her teachers
taught her that mass transportation is good because it saves
energy. I explained to her that it might be worth sacrificing

some energy in exchange for the comfort of a private car. Her teachers taught her to recycle paper so that wilderness is not converted to landfill space. I explained to her that it might be worth sacrificing some wilderness in exchange for the luxury of not having to sort your trash. In each case, her five-year-old mind had no difficulty grasping the point. I fear that after a few more years of indoctrination, she will be as uncomprehending as her teachers.

In their assault on the minds of children, the most reprehensible tactic of environmental extremists is to recast every challenge to their orthodoxy as a battle between Good and Evil. The Saturday morning cartoon shows depict wicked polluters who pollute for the sake of polluting, not because polluting is a necessary byproduct of some useful activity. That perpetuates a damnable lie. American political tradition does not look kindly on those who advance their agendas by smearing the character of their opponents. That tradition should be upheld with singular urgency when the intended audience consists of children. At long last, have the environmentalists no decency?

Economics in the narrowest sense is a science free of values. But economics is also a way of thinking, with an influence on its practitioners that transcends the demands of formal logic. With the diversity of human interests as its subject matter, the discipline of economics is fertile ground for the growth of values like tolerance and pluralism.

In my experience, economists are extraordinary in their openness to alternative preferences, life-styles, and opinions. Judgmental clichés like "the work ethic" and the "virtue of thrift" are utterly foreign to the vocabulary of economics. Our job is to understand human behavior, and understanding is not far distant from respect.

Following our graduation day confrontation, I sent my daughter's teacher a letter explaining why I had declined her invitation to engage in theological debate. Some of the opinions in that letter are more personal than professional. But the letter is above all a plea for the level of tolerance that economists routinely grant and expect in return. Therefore I will indulge myself by reproducing it, as an example of how the economic way of thinking has shaped one economist's thoughts.

Dear Rebecca:

When we lived in Colorado, Cayley was the only Jewish child in her class. There were also a few Moslems. Occasionally, and especially around Christmas time, the teachers forgot about this diversity and made remarks that were appropriate only for the Christian children. These remarks came rarely, and were easily counteracted at home with explanations that different people believe different things, so we chose not to say anything at first. We changed our minds when we overheard a teacher telling a group of children that if Santa didn't come to your house, it meant you were a very bad child; this was within earshot of an Islamic child who certainly was not going to get a visit from Santa. At that point, we decided to share our concerns with the teachers. They were genuinely apologetic and there were no more incidents. I have no doubt that the teachers were good and honest people who had no intent to indoctrinate, only a certain naïveté derived from a provincial upbringing.

Perhaps that same sort of honest naïveté is what underlies the problems we've had at the JCC this year. Just as Cayley's teachers in Colorado were honestly oblivious to the fact that there is diversity in religion, it may be that her teachers at the JCC have been honestly oblivious to the fact that there is diversity in politics.

Let me then make that diversity clear. We are not environmentalists. We ardently oppose environmentalists. We consider environmentalism a form of mass hysteria akin to Islamic fundamentalism or the War on Drugs. We do not recycle. We teach our daughter not to recycle. We teach her that people who try to convince her to recycle, or who try to force her to recycle, are intruding on her rights.

The preceding paragraph is intended to serve the same purpose as announcing to Cayley's Colorado teachers that we are not Christians. Some of them had never been aware of knowing anybody who was not a Christian, but they adjusted pretty quickly.

Once the Colorado teachers understood that we and a few other families did not subscribe to the beliefs that they were propagating, they instantly apologized and stopped. Nobody asked me what exactly it was about Christianity that I disagreed with; they simply recognized that they were unlikely to change our views on the subject, had no business trying to change our views on the subject, and certainly had no business inculcating our child with opposite views.

I contrast this with your reaction when I confronted you at the preschool graduation. You wanted to know my specific disagreements with what you had taught my child to say. I reject your right to ask that question. The entire program of environmentalism is as foreign to us as the doctrine of Christianity. I was not about to engage in detailed theological debate with Cayley's Colorado teachers and they would not have had the audacity to ask me to. I simply asked them to lay off the subject completely, they recognized the legitimacy of my request, and the subject was closed.

I view the current situation as far more serious than what we encountered in Colorado for several reasons. First, in Colorado we were dealing with a few isolated remarks here and there, whereas at the JCC we have been dealing with a systematic attempt to inculcate a doctrine and to quite literally put words in children's mouths. Second, I do not sense on your part any acknowledgement that there may be people in the world who do not share your views. Third, I am frankly a lot more worried about my daughter's becoming an environmentalist than about her becoming a Christian. Fourth, we face no current threat of having Christianity imposed on us by petty tyrants; the same can not be said of environmentalism. My county government never tried to send me a New Testament, but it did send me a recycling bin.

Although I have vowed not to get into a discussion on the issues, let me respond to the one question you seemed to think was very important in our discussion: Do I agree that with privilege comes responsibility? The answer is no. I believe that responsibilities arise when one undertakes them voluntarily. I also believe that in the absence of explicit contracts, people who lecture other people on their "responsibilities" are almost always up to no good. I tell my daughter to be wary of such people—even when they are preschool teachers who have otherwise earned a lot of love.

Sincerely,

Steven Landsburg

APPENDIX

Notes on Sources

This book contains many ideas and arguments that I lifted from other people. My memory is not good enough to accurately acknowledge them all. In this appendix I will do the best I can.*

The Power of Incentives: Sam Peltzman's work on auto safety was published in the *Journal of Political Economy* in 1975. Isaac Ehrlich's work on capital punishment was published in the *American Economic Review*, also in 1975. Ed Leamer's article on taking the "con" out of econometrics was published in the *American Economic Review* in 1983. The experiments on rats were reported in several journals including the *American Economic Review* in 1981.

Rational Riddles: The explanation of dressing for success comes from Alan Stockman. The riddle about sports betting comes from Ken McLaughlin. Don McCloskey talks about scattering in *Markets in History*, published by the Cambridge University Press in 1989.

Truth or Consequences: The observations about smoking come from a paper by Eric Bond and Keith Crocker in the *Journal of Political Economy*, 1991. The discussion of why employers give productive fringe benefits is inspired by work of Paul Yakoboski and Ken McLaughlin. The discussion of why we don't buy our jobs (and of how to

*The sources listed here are often quite technical. If this book leaves you feeling inspired to learn more about economics, and if you would like to see a presentation of economic ideas at a level intermediate between this book and those sources, I commend my own textbook, *Price Theory and Applications*, available from the Dryden Press division of Harcourt, Brace, Jovanovich until some time in 1994, and from West Educational Publishing after that. Another textbook that I think is a lot of fun to read is *Price Theory* by David Friedman, available from Southwestern.

split a check) is inspired by work of Ken McLaughlin. The idea of using Joseph Conrad to illustrate truth-revelation mechanisms is due to Gene Mumy.

The Indifference Principle: Hanan Jacoby pointed out that sex scandals need not be bad for politicians. When I asked him why farmers are subsidized and grocers are not, Mark Bils responded by asking me why motel owners are not paid to keep rooms vacant. David Friedman suggested the answer.

Why Taxes Are Bad: The story of the lost dollar bill is a fiction but could have been a truth. When I presented David Friedman with the airline ticket conundrum from the end of the chapter, he immediately responded by telling me that if I believed in an efficiency standard for personal conduct, I was honor-bound not to retrieve the next dollar bill that I dropped.

Of Medicine and Candy, Trains and Sparks: The entire chapter is inspired by Ronald Coase's article on social cost, published in the *Journal of Law and Economics* in 1960.

Sound and Fury: James Kahn pointed out to me the irony of Al Gore's timing.

How Statistics Lie: The observation about Star Market's misleading advertising is due to Walter Oi.

The Policy Vice: The observation that the possibility of "scoops" might justify either taxing or subsidizing inventors is due to Marvin Goodfriend. The colleague who worries about Styrofoam peanuts is Bruce Hansen.

Some Modest Proposals: I believe, but am not certain, that the idea of allowing people to sell their punishment rights arose from a conversation with Alan Stockman.

Why Popcorn Costs More at the Movies: Most of the ideas in this chapter are lifted from an article by Walter Oi in the *Quarterly Journal of Economics* in 1971.

Courtship and Collusion: The analysis of polygamy derives from work of Gary Becker. The observation in footnote 3 came from Mark Bils. I learned the story about the bargemen from Walter Oi.

Cursed Winners and Glum Losers: The theory of disappointment is due to Jack Hirshleifer. I learned it from Alan Stockman. There is an excellent overview of auction theory, by R. P. McAfee and J. McMillan, in the *Journal of Economic Literature*, 1987.

Was Einstein Credible? This entire chapter is based on original research that I have done jointly with James Kahn and Alan Stockman. A paper reporting on that research will appear in the *British Journal for the Philosophy of Science* in 1993. Another, more technical paper has been provisionally accepted for publication in the *Journal of Economic Theory*.

New, Improved Football: I learned the football analogy from Chuck Whiteman; I believe (but am not certain) that it originated with Tom Sargent. Milton Friedman's insight that inflation could affect unemployment by fooling people about the real value of their wages comes from a paper on the role of monetary policy that appeared in the *American Economic Review* in 1968. Lucas's work is reported in the *Journal of Economic Theory* in 1972.

INDEX

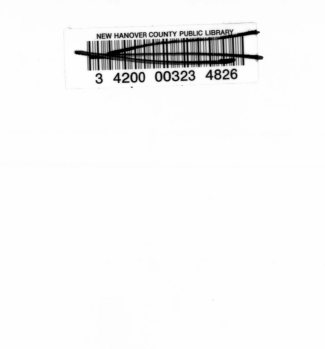